Praise for
Selling the Intangible Company

"This is an encyclopedic work that deserves multiple readings. I found a great number of familiar situations in the book from my many years as a high-tech company executive. An excellent resource for anyone considering the sale of their company."

—*Phil Herres, President, Haydrian Corporation*

"Tom's book reveals the secrets of how entrepreneurs can get the most value for their business at the best time. Anyone who does not read it will leave a lot of money on the table when they sell."

—*John R. Castle, Sc.D., Lecturer in Entrepreneurship, Foster School of Business, University of Washington*

"*Selling the Intangible Company* is a comprehensive resource that describes not only the technical issues associated with valuing, marketing and selling a business, but also the interests and biases of those who influence the process. This is a must read for entrepreneurs, chief executives and their key advisors."

—*Douglas W. Brown, President and CEO, All Star Directories, Inc.*

Selling the Intangible Company

Selling the Intangible Company

How to Negotiate and Capture the Value of a Growth Firm

THOMAS V. METZ, JR.

WILEY

John Wiley & Sons, Inc.

Published by John Wiley & Sons, Inc., Hoboken, New Jersey.
Published simultaneously in Canada.

For general information on our other products and services or for technical support, please
contact our Customer Care Department within the United States at (800) 762-2974, outside
the United States at (317) 572-3993 or fax (317) 572-4002.

Wiley also publishes its books in a variety of electronic formats. Some content that appears in
print may not be available in electronic books. For more information about Wiley products,
visit our web site at www.wiley.com.

Library of Congress Cataloging-in-Publication Data:

Metz, Thomas V., 1951-
Selling the intangible company : how to negotiate and capture the value of a growth firm /
Thomas V. Metz, Jr.
    p.   cm. – (Wiley finance series)
    Includes bibliographical references and index.
    ISBN 978-0-470-26137-8 (cloth)
    1. Venture capital–Marketing.   2. Selling.   I. Title.
HG4751.M483 2009
658.1′64–dc22   2008022830

Printed in the United States of America

10   9   8   7   6   5   4   3   2   1

With gratitude, I dedicate this book to my parents,
Joanie and Tom.

Contents

Preface

I have always been intrigued by doing deals. When I was a young man I would sell my current car for a profit and figure out a way to get a good deal on a newer car. I was very tuned in to the market and I could spot a bargain. A deal is a deal. A small deal is just as exciting as a big deal. The fee is not as large, but the problems are just as real and often more difficult. Sometimes small deals require solutions that are much more creative.

Selling the intangible is a natural extension of this interest. The value of many technology and software companies is intangible; it is based on their software and technology, not on the company's earnings. This is a challenge when selling a company, because there is no way to effectively value the firm. So how do you negotiate the sale of a company when the value is intangible? You will find the answers in this book.

I have been selling technology and software companies for more than 25 years and have managed more than 100 transactions as the chief negotiator. This narrow specialty has enabled me to work with clients all over the world—including North America, Europe, and Asia. In selling companies I have tried a variety of approaches and techniques in an attempt to determine the best way to sell companies whose value is strategic. Sometimes these methods may appear contrary to conventional wisdom in the merger and acquisition business. In many cases I started my approach using typical methods but discovered that they were not very successful. So I had to go back to the drawing board and find other ways to be effective in closing those transactions.

I have always gravitated towards philosophical thinking. It intrigues me to figure out why things are the way they are and to postulate some overarching theory that can help explain matters. Sometimes it leads me to discover a better way to do things. At the same time, I consider myself a very practical person, so my approach to investment banking is a pragmatic one, guided by a philosophy or a set of principles that help me deal with the realities of the market.

Perception is more important than analysis when selling a company that has strategic value. Many CEOs of technology companies have strong analytical skills and they place a lot of stock in these abilities. In my experience, perception is the hard part. Perception means clearly seeing the market as it is. It means perceiving the real needs of the buyers. It means perceiving the nuances and subtleties in the midst of negotiations.

This book is designed to help entrepreneurs, venture capitalists, and CEOs to better understand the process and nuances of selling a company whose value is strategic. It addresses the issues surrounding the sale of a company in which the value is in its technology, its software, and its know-how, and has not yet shown up in earnings or on its balance sheet.

The target audience for the book includes entrepreneurs, CEOs, and boards of directors of companies with strategic value that will one day need to sell. Venture capitalists, founders, and individual shareholders should also benefit from the concepts in this book. Lastly, I think that attorneys, accountants, and other professionals involved in the transaction will find this book informative.

There are a number of good books on mergers and acquisitions. Many are written by attorneys and academics and they do a fine job of describing the structuring and legal aspects—purchase agreement, transaction structure, letter of intent, due diligence, and so on. Many include checklists and sample agreements which are helpful. My observation is that CEOs and venture capitalists have a good understanding of the overall process of selling a company, but that some of the nuances and subtleties of selling an intangible company are missed. Few books address the sale of a company from the market perspective, which addresses questions such as: Why are adjacent markets important? In which sectors can the best buyers be found? How will a buyer view the acquisition? How does the buyer perceive value? These are questions that I explore in the book.

Almost every business will transfer ownership at some point in time. Only a small fraction will actually complete a public offering. The vast majority of companies will achieve liquidity for their shareholders through a sale of the company.

Acquisitions can have strategic or financial motivations. A financially motivated transaction is one in which the price is based on the company's record of profits. The buyer is purchasing a stream of profits in the future and the value can be calculated using standard valuation methods. A strategic transaction is one in which the buyer makes the acquisition because of the target's special capabilities, technology, or know-how.

In a sense, all deals are strategic; however there are different degrees of strategic. An industry consolidation acquisition is not as strategic as the acquisition of a company to gain key technology or to penetrate a new market. Strategic value is a moving target. This is one of the reasons that selling these kinds of companies is so interesting.

My perspective is that of a boutique investment banker and my role is to manage the process and get the deal closed at the best price with the best buyer. Throughout my career, working with entrepreneurs is one of the aspects that has been the most fulfilling. I have great respect for entrepreneurs. It takes courage, because the possibility of failure is all too real. Entrepreneurs do not take the easy road. They can be stubborn and difficult to deal with; but they are terrific.

It is a source of great satisfaction for me to help entrepreneurs realize their dreams and capitalize on their hard work and ingenuity. Almost every single client truly needed my help and I was honored to assist them with the sale of their company. I view my mission as an important one, helping entrepreneurs gain liquidity and achieve their goals.

OVERVIEW OF THE BOOK

Companies with strategic value exist in a variety of industries, but they are predominantly found in the technology, software and service industries, and in an emerging category that I term tech-service. Most have a value less than $30 million and I call these "sub-30" companies.

We begin by examining the kinds of companies that are characterized as intangible companies and why these traits are important. We investigate the reasons that companies consider selling and the best time to think about selling. We look at the nuances surrounding the sale of companies whose value is strategic, such as why small transactions have different dynamics than large transactions and how selling a company with strategic value is different than selling a company with financial value.

Many myths surround the sale of a company that has strategic value. In Chapter 2 I debunk eight myths that arise in the sale process. Multiples of revenue is one of these myths and I explain why these multiples are problematic.

The process for selling a sub-30 company is different from selling a $50 million company or a $100 million company. The approach for selling a company is described in Chapter 3. We compare the two-step auction and the negotiated sale. I also lay out the transaction time line and discuss how confidentiality affects the process.

Preparing a company for the sale process ahead of time can pay big dividends in terms of getting the best price and making the transaction come together with fewer problems. Chapter 4 poses some good questions that will help companies undertake the right actions prior to a sale.

Many times the best buyers reside in adjacent markets and I will describe the importance of tangential markets. How does market stage affect the sale process and impact value? Chapter 5 answers these questions as well as addresses how a buyer will assess the value of an acquisition target.

Selling to a public company and selling to a private company have different dynamics and I contrast these differences in Chapter 6. Sometimes selling to a privately held company can ultimately give the shareholders a greater return.

Value is one of the most misunderstood issues regarding the sale of a company. In a financially motivated transaction, three valuation approaches are typically used to determine value. Chapter 7 explains these methods and discusses how they apply or do not apply to the sale of a company with strategic value. Optimum price is closely correlated with the stage of market development. Recognizing the pre-tipping point is critical for obtaining the best price. This chapter describes how to determine the best time to sell a company from a market perspective.

Negotiating the price of an intangible company is very much like a poker game. I discuss the opening gambit, game theory, knowing your opponent, and a few rules and tactics. I also point out several common negotiating mistakes. Managing and generating alternatives is an important part of getting the best price. How does one negotiate when value is intangible? Chapter 8 answers this question and discusses the nuances of negotiating a deal with strategic value.

There is no end to the variety of difficulties that can impede a transaction. Every transaction will encounter obstacles and roadblocks. Chapter 9 discusses the challenges and the opportunities of selling a company with strategic value. Shareholders and management issues can also hinder the deal. We address some intriguing questions such as: Why would the sale of a company not be successful and how should a company respond to an unsolicited offer.

The CEO has a strong impact on the transaction process. Sometimes this can be positive and sometimes it can be negative. I discuss the CEO's involvement and problems that can arise. Chapter 10 also includes a section entitled *18 Reasons a CEO Should Not Sell His or Her Own Company*.

Tech hubris is a phrase that describes an attitude that pervades many technology and software companies. I expose this issue in the hopes that technology people will recognize certain personality traits and actions that are not productive and that can negatively impact the sale process. Many technology people try to outthink the market and this cannot be done.

In Chapter 11 we look at transaction structures and examine the pros and cons regarding the sale of stock versus a sale of assets. We also look at transaction currency alternatives and how creative structuring can overcome unusual deal problems. I also comment on consulting contracts and noncompete agreements. As a transaction moves forward the buyer will usually issue a letter of intent. I discuss the advantages and disadvantages of using a letter of intent. I also explain the due diligence process. What are the key issues and how long should it take? We also investigate the purchase agreement in Chapter 12. This is the definitive document that delineates the transaction details.

Earnouts can be an attractive alternative for the right situation. However not all situations lend themselves to the earnout structure. In Chapter 13 I discuss when earnouts are appropriate and when they are not. In addition, I present six tips for structuring effective earnouts.

Many companies pride themselves on being self-sufficient and they often do not understand how they can benefit from utilizing an experienced intermediary. In Chapter 14 I discuss how an investment banker adds value to a transaction. Many tech CEOs view the banker's role as one of a finder. Certainly identifying buyers is important, but driving the process and negotiating the best price is really the heavy lifting. In addition I comment on how to work effectively with an investment banker. Deal skills are an issue that I explore because they are both subtle and indispensable. Misconceptions abound regarding which deal skills are the most important. In my opinion, the most critical deal skill is understanding and reading people. This ability has helped me more than any other skill in successfully negotiating and closing transactions.

The search for small acquisitions can be a window into new growth areas and niche markets. Small deals have a number of advantages and Appendix A explores the beauty of small acquisitions from the buyer's perspective. International aspects of selling intangible companies are reviewed in Appendix B and Appendix C explores how a company should go about selecting an investment banker and includes some relevant questions to ask candidates.

Throughout the book you'll find numerous examples, or war stories, that illustrate concepts from actual transactions that I was involved in.

AN ADVANCE APOLOGY

I tend to pick on founders and CEOs a little bit, so I apologize for any broad categorizations. However, I deal a lot with founders and CEOs of technology companies so I have had significant interaction with them. One of the reasons I bring up the points about tech CEOs is to help them recognize that they may act in a certain way or express certain traits that may not be productive. If they alter their actions they can be more effective running their companies.

It's all about effectiveness. Effectiveness does not result when CEOs have problems with ego or if they must do everything themselves. One of the most effective things that any CEO can do is ask the right questions.

Many of my remarks are directed at CEOs with the intention of helping them ask better questions, make better decisions, and be more effective.

Technology people need to become businesspeople. The transformation from a technology-oriented viewpoint to a business viewpoint will help them be better entrepreneurs, better managers, and make their companies worth more money. Plus, it will eliminate a lot of frustration that tech people encounter in running their businesses.

You may notice that I use the term 'we' a lot in the book. This is simply one of my habits; I hope it is not confusing to the reader. By 'we' I am either referring to my firm or in other cases to you and me, the reader and me, as we explore a topic in the book.

Acknowledgments

I would like to express my gratitude to a number of individuals who helped me with this project. First I would like to thank two critical readers, Phil Herres and Jon Birck, who invested many hours reading the early drafts of the manuscript and advised me on where I needed to make improvements. I appreciate their judgment, frankness, and insight.

Individuals who reviewed sections that I was struggling with include: Chuck Gottschalk, George Textor, Bob Carroll, Keith Cochran, Hal Beals, and John Castle. I also owe thanks to those who gave me their input on a number of topics. These include: Kim Levinson, Larry Schwartz, Doug Seto, Doug Brown, Tom Simpson, Mike Hurt, John Weintraub, Ivor Frieschknecht, Shahan Soghikian, Christina Seelye, Josh Friedman, Jill Mogen, Rob McIntosh, Gary Blitz, and Wayne Wager.

I would like to thank Emilie Herman at John Wiley & Sons for her thoughtful editing. She is a real pro and her input was invaluable. Thanks to Bill Falloon for taking on this project, Laura Walsh for her editing, and to Kevin Holm for his production editing.

I would also like to thank the employees who worked for me over the years who asked me interesting questions. It caused me to pause and reflect upon why I thought a certain way and helped me learn to express a clear answer. I appreciate this.

In addition I want to thank my father, Thomas V. Metz, who taught me to be an independent thinker.

Selling the Intangible Company

CHAPTER 1

Intangible Companies— Who are These Guys?

An intangible company is a real company, one with real employees, and with real products and services that it sells to its customers. An intangible company is just like other companies except for one thing—the company's value is strategic. The value is strategic because the company has strategic assets such as technology, software, intellectual property, and know-how. This strategic value might also be called intangible value; and a company whose value is intangible is termed an intangible company.

An intangible company can be any size, but most have less than $30 million in revenues. These companies are typically in the software, technology, and the service industries. More and more of these technology companies are providing services to their customers rather than selling technology to them.

In this chapter we explore the concept of intangible value and examine the reasons that intangible companies are sold, when they are sold, and what are their sources of value. We will also take a look at the nuances of selling an intangible company and how these deals differ from other types of transactions.

Many intangible companies sell early in their life cycles. Companies sell for a number of reasons including shareholder reasons, market reasons, and management reasons. In addition to the good reasons to sell, there are some bad reasons to sell; there are also bad reasons *not* to sell.

The best time to sell is when the market is hot and buyers are willing to pay top dollar. Many companies wait too long before they consider selling. The first company to sell in a particular market sector will have an advantage because there are more good buyers who need those strategic assets. Of course, the best situation is to have multiple buyers.

The nuances of selling an intangible company are interesting and we will explore several examples. Small transactions, those under $30 million, are different from large transactions for a number of reasons.

WHAT IS AN INTANGIBLE COMPANY?

An intangible company has special sauce of some kind. Its strategic assets include items such as technology, software, patents, intellectual property, know-how, brand name, market position, customer relationships, development team, etc. For an intangible company, the value of the strategic assets is greater than the financial value that is based on the firm's profits. These firms are often young and have not had time to translate their technological edge and market insight into profits. To be exact, the company itself is not intangible, but rather its value is intangible.

A software firm is probably the most typical intangible company. Its primary assets are its software technology and its development team. A company that manufactures instruments incorporating proprietary technology is also an example of an intangible company. A shoe company that has innovative designs is an intangible company as well. A consulting company with proprietary best practices on how to convert manufacturing companies into 24-hour operations is an intangible company. The common thread among these types of companies is that they have significant value in their technology, know-how, and customer relationships.

Intangible Value and Elvis' Guitar

Intangible value is like the value of Elvis' guitar. How does one measure this kind of value? Is there an objective measure? What *is* the value of Elvis' guitar?

Intangible value is truly in the eye of the beholder. The value is extrinsic. The guitar's value is not a function of its "guitarness" but a function of how badly a collector wants to own it. The market for one of Elvis' guitars is not just collectors of Elvis memorabilia; it also includes people who wish to *become* collectors of Elvis memorabilia.

The value of technology depends on how effectively a buyer can incorporate that technology into its products and services and then sell those products and services in the market. The size of the market also impacts the value.

Similarly, value is extrinsic for an intangible company. If a company's value is intangible there is no objective way to place a value on the company. For most companies, tangible companies that is, value is a function of the company's profits, its rate of growth, and its risk. This value can be determined by comparison to other companies with similar profitability, growth potential, and risk. However, it is difficult to compare two intangible companies because there are too many differences between them. Even if two intangible companies are similar, valuation comparisons are difficult because the markets change too quickly. Chapter 7 will explore the concept of value in more depth.

By the way, Elvis' guitar sold for $180,000.

How Big Is an Intangible Company?

Most intangible companies sell for transaction values less than $30 million. Occasionally companies with revenues from $30 to $100 million will have significant intangible value and will sell for a price that reflects the importance of these intangible assets. Once in a while a company with revenue greater than $100 million will sell because of its intangible assets; however this is generally the exception.

Most companies with $30 million or more in revenue have been in business for a number of years and they likely are generating meaningful profits. A company with $3 million in operating earnings (earnings before interest and taxes) certainly has meaningful profits. Such a company will be of considerable interest to buyers from a financial standpoint. Its financial value will most likely be greater than its intangible value. This is the crossover point where the value shifts from intangible to tangible.

The Tech-Service Company

Software, technology, and other intangible companies have been shifting to become more service-oriented than in earlier years. This shift to service will continue. In my opinion, software is essentially a service. That is how most customers view it. It makes no difference whether the words and images that appear on their computer screens are delivered from their own hard disks or over the Internet from a provider's hard disk.

Two aspects of technology companies distinguish them from non-technology companies—invention and change. A technology company invents new types of technologies: hardware, software, and other varieties of technology. The second characteristic of a technology company is rapid change. By rapid change I am referring not just to the company's technologies but also to the company's rapidly changing markets.

Many companies invent and apply technology in a wide variety of industries and application areas—chemicals, instruments, biotechnology, plastics, automobile technology, and even clothing. It is important to think of technology companies not just with respect to computer-related technology companies.

More and more technology companies are providing their customers with the benefits of their technologies not by selling the technologies but by providing services that utilize them. A good expression for these companies is tech-service companies. A tech-service company is a technology firm that has a large service component to its business. Software as a service is the quintessential example of a tech-service company. Now it even has an abbreviation—SaaS.

The success of Salesforce.com underscores the escalating popularity of software as a service. Salesforce.com exemplifies the tech-service company because all of its revenues derive from the service aspect. The company is a leader in customer relationship management (CRM) services and has changed the way that customers manage and share business information over the Internet.

It has taken years for customers to get comfortable with the idea of software as a service, but it is catching on and will continue to become more prevalent. This business model also makes better sense for the software companies. It provides them with ongoing service revenue, which is preferable to the old model in which software firms regularly released new versions. Many software firms could not release versions fast enough to generate sufficient revenue. This model created grief for customers as well because they had to install new software on a regular basis. Software as a service will continue to gain acceptance because it is better for all parties.

Even IBM is a tech-service company. In recent years the service component of IBM's business surpassed the sale of its hardware and software products. IBM's Global Business Services Division, which includes technology services and consulting, now accounts for more than 50 percent of the company's revenues.

The Service Model

Selling a service is a more subtle and sophisticated business model than selling products. As the American economy matures, more and more companies will be providing services rather than just selling technology. There are a couple of reasons for this: one, services are what the customer wants. The customer wants their problem solved. Second, customers are gaining trust in service providers to maintain the accuracy and confidentiality of their data. A few years ago many customers did not want an outside company to be in control of their data. Now customers are more comfortable with this idea. In addition, the service provider can probably do a better job of keeping the data secure than the company can itself. The provider has better backup systems, better redundancy, and more sophisticated data management software.

A good example of this shift to service is an e-mail direct marketing company. Initially this particular company sold its software to customers so that the customers could perform their own e-mail marketing. The company usually provided the service for the first six months to get the customers up and running. Six months later when the time came for the companies to take on the work themselves, they preferred to let the software company continue providing the service. At the outset customers bought the software fully intending to utilize it in-house. However, very few of the company's clients ever performed their own e-mail marketing; they continued to let the software company perform their e-mail activity. It was much easier to simply pay for the service.

WHY ARE COMPANIES ACQUIRED?

Let's look at the sale process from the buyer's eyes for a moment. An intangible company may be acquired for a price greater than $100 million or possibly greater than $200. However most of the time intangible companies will sell for less than $30 million; I regard these as small acquisitions.

Making a small acquisition can be an excellent strategy for an acquirer to gain a foothold in a niche market, gain new customers and new talent, acquire new capabilities and technologies, and serve as a platform to build upon. Small acquisitions are less expensive, easier to integrate, and often simpler to transact than large acquisitions.

A $5 or a $10 million acquisition will be important to a company with $175 million or less in revenue. To a $500 million company, a $10 million acquisition is usually too small to get their attention. Only if the assets or technology are highly strategic will a very large company acquire a small firm.

The market opportunity for small acquisitions is significant. Many small companies need be part of larger companies in order to grow and thrive and to gain economies of scale in marketing and sales. Often the best firms are not seeking to be acquired and may be under the radar. The market for small acquisitions has not been picked over. The smart play for an acquirer is to make a small acquisition, get a foothold in a niche market, and then grow it.

The search for small acquisitions can provide a resourceful window into new growth areas. Even if an acquisition is not completed, the search process brings new market knowledge. Appendix A illustrates the beauty of small acquisitions in more detail.

WHY ARE COMPANIES SOLD?

A company that is thinking about selling needs to examine the reasons that it is considering a sale. These reasons may be shareholder reasons or market reasons. A primary driver for the sale of a company is that the shareholders desire liquidity for their shares. A second reason is that the company lacks the capital for effective marketing and sales and it can grow faster as part of a larger company with established sales channels. A third reason, although less common, is management problems. Timing is a critical aspect of the decision to sell. Some companies wait too long to consider selling and others sell for the wrong reasons. Let's examine the reasons to sell.

Shareholder Reasons

Shareholders include the founders, individual investors, and venture capital firms. Each group has both similar and different objectives in seeking liquidity. If the founders are the major shareholders, they may desire liquidity because they've been working for a long time and they would like to pursue other challenges or retire. This period of time may be as short as five or six years or as long as 10 to 15 years. The founders would like to cash in on their efforts; plus many are simply ready for a change.

If a company has been performing extremely well, the shareholders may think it is a good time to sell the company and realize an excellent return on their investment. They will likely hire an investment banking firm to assist with selling the company and negotiating a transaction. In some cases a buyer will approach the company out of the blue. The company may end up selling to that buyer or it might approach other buyers as well. A company with exceptional performance is in a strong negotiating position and it can command a top price. A top-performing intangible company with revenues from $15 million to $30 million might sell for a price of $30 million to as much as $150 million.

The second situation is one in which there are outside investors: either individual investors or venture capital investors. If individual investors are the primary shareholders they may desire liquidity because they invested a number of years ago and now it is time to recognize a return on their capital, even if it is not a stellar return.

In some cases companies have both angel investors and venture capital investors. The situation in which the company has venture capital investors is a little different than a company with only individual investors because venture capital firms tend to own a greater percentage of the company's equity than do individual investors. The result is that the venture capital firms will often have a greater influence on the decision to sell the company.

Venture capital investors seek liquidity for three primary reasons. First is that the company has achieved spectacular results and a sale enables the venture capital firm to cash out and realize a return on its investment. In this situation it is likely that the company was approached by a strategic buyer who made an extremely attractive offer to acquire the company. The second reason is that the venture capital investors do not want to invest additional capital in the company. They may be weary of the investment and do not see the company becoming a major success. The third reason is that the venture capital fund is at the end of its life and it must return the funds to its limited partners.

Let's take a closer look at these reasons to sell. The venture capital backers may have decided that they are unwilling to invest additional capital in the company. It is their judgment that the money will not generate a sufficient return given the upside potential and the risk involved. Investing additional capital raises the bar and requires the company to be even more successful in order to generate the required return to the venture firm.

Venture capital firms may have invested $10 million in a company to develop its technology and now the company is seeking an additional $10 million to build out its marketing and sales capabilities. At some point almost every company must become a sales- and marketing-driven company. This significantly raises the stakes to the venture capital firms because now they will have $20 million invested in the company. This means that the company must be an even greater success in order to provide an adequate return to the venture capital investors. Now the company must sell for $200 million rather than $100 million, for example, to provide the desired return.

The venture capital backers decide at this point that they would rather earn a moderate return and not invest additional capital in that particular company. So, they instruct management to sell the company. If the venture capital backers own more than 50 percent of the company, they can dictate that management go forward with the sale. If the venture capital firm owns less than 50 percent, they can still have significant leverage. The terms of the shareholder agreement can also give the venture capitalists more clout.

A venture capital firm may also want to achieve liquidity because it is losing patience with the company. It realizes that the company will never be a home run. The venture fund may have maintained its investment in the company for five or six years and is becoming weary of the investment. The venture capital partners no longer want to spend time overseeing the investment and attending board meetings for a portfolio company that will generate only a mediocre return. They would rather focus their limited time and energies on portfolio companies with greater promise.

A venture capital firm may be closing down an older fund that has reached the end of its economic life. A venture capital partnership typically has a life of eight to ten years with an option to extend it for another two years. At the end of the partnership's life, the general partners are required to return the capital to their limited partners. A venture fund that is near the end of its life will seek to liquidate the remaining companies in the portfolio.

I have worked on a number of transactions in which the primary driver for the sale was that the venture fund was nearing the end of its life.

Market Reasons

Many intangible companies sell because the firm has reached an inflection point at which it needs to either expand its sales force or join a larger company that already has a sales and distribution infrastructure. The problem is that they don't have sufficient marketing and sales resources to penetrate their markets in an aggressive and meaningful way.

The most common situation is a company that has developed technology, often quite successfully, but does not have adequate sales capabilities. Cash flow may cover operating expenses but not much more. Any extra cash is spent improving the technology or developing new products. The company does not have the cash to hire additional salespeople, which is what it really needs to generate greater revenues. The company lacks the capital for growth. The firm may have spent $8 million to develop its technology and now it needs an additional $8 million to take it to market. Lack of growth capital is a good reason to sell.

Often these are one-product or two-product companies. The founder might be the sole salesman in a small intangible firm. It is not viable to have a large sales force with only a couple of products; there are no economies of scale. At some point in the company's life, management can become frustrated with its efforts to grow the company, to build revenues and profits. The alternative is that they must either sell the company or else limp along. Selling to a larger firm enables the acquired company to make deeper inroads in the market. The acquirer usually has capabilities that the target company lacks. The selling company can now take advantage of the buyer's greater marketing, sales, and distribution resources and dramatically boost its revenues.

When a company is acquired, its risk level changes. As part of a larger firm with greater resources the target's operating risk is significantly reduced. This can be very attractive to an entrepreneur who has endured a high degree of risk for a number of years. The entrepreneur has the opportunity to continue building the company as a division of a larger firm—a much less risky alternative.

Management Reasons

A third reason for a company to sell is management issues. Management problems can occasionally escalate to the point where the company has no other alternative but to sell. The founder may have outgrown his role as inventor or technologist and the CEO role is not being adequately filled. In other cases there may be a conflict between management and the venture capital backers.

In one transaction that I was involved in, the founder and the VCs were not getting along. Not only were there conflicts between the founder and the venture capital backers, there was mistrust on both sides and the parties had differing agendas. The founder wanted to build the company at all costs and did not want to consider selling. This was his baby and his ego was closely tied to the success of the company. Selling was anathema to him. The venture capital firm had been an investor for several years and did not want to invest additional capital in the company, primarily because of the problems with the founder.

Sometimes an intangible company will sell because it is an alternative to raising capital. Being acquired by a larger firm might provide the company with the same resources that it would have purchased with additional capital. In one case in which I was working with a buyer to identify attractive acquisitions, I contacted a company that just happened to be in the middle of raising capital. The amount of dilution that the shareholders would have experienced in the financing transaction was significant. In addition, the buyer had all the resources and distribution channels that the seller was seeking to build. The shareholders decided that they were better off being acquired than raising capital and continuing as an independent company.

Bad Reasons to Sell

The worst reason to sell is because the founders or shareholders simply desire a high price. The sellers will be disappointed most of the time. Such a sale is motivated by an external financial objective not by market conditions or the company's current growth situation. In addition, the desired price can be extremely high and often unrealistic. Of course, if a buyer makes an unsolicited offer, that is a different story. This situation is discussed in Chapter 9. Once in a rare while an offer may come in out of the blue that is simply too good to pass up.

WAR STORY: DANGEROUS MOTIVATIONS

This was an unusual company. It had excellent technology but the management team had some serious issues. The two founders were

(Continued)

the majority shareholders. In the third year of operation the founders brought in both a new president and a VP of marketing and sales. The new management people made an agreement with the founders when they came on board. The deal was that if they could sell the company for at least 4 times revenues, then the founders would be required to sell the company. They even signed a written agreement to this effect. This situation could easily encourage management to take unnatural actions in order to achieve the threshold amount. I declined to accept this assignment. The last I heard the company had not sold. This kind of deal is fraught with danger.

Why Not to Sell

A company should not sell if it can create more value by continuing to grow as a stand-alone business. The company should continue on its own when the value being created outweighs the risks of staying independent.

Bad Reasons *Not* to Sell

On a related topic, there are also bad reasons *not* to sell. The primary bad reason not to sell is that the CEO has a personal agenda that is not aligned with the shareholders' objectives. He may enjoy running the company. He is getting a very good salary, nice perquisites, and he likes being in charge. Also, the CEO is not usually playing with his own money. At least most of it is not his money. His attitude is, "Just give me more money and a little more time. I can make it a success." The problem is, however, that he has already had plenty of time and spent plenty of money. He cannot bring himself to accept defeat or even mediocrity. Success is always right around the corner so he never wants to sell.

Another bad reason not to sell is the "lifestyle company." A lifestyle company is one in which management draws attractive salaries without regard to returning capital to the shareholders. I have run across a number of companies that fit this description. The shareholders either do not have the voting power to effect change or the value of their holdings has diminished to a point where they simply do not care. There is no impetus to change; management is happy with the status quo. I have suggested a sale of the company in situations such as this, however management usually responds with the same platitudes about greater revenues and profits being right around the corner.

Alternatives to Selling

A company almost always has alternatives to selling. It is important that a company recognize that it has options. Not selling and continuing down the present path is an alternative. Growth is another alternative. Existing shareholders can contribute additional capital to keep the firm alive or to grow it aggressively as the case may be. The company can raise venture capital and expand the business. If a single owner or founder wants to spend less time working, he or she can hire a professional manager and the owner can step back. There are always several alternatives to selling.

WHEN ARE COMPANIES SOLD?

Timing is critical when selling a company. It is one of the primary drivers for getting the best price. When is the best time to sell? There are two types of timing: internal timing and external timing. Internal timing is based on the company's specific issues, unrelated to any situation in the market. External timing is based on the market and the needs of companies in the market.

The pace of innovation and change is rapid in the technology industries and it is common for a technology company to be sold at an early stage in its development. An attractive return for shareholders may be realized before the company has invested significant dollars in sales and marketing.

As we mentioned above, a company should not sell when it can continue building significant value without taking undue risks. From this statement we can back into the right timing to sell. The right time to sell is when the risks associated with growth are escalating beyond a reasonable level. Another good time to sell is when the company is struggling to achieve growth. Temporary downturns and slack periods are one thing but when a company has a systemic problem with maintaining its growth it might be time to sell the company. A company should also sell when it has experienced a period of strong growth and can demonstrate additional growth prospects for the future. This is when the firm can sell for top dollar. One of the cardinal rules of mergers and acquisitions (M&A) is that a company should always sell before it needs to sell.

External timing is based on market reasons. The market dictates the best time to sell. The difficulty is recognizing the market situation, particularly if one is focused internally on the company's issues and problems. Markets are always in flux. As a result it is not an easy task to recognize the perfect time to sell from a market standpoint. Chapter 7 addresses this topic in more depth.

The best time to sell is when the market is hot—when buyers are willing to pay top dollar. The timing that matters is the timing of the potential buyers, not the timing of the seller. Are the likely acquiring companies at a stage when making acquisitions makes sense for them? Do they need the technology now? Will they pay top dollar now?

A good example is the acquisition of Skype by eBay for $2.6 billion. eBay's core auction business had flattened out and eBay was looking for a new growth area. Skype was only three years old with revenues of $7 million, but eBay was in the mood to buy. Skype was smart to sell early in its life cycle and capitalize on this market situation.

Think for a minute about the opposite situation. The market does not need this technology now because the technology is too early. Or, the supporting infrastructure has not yet been developed. At the other extreme, it could be too late. The likely acquirers have already developed or acquired substitute technology; they have found other solutions. This is the problem when companies wait too long to sell.

Market timing can be segmented into two categories—broad-market timing and the timing of a specific buyer. Broad-market timing refers to the overall situation in a market. In many markets competitors develop along similar time lines and experience similar stages of maturity.

For example, let's take a look at the market for software applications that run various aspects of municipal government. Historically this has not been an attractive market sector because there are significant barriers to entry and the sales cycle is long. For a software development company other markets are clearly more attractive. But for the software company that is willing to put in the time and effort to penetrate this market, the market is a good one. It is usually the smaller software firms that achieve early success serving this market.

After a number of years the more mainstream markets become saturated and competition increases. The larger players begin to look for additional market opportunities and now they may notice that the government software market appears attractive. This is a dangerous time for the smaller software development companies. The small firm can continue in this market and compete with the larger companies who are entering the space. However, the shrewd smaller company will sell, often at an attractive price, to one of these larger firms who is moving into the government software market.

The losing strategy is that of the smaller software company who goes head-to-head with the much larger competitor. In this case the smaller company has the mindset that they know the market better than the large competitor (which is usually true) and that their software is better and more on target with their customers (which is also likely to be true). However, in the long run the smaller company will lose out to the bigger company. The bigger company can simply throw more resources on a project and attack the market with significant sales and marketing power. The large company can also offer a bundle of products and services that smaller firms simply do not have. Municipal governments are more likely to choose the large company as its vendor of choice.

The second kind of market timing is the timing of a specific buyer. In this case the broad market picture is not as important as an individual buyer's stage in its life cycle. Regardless of what's going on in the market, if this particular company recognizes that it needs to branch out into new or adjacent markets, it will have an acquisitive mindset. This type of company is an excellent candidate to acquire smaller firms in adjacent markets. Chapter 5 discusses market timing and its correlation to selling at the optimum price.

WAR STORY: DO THE MATH—MAYBE YOU SHOULD SELL EARLIER

Sometimes an intangible company will sell early in its life cycle. Let's take the example of Lambda Medical Technology, a small firm that had developed great technology for solving a specific medical condition. The founder was a doctor and a well-known expert in this particular medical area. The product and technology worked quite well and the company expected to receive FDA approval within a month.

The company had spent $5 million to develop the technology and product. This capital had been provided by a Small Business Innovation Research (SBIR) grant from the National Institute of Health. Now the company was at a crossroads. Lambda calculated that it needed about $3 million to undertake a reasonable marketing and sales effort to roll out the product to the broad market. Unfortunately, $3 million is a difficult amount of money to raise. It is significantly less than what venture capital firms prefer to invest and it is a large amount to obtain from individual or angel investors. Initial meetings with angel groups showed promise but it did not look like the company could obtain close to $3 million.

I spoke with the founder about the situation. We both thought the company's current value might be in the $3 million to $5 million range. The company had told investors that its pre-money valuation was $4 million. The founder calculated his potential capital gain if he

(Continued)

sold the company now and compared it to the gain he might achieve if he raised capital, grew the company, and sold the firm in five years. Here is how the math worked out:

- Current market value: $4 million.
- Founder owns 75 percent of the company. Founder's value: $3 million.
- Investors contribute $3 million at a pre-money valuation of $4 million. Thus, investors will own 3/7 or 43 percent of the company.
- After the financing the founder will own 75 percent of 57 percent, or 42.8 percent of the company.
- If the company is sold in five years for $12 million, the founder's portion will be $5.1 million. (This assumes the investors do not have any special preferences regarding liquidity.)

Even with great technology, generating market acceptance for a product is a long, uphill battle. The founder does not have a background in sales and marketing. There is also the possibility that the company might require even more capital for growth, in which case the founder would be diluted further.

The result of this analysis is that the founder's shares are worth about $3 million at the current time. If the company sells in five years for 3 times its current value, or $12 million, the founder's shares would be worth about $5 million. Should the founder cash out now for $3 million or wait an additional five years in order to achieve a $5 million payout? Is it worth waiting five years? Is it worth the risk?

At the time of this writing, the founder is considering his alternatives while he waits for the FDA approval. He is strongly inclined to cash out now, in part because of the timing and in part because of the risk.

Waiting Too Long to Sell

In my experience many sellers wait too long before selling. There is always some excuse that keeps them from executing the sale process. They just want to get revenues up a little more, get the latest version of the product developed, attend the next industry trade show, or whatever. There is always a reason not to sell. Venture capital firms are guilty of waiting too long as well. Most venture capitalists are in the business to hit home runs, not singles or doubles. So they typically wait too long to sell, waiting for that home run.

It takes courage to sell. It takes courage to change direction and make a decision and move forward with it. Perhaps the CEO does not really want to sell at all. Maybe he is afraid of going down a road that he is not familiar with (i.e., the sale process). In any case, companies often wait too long before selling. Here are some of the reasons.

Many CEOs and founders want to continue growing the company. If the company is performing well, the CEO wants to grow revenues to a higher threshold. If the company is performing moderately, the CEO wants to boost profits. If the company is struggling, the CEO wants to dig himself out of the hole and achieve break-even profitability. The company will always do better down the road. There is no shortage of optimism in the entrepreneurial environment. There is always a reason to wait. This mindset can be a problem.

For a company whose value is strategic these are not good reasons. The sale of an intangible company will always be a strategic transaction. The buyer is buying technology and capabilities, not revenues or cash flow. If a larger company needs your technology because it complements their products, there is a better chance at selling it for top dollar now, not down the road when you have improved your cash flow. Although better financial performance certainly doesn't hurt, the deal does not hinge upon the financial performance. The strategic asset is unchanged, even if revenues are slightly higher. Remember, the deal is strategic, not financial.

Don't milk the company dry. Do not try to wring every last dollar out of the market. Sell the company when there is still good growth left for the buyer to realize. This is how a company cashes out for top dollar. For one, buyers tend to be reasonably smart about the markets. Sooner or later the buyer will realize that the company has milked the market dry. If they do go forward and make an offer to acquire the company, it will be a low offer.

Do not try to sell at the top or even just before the top. Why not? Because you will never know where the top is. This is an impossible question to answer. It is similar to trying to sell a stock at the top of the market. Market timing is impossible to predict.

The other side of this coin is that the risk does not diminish. Markets are not static, they are always changing. As a result the price that a company might command at one point in time may be very different from the price it commands a year later, even if the company is unchanged.

Entrepreneurs and CEOs are optimists and they believe they can grow their companies to the stars. The most dangerous ones can be blinded by their optimism. The smart sellers are ruthlessly realistic about the market. They recognize early on when larger competitors are entering their markets putting pressure on prices and margins. The right time to sell is when the market is ready.

First Seller Advantage

First seller advantage is akin to musical chairs. In musical chairs, the last person standing loses. This concept is similar to that of "First Mover Advantage." I like to call it "First Seller Advantage" and "Last Seller Disadvantage."

The concept is this—the first company to sell in a particular market niche has a significant advantage because there are more buyers that need its software or technology. The first company to be acquired is likely to receive the best price because there is more competition among more buyers.

A good example of First Seller Advantage is Google's acquisition of YouTube, Inc. for $1.65 billion in stock. YouTube only had 65 employees and did not have a profitable business model. Analysts regarded the acquisition as a defensive move on Google's part. In other words, Google wanted to keep YouTube out of the hands of competitors. (There were rumors that Yahoo also bid for the company.) A Google vice president commented that the transaction's value to Google was not determined on a stand-alone basis, but was based on synergies with Google's existing business. This is typical for the acquisition of an intangible company.

In the technology markets it is unlikely that there will be 10 or 20 good buyers for a company that is seeking to be acquired. Typically there are between one and four truly good buyers for a target company. So, in the Internet video market space, other sellers will have a more difficult time finding good buyers when they decide to sell. Yahoo is a likely buyer, but who will bid against them? The next sale will likely be for a lower price.

The antivirus or security software market is similar. There was a time when few companies had antivirus software, then a handful of companies had it, and now of course almost all applications have some sort of antivirus or security software. Sometimes large software companies develop this software in-house but more commonly they will acquire a smaller firm that has developed specialty technology. The first company to sell has an advantage because there are more potential buyers in the market.

THE NUANCES OF SELLING AN INTANGIBLE COMPANY

If you are thinking about selling, the first task is to examine your company. What are your reasons for selling? Why are you considering it? Take a look at your sources of value. What are your key assets? A keen understanding of your company's strengths is imperative. What are the drivers of value in your company? Is it the technology? Patents? What people strengths do you have? What about development capability? Is your customer base a key asset? Can you quantify these strengths in any way?

What strengths will you bring to a buyer? What additional revenues will you contribute? What about recurring or maintenance revenues? Are there cross-selling opportunities? Does your technology offer key strategic value to a buyer? Can the buyer find similar technology elsewhere? Try to estimate the dollar value of incorporating your technology into their products.

In many cases it is difficult for an owner or management to be objective about these issues. That is why it is helpful to seek the advice of a third party such as an investment banker. A banker will have a broader purview and can usually offer practical advice about the depth or breadth of the company's components of strategic value. Management should make a point to listen to the advice, even when it may not be what it wants to hear. In Chapter 14 we explore the concept of using an investment banker to assist in the sale of a company and Appendix C discusses how to select an investment banker.

First let's discuss the sale of a *tangible* company. The value of a tangible company is real; the company's earnings are factual. The company has a record that cannot be altered. The historical earnings are the historical earnings, period. For a tangible company if the earnings are X, the value is Y. There is little opportunity for imagination or vision to negotiate a better price.

Let's consider a hypothetical tangible company. Let's say the firm has been in business for a number of years, its earnings have been consistent from year to year, and there are no surprises. This business is transparent as to what it is. There are no wildly optimistic projections for future earnings. It will perform in the future very closely as it has in the past and the price will be a function of its profits. The most likely valuation yardstick is 5 or 6 times operating income. So, if the company has operating earnings of $1.5 million, the value of this company will be between $7.5 and $9 million. This range will be narrowed further by examining the risk characteristics of the company. There is minimal growth so there is no premium paid for growth.

In contrast, selling an intangible company means selling a vision of what the potential growth *might* be. The value is not a function of its profits but a function of its technology and other strategic assets. It can be easier to get an exceptionally high price for an intangible company than for a tangible company.

The following sections explain a few of the other nuances surrounding the sale of an intangible company. A valuation is not necessary—the parties simply need to agree to a deal. Sometimes there are multiple buyers and sometimes there is only one good buyer. In addition we explore why small deals have characteristics that are different from large transactions.

Agreement is the Goal

The key to closing the sale of an intangible company is to get the parties to agree on the price and terms. The parties do not need a valuation; they do not even need to agree on value. They simply need to agree on the price.

If I trade you my bike for your skateboard, we do not need a valuation. If we are both happy with the trade then it is a successful transaction. Think of it as a barter economy. There is no money in a barter economy. All deals are done by trading one asset for another asset. There are no valuations. If someone wants to trade four pigs and one goat for two cows and each side is happy with the trade, then it is a successful transaction. A valuation is not required.

Similarly for the purchase of an intangible company—it is a trade. Unless it is a cash deal, the players are trading shares of one company's stock for shares of another company's stock. The buyer is trading 14 percent of its stock for 100 percent of the target's stock. Expressed in number of shares it may be something like trading 1.3 million shares of the buyer's stock for the 2.4 million outstanding shares of the selling company. There is no accurate valuation for either company (unless the buyer's stock is publicly traded). As long as the principals on both sides agree on the ratio of shares to be exchanged then a successful transaction can be concluded.

Multiple Buyers versus One Buyer

There are two situations to consider. The first—and best—situation is when there are multiple buyers. Having multiple buyers is the best way to ensure that the shareholders of the seller will achieve the best price for the company. The second situation is when there is just one viable buyer for the company.

When multiple buyers are in the picture it is possible to go back and forth to make sure that each buyer is offering the highest price that it can. Then the seller simply chooses the highest offer. The seller might choose the second place offer if the terms are more favorable or if there is a better management fit. Otherwise the choice to select the highest offer is an easy one.

When there is only one buyer it is a little trickier. I have had good success over the years negotiating deals when there was only one buyer. In most cases the alternative for the buyer is to develop the technology in-house. It is imperative for the seller and its intermediary to have an in-depth understanding of the buyer's situation. The seller needs to know specifically how important the technology is to the buyer. It is only through this knowledge that the seller can negotiate a top price.

Small Deals are Different than Big Deals

Why would a small transaction be any different than a large transaction? A deal is a deal. Some think that small deals are just as complicated as big deals. They can get complicated, but they do not need to be. Small transactions have a number of characteristics that differ from large transactions.

The buyers for an acquisition under $30 million are smaller companies with revenues between $15 and $175 million. For a large transaction there may be 40 or 50 potential buyers, versus 150 or more for a small acquisition. The universe of buyers is different. Small acquisitions are often made with market entry as a motive, so the search process can require more creativity to investigate adjacent markets.

Small technology companies are not usually fully developed, not "cast in concrete." A company with $100 million in revenue is fairly well-defined. A company with $7 million in revenue is much more adaptable. A young intangible company can fit with more buyers and its technology can be employed in more contexts.

The sale process for a sub-30 company is different than the process for selling a larger company. The two-step auction process used for large transactions does not work well for transactions less than $30 million; a negotiated sale is much more effective. Chapter 3 discusses the advantages and disadvantages of the two-step auction process versus the negotiated sale.

Not only are small deals less expensive, they can have simpler transaction structures. In many cases the buyer simply purchases the seller's assets and assumes selected liabilities. If stock is not being acquired, there is reduced due diligence and less concern about hidden liabilities. With a small acquisition there are fewer integration issues because there are fewer people to bring on board and no "culture" that must be integrated.

In some ways, small transactions can be more difficult. Deal structures can be more diverse with notes, earnouts, royalties, etc. A consulting agreement may account for a material portion of the transaction value. A small glitch can be a significant problem in a sub-30 deal. In addition, the participants are generally less sophisticated on small transactions. The buyer might have never made an acquisition before and it may not have an experienced investment banker or attorney advising it. For a more in depth examination of the differences between small transactions and large transactions please see Appendix A.

A Few Other Nuances

One of the problems with selling an intangible company is that management and shareholders do not know what it is worth ahead of time. Most CEOs and board members find this a bit frustrating. Generally the board of directors wants to have a clear valuation range in mind before they begin the sale process. This can be difficult to achieve. For one thing the selling company does not need a value range up front. There is no decision that the company will make or not make that depends upon the value range.

The decision to go forward with the sale process should not be based on an expected value but rather on strategic business reasons or shareholder reasons. In doing this, the company shouldn't try to outthink the market. The seller may decide not to accept an offer, but that occurs later, after it has gone through the sale process and generated offers. Even though the company might have an idea ahead of time about the price, it really will never know until it goes to the market and finds out. The price is determined solely by the market.

This is particularly problematic when an offer comes in out of the blue. The board does not really know if it is a good offer or not, as they have nothing to compare it to. Chapter 9 discusses unsolicited offers in more depth.

Intangible deals are usually not accretive. Accretive means that the seller has earnings and these earnings will increase the buyer's earnings per share. A selling company with excellent technology but minimal profits will not be an accretive acquisition. Most sales of intangible companies are not accretive. Publicly traded buyers will almost always state that any acquisition must be accretive. This is part of their acquisition criteria. However a buyer will break this rule if an acquisition truly adds strategic value or a key technology. A strategic acquisition may not add to earnings immediately but it will increase earnings over the long term by enabling the buyer to take advantage of new technologies or to enter new markets.

SUMMARY

Intangible companies are interesting creatures. In this chapter we reviewed the reasons why these types of companies sell and we noted that intangible companies may be acquired early in their life cycles. Many intangible companies sell because they need additional resources to reach the next level of growth. Since their value is strategic, the timing of the sale with respect to the market is more critical than it is for financially valued companies. The transaction dynamics regarding the sale of small intangible companies are different than those involving larger companies or companies with financial value.

There are a number of widely held beliefs regarding the sale of intangible companies that are more myth than fact. In the next chapter we take a look at these myths and discuss why they are not true.

CHAPTER 2

Debunking the Myths of Selling the Intangible

When I think of myths, the first one that comes to mind is the age old myth that the sun revolves around the earth. As an earthling, this makes sense to me. As one who has studied science, of course, I know the opposite is true. But for purposes of living on the earth, there is not much harm in believing that the sun revolves around our planet. We still say the sun comes up or the sun goes down when in reality the sun is not going anywhere.

Myths regarding the sale of an intangible company however are a different story. Believing in these myths *can* have a negative impact on the situation. These myths are much more subtle. What we mean by myths in this context are the so-called truths that most people believe about the sale process. In this section I point out why these myths are not true and I illustrate how they can have a negative effect on the sale process.

Myths perpetuate in the merger and acquisition field because people do not pause to challenge their assumptions or question established beliefs. This chapter debunks eight myths that surround the sale of intangible companies. They are:

1. The Myth of Intrinsic Value
2. The Myth of a Narrow Value Range
3. The Myth of Revenue Multiples
4. The Myth of Liquidity
5. The Rolodex Myth
6. The Myth of Big Buyers
7. The Myth that Small M&A is like Big M&A
8. The Myth that the CEO Should Sell the Company

THE MYTH OF INTRINSIC VALUE

Myth: The value of a company is intrinsic.
Reality: The value of intangible companies is extrinsic, not intrinsic.

This myth is based on the assumption that a firm's value is intrinsic, that it is a function of the selling company's technology and other assets. The reality is that an intangible company does not have intrinsic value. Value is *extrinsic*, and it exists only in the context to the marketplace. Put another way, the value is simply how much a buyer is willing to pay.

Almost every asset that we own has an intrinsic value: our car, our house, our CD collection. Nonphysical things also have values: a round of golf, a movie, a play, etc. A thing has value if there is a market for those things, and there is a market for most material goods. Craigslist and eBay have created markets for almost everything one can imagine.

The same is not true for a software company, a technology company, or many service companies. A software firm may have spent $10 million developing a specific software application, but if no buyer wants to acquire this software, then the value is zero. The value is what the market is willing to pay.

Intangible companies have a limited number of potential buyers. For intangible companies selling for less than $30 million, there are probably at most five or six companies in the world that are truly good acquirers; 10 at the very most. This is an *extremely* limited number of buyers. This is not enough buyers to call it a market. There will be no market price. And this is why the value range varies dramatically.

Remember that we are talking about strategic transactions, not financial transactions based on profits. For companies with financial value there are many buyers, particularly private equity groups. Private equity groups, or leveraged buyout (LBO) funds as they were formally called, obtain capital from institutional investors to acquire companies. The number of private equity groups has risen dramatically in the last decade. As a result there might be 200 potential buyers for a financial acquisition.

There is no market for technology companies per se. With only five or six legitimate buyers, a market does not exist. As such, there is no market price. Thus, there is no intrinsic value for intangible companies. Value is solely a function of how much a buyer is willing to pay. This leads to our next myth.

THE MYTH OF A NARROW VALUE RANGE

Myth: Value falls within a narrow range.
Reality: The value of an intangible company can vary dramatically.

For most of the assets in our lives a market *does* exist and the value *does* fall within a relatively narrow range. For example, the market value of your house may range between $800,000 and $925,000. The value of your two-year-old BMW 5 Series is from $40,000 to $45,000 depending on the mileage. The range from low to high is relatively small. In these examples the high value is about 15 percent greater than the low value. People are used to value falling within a narrow range.

Now let's consider the value range for an intangible company. The range in price for the sale of an intangible company can be extreme. An intangible company may receive offers of $3 million, $8 million, or $12 million depending on its strategic importance to the buyer. This is a range of 4 times, or 400 percent. Another company may range in value from $60 to $100 million. This is a huge difference.

The reason for this wide range is that the sale of an intangible company is always a strategic deal. A buyer will offer a price that reflects the company's strategic importance to them. The price is not a function of profits, but of how badly the buyer needs the technology and how important the acquisition is to the buyer's growth. As a result, the price can vary widely.

THE MYTH OF REVENUE MULTIPLES

Myth: A multiple of revenues is a good way to value a company.
Reality: Multiples of revenues are totally spurious.

The term multiple of revenue showed up a few years ago and just will not go away. This myth is insidious because it is so easy to calculate. One can calculate this ratio in one's head without too much trouble.

One of the reasons that this myth is so popular is that people love rules of thumb and they dislike uncertainty. The myth is perpetuated by man's need to have a number for value. Human beings are not good at dealing with ambiguity and uncertainty. Not having a value is particularly unsettling to technology types who are highly analytical and are used to coming up with answers. It is discomforting not to have an answer for the value question. So they will do strange things including multiplying revenues in order to appease their need for certainty.

"What is the latest multiple of revenue for a company in our market space?" I am asked this question all the time. This is a bogus metric. You might as well calculate a company's value as a multiple of the average employee weight.

There are four major problems with revenue multiples:

1. The range is too wide to be helpful.
2. The multiple is not comparable to other transactions.
3. The multiple does not consider expenses, pricing, profitability, or growth.
4. There is a limited number of strategic buyers therefore there is no definable market price.

Too Wide a Range

First let's consider the value range. The major problem is that the range is extremely wide. To be useful, a multiple of any kind must fall within a fairly narrow range. Multiples of revenue typically range somewhere between .4 times to 3.5 times revenues. What can one do with this information? How does it help determine value? It is like telling someone their house is worth between $400,000 and $3.5 million. This range is so wide that it is basically useless. A seller would have no idea what price to list their house for.

Not Comparable

Now let's address comparability. The problem is that the multiple from one transaction is not comparable to other transactions. For a multiple of any kind to be useful it must be comparable to other transactions and other companies. And the comparison must be valid. A valid comparison is one in which the companies are very similar. What do I mean by one multiple is not comparable to other transactions? In other words, just because one company sold for 1.5 times its revenues does not mean that another company will also sell for 1.5 times its revenues, even in the same industry.

Let's take the software industry for example. Software companies are not commodities. Even if they operate in the same sector of the market, the companies are typically quite different. In other words, each software company is unique so it is not reasonable to apply the multiple for one company to another company. The buyers are not commodities either. A buyer may have paid a high price for an acquisition because it desperately needed certain software technology. This does not mean that other buyers need to acquire similar technology or that they would be willing to pay a high price.

A software company's primary asset is its proprietary technology and the value of that company will be due to this proprietary software. Whether the revenues are $2 million, $4 million, or $6 million, the software technology is the same. Sure a few more revenue dollars are good; it shows that customers are willing to purchase the software. However, if the company is acquired it will be because of its proprietary technology. The buyer will determine price based on the strategic importance of that technology to them. The buyer does not determine price on the basis of some revenue multiple.

Let's presume that Microsoft had been successful with its acquisition of Intuit, Inc. Intuit is the developer of the checkbook software Quicken. (The U.S. Department of Justice prohibited the transaction from going forward on anticompetitive grounds.) The price would have been 6 times revenues. Does this imply that other checkbook software companies competing with Intuit are also worth 6 times revenues? Actually, had the merger been completed, competitors would probably have a value of about zero. Who could compete with Intuit, especially if it were owned by Microsoft? This valuation reflected the importance of Intuit's market position and installed base to Microsoft. The price was negotiated on this basis. Comparing this revenue multiple to other situations is simply not meaningful. Value is not a function of revenues.

To be useful, a multiple of any kind must be comparable to other companies and other transactions. In the technology and software fields this is simply not the case. Just because one company sold for 3 times revenues does not mean that another company in the same business will sell for 3 times revenues. The value is based on strategic need, not on revenues.

Expenses, Pricing, Profitability, and Growth

Companies have different growth rates, different cost structures, and different pricing structures. Each of these factors will have a substantial impact on the company's value. A multiple of revenue does not include any of these factors. Even within one industry, say the software industry, which is a diverse industry, the companies are not particularly comparable. Comparing a fast-growing company with a slow-growing company is not valid. Neither is comparing a company with older technology to one with new technology.

Comparing companies with dissimilar cost structures is not valid either. Different cost structures will produce different profits and therefore different company values. One simply cannot compare companies with different cost structures and assume they are the same.

Even if two software companies have similar cost structures, they most likely will not have the same pricing structures. Development costs for an application may be similar, but one application may be more valuable in its market sector than a software application in another sector. As a result, the product may command a higher price. The problem it solves may be a more critical problem and a more costly problem, and therefore the higher price is justified. Company Alpha, with a high price for its software, will produce greater profits than Company Beta that has a lower price, even assuming the same cost structures. Thus, Company Alpha and will have significantly greater profits and therefore a greater value.

In a conversation with one CEO regarding revenue multiples I commented on the wide range and comparability problems. The CEO stated that what should be done is to adjust the revenue multiple depending on the company's profitability and rate of growth. Well sure, you can adjust the revenue multiple for profitability, growth rate, and a host of other variables but now it is no longer a multiple of revenues. It has become a made-up number that is comparable to nothing.

Limited Number of Strategic Buyers

There are a limited number of strategic buyers for a specific intangible company. Financial transactions can potentially be sold to one of many hundreds of financial buyers. But a strategic transaction, one in which the value is intangible, has a very limited set of buyers. These buyers are the companies who can truly benefit from that particular strategic asset or technology. Rarely are there any more than five or six good strategic buyers for an intangible company.

Buyers do not have static needs. At one point in time a buyer may have an immediate need for a specific technology. A year or two later it most likely will not have a need for that technology because it will have developed the technology internally or acquired it elsewhere.

Let's take a hypothetical example. If a company that makes antivirus software recently sold for 2.5 times revenues does that mean that your antivirus software company is worth 2.5 times its revenues? Maybe, but maybe not. If other companies need to acquire an antivirus company then there is a good chance you can sell for a similar multiple. However, if all of the best buyers already have antivirus software then there is no market for an antivirus software company. So the last few antivirus software companies will have a very difficult time being acquired, and certainly not for a good price.

How do we resolve the value issue? Well, actually there is no value issue; there is only a price issue. This brings us to one final and important point: a number for value is not necessary for the sale of an intangible company. We do not need a price tag to successfully complete a transaction. We ask the buyers to make offers. We attempt to get as many offers as we can; we negotiate with the buyers, and then we accept the highest offer. My experience has taught me the lesson that this is the best method for successfully selling an intangible company. Multiples of revenue are simply not valid or appropriate.

WAR STORY: WHEN A MULTIPLE OF REVENUES *IS* APPROPRIATE

This was my first attempt to herd cats. I was negotiating a deal to combine six garbage collection companies into one entity in order to compete with Waste Management. Waste Management was coming to town and putting a scare into the local garbage collection companies. The company was changing the industry; it had already made more than 100 acquisitions.

When Waste Management came to town it offered to acquire any garbage route for 20 times monthly revenues. It did not matter how many trucks the route used, how old the trucks were, how many men per truck there were, or what the overhead was. They were simply offering 20 times monthly revenues for a company. They were really after the routes or the customer bases. After a company was acquired, Waste Management would operate the business according to its own practices and impose its own cost structure. As such, the multiple of revenues *was* an appropriate measure of value. Waste Management was not really acquiring a business, but rather a garbage route.

As a side note, this herding of cats business does not work so well. These garbage operators are extremely independent. We never could get all six operators to agree on the best way to move forward. Eventually two of the garbage companies merged and combined operations. Later on this firm acquired one of the other garbage collection operators and the company ultimately achieved significant profitability.

THE MYTH OF LIQUIDITY

Myth: When a company sells, its shareholders achieve liquidity.
Reality: The sale of an intangible company may not be a liquidity event.

In the sale of many intangible companies shareholders may not receive cash, but rather stock from the acquiring company. Many acquirers of intangible companies are privately held firms. Even if the acquirer is publicly held there may be restrictions on the stock so that it cannot be sold for some time. If the shareholders of the selling company receive shares of privately held stock, they will not be able to sell the stock, at least for a period of years until the company goes public or is itself acquired.

Many times, investors, particularly individual investors, prefer to receive stock instead of cash. They would like their investment to continue to increase in value. Plus, wealthy investors do not actually need the money back.

In one transaction that I completed, the selling shareholders received shares of stock in the buyer which was a privately held company. The buyer was an exceptional company and was growing rapidly. The selling shareholders were happy to receive shares in this firm because it looked like the stock would appreciate. In this case the seller sold for a price that was less than the amount that the investors had invested. So when the transaction closed it was not cause for a big celebration.

Two years later the buyer was acquired at a very attractive price. The investors in the original selling company recognized a return of 3 times the value of their shares, so, overall the shareholders doubled their money. (Here is the math: $3 million invested. The company sold for $2 million of the buyer's stock. The buyer's stock rose in value by 3 times. So when the buyer was sold, the investors' shares were worth $6 million. So the investors doubled the value of their original $3 million investment.) It took an extra two years but the shareholders were happy to stay invested and achieve a much higher return.

THE ROLODEX MYTH

Myth: Contacts and relationships are the key to selling a company.
Reality: Contacts are the easy part; getting the deal closed is the hard part.

There is a pervasive myth that contacts and relationships or "knowing a space" is the key to success in selling a company. I am frequently asked: "Do you have any contacts in the XYZ industry?" or "What space have you worked in lately?" Many CEOs, boards of directors, and VCs mistakenly believe that successfully closing transactions is all about contacts and relationships. The reality is that success results from exceptional deal skills, disciplined execution of the process, and experience in getting transactions closed.

To some degree this myth may be perpetuated by the large New York investment banks. A key element of their sales pitch is that they have access to the CEOs and decision makers of the potential buyers. The large investment banks sell their services in this manner, touting their contacts and relationships. This may well be true for deals over $100 million, but it is not true for sub-30 deals.

The large investment banks are organized along industry lines: there is the telecommunications group, the semiconductor group, the consumer goods group, the manufacturing group, etc. Each of these industry groups is a like a private club and having connections with the right people is important. The banker has access to management and good relationships are beneficial. This is a key part of their pitch.

The landscape for deals under $30 million is an entirely different situation. The software and technology market space is like the Wild West. The landscape is huge and things are changing rapidly. Companies sprout up all the time; companies are acquired, and companies go out of business. Many of the CEOs who were running the companies three years ago are long gone.

The sub-30 acquisition marketplace is no private club. Rapid movement and blurry market sectors are the rule, not the exception. Access is not a problem. CEOs of technology companies are interested in knowing which companies are for sale. They will respond if they are interested. Making the contact is simply not the problem.

Can contacts and relationships help? Sure, of course they are helpful. However, the key competencies that an investment banker brings to a transaction include executing a disciplined process, overcoming the difficulties that arise, negotiating the deal, and driving the transaction to a successful conclusion. Making contacts is the easy part.

WAR STORY: THE SHORT HALF-LIFE OF CONTACTS

Let me give you an example that illustrates the short half-life of contacts. A few years ago, I sold a company in the network security market. About 20 months later I received a call from one of the potential buyers that I had contacted earlier. They had decided to sell their company and they engaged my firm to handle the transaction. This new assignment was in the exact same market space that I had examined less than two years earlier.

As I moved forward with the transaction I discovered that two-thirds of my original contacts were gone. Either the people had changed

(Continued)

jobs or the companies were gone. A third of the companies had been acquired, merged, or had gone out of business. For those that remained, my contacts were no longer working at about half of the companies. Looking at it another way, only 30 percent of my contacts were still in place 20 months later.

A sidebar to the Rolodex myth is the mini-myth of "knowing a space." The issue is that tech founders and CEOs think that industry knowledge is a primary driver for achieving success in closing a transaction. Once again, this may be true for the big deals but it is not true for sub-30 deals.

One of an investment banker's primary skills is knowing how to drill down into an industry, to quickly get up to speed on who the players are, who is growing rapidly, who is experiencing problems, etc. All industries have these dynamics. The experienced investment banker understands these dynamics even though the details may differ from sector to sector. Bankers are highly skilled at researching and analyzing market sectors. The banker gathers the requisite industry knowledge as he researches the industry, identifies companies, and puts together a list of potential buyers.

Transactions fall apart all the time. There are far more failed transactions than successful transactions. Deals are completed successfully because of superior deal skills, not contacts and relationships or knowing a space. Getting a transaction closed—in which one party wants to get the highest price and the other party wants to pay the lowest price—requires strong deal skills.

Deal skills involve knowing how to work with different types of people; how to read people, how to respond to them, how to question them, how to work with their egos, how to motivate them, how to tell when they are stretching the truth, and how to negotiate the best price. Industry knowledge is important; however the banker gathers the detailed industry knowledge as he progresses with the transaction process. A rich background of experience, however, produces the comprehensive set of deal skills that successfully solve the problems and get the transaction closed at the best price.

THE MYTH OF BIG BUYERS

Myth: Big companies are the best buyers.
Reality: Smaller buyers are the best buyers for intangible companies.

This myth is the belief that big companies are the best buyers. The reality is that this is the exception rather than the rule. Big buyers are the best buyers for large transactions but they are not good buyers for small transactions.

Big buyers (companies with revenues greater than $500 million) are certainly the best prospective acquirers for a transaction greater than $100 million in value. Big buyers may also be good candidates to acquire a company with $30 million to $100 million in transaction value. However most acquisitions of intangible companies are for less than $100 million and the vast majority are for less than $30 million.

For many sellers, ego plays a role in the desire to sell to a large buyer. A technology entrepreneur would much rather tell his friends or his golf buddies, "I sold to Google," or "I sold to Amazon," than he would, "I sold to arcPlan or Systems Union." There is nothing wrong with a little ego in this area, but the danger is that it can lead sellers down the wrong path.

The best buyers for a company with a value of less than $30 million are companies with revenues of $25 million to $175 million. The primary reason is that a small acquisition will be important to them. They will care about an additional $5 million or $10 million in revenues. Every $50 million company wants to be a $100 million company. And every $125 million company wants to be a $200 million company. A $1 billion company will rarely care about acquiring a company with $5 million or $10 million in revenue. It is simply immaterial to them. If a very large company does acquire a very small company it is for one reason: the seller has essential technology that the buyer needs.

Another reason that the myth of big buyers persists is because the big buyers are obvious. They stand out. The sellers have heard of them. Smaller buyers are less well-known; they are not obvious or noticeable. In one quarter to one third of the transactions that I have completed, the seller was not aware of the buyer. In the sale of an intangible company the best buyers are usually small companies or midsized companies, not large companies.

THE MYTH THAT SMALL M&A IS LIKE BIG M&A

Myth: The sale process for small transactions is the same as for large transactions.
Reality: The process for selling a sub-30 company is not the same as that used for large transactions.

Many venture capitalists and technology CEOs assume that small M&A is similar to large M&A. Many of these players have experience in the big

M&A arena, either from working for a Wall Street investment bank or from working at a large technology company like Cisco, Intel, or Computer Associates. They know how big M&A is done. They assume small deals are just like the big deals, but with a few less zeros. Why would small deals be any different? A deal is a deal. Well, that is simply not the case. Sub-30 deals are very different.

The two-step auction process works well for transactions greater than $30 million. The sale moves forward at a well-defined pace and a transaction can generally be concluded in a reasonable time frame. The universe of buyers is much smaller for large deals, maybe 30 or 40 companies, whereas on a small transaction it may be smart to contact 125 potential buyers. The auction process is a successful method when companies are profitable. A smaller company may have minimal profits but excellent technology. These types of deals do not lend themselves to the auction process. Small transactions are more customized. In addition, smaller buyers do not have the in-house M&A resources to easily respond to the auction process. In the next chapter we will examine the two-step auction process in more depth.

THE MYTH THAT THE CEO SHOULD SELL THE COMPANY

Myth: CEOs assume they are the best person to sell their companies.
Reality: A CEO should never sell his own company.

Many CEOs believe that it is their job to negotiate and sell their companies—they know their market space, they know their company, and they like doing things themselves. CEOs typically contact only a small set of buyers. They think they know at the outset who the best buyers are and they rarely reach out to adjacent markets to contact the nonobvious buyers.

Selling a company is a full-time endeavor. A CEO cannot execute a comprehensive and disciplined sale process and at the same time run the company effectively. In addition, a CEO cannot be objective about his own company. Negotiating and overcoming the problems that inevitably occur are better handled by an experienced third party. Chapter 10 examines this topic in more depth and I outline 18 reasons why a CEO should never sell his own company.

SUMMARY

The CEO and board of directors of an intangible company that is thinking about selling should be careful about how they think about value. The value of an intangible company is strategic value and it is truly in the eye of the beholder. It is worth whatever the buyer is willing to pay. Strategic value can vary widely depending on how well the buyer can capitalize on the seller's strategic assets.

Do not be deceived by revenue multiples; for most purposes they are irrelevant. Revenue multiples are rarely comparable from one transaction to another and they ignore some key business concepts—profits, pricing, expenses, and growth.

The sale of an intangible company may not be an immediate liquidity event for the shareholders. In many transactions, the stockholders simply trade their shares for the shares of the buyer. Hopefully, this is a good trade and these shares will have a greater chance for appreciation and liquidity.

The best buyers for an intangible company are small and midsized companies, not the larger companies. The negotiated sale is a more effective process for selling a sub-30 intangible company than is the auction process that is used on large transactions. And finally, a CEO should never attempt to sell his own company. He is too close to be objective and he cannot possibly execute a disciplined sale process and run the company effectively at the same time.

Now let's examine the sale process that is most effective for selling an intangible company.

CHAPTER 3

The Sale Process

The merger and acquisition process takes many twists and turns on the road to a successful conclusion. And there can be some surprises as well. Sometimes the surprises are good but most of the time surprises are bad. The key to the sale of any company is applying a disciplined process.

In this chapter we will review the sale process and the typical time frame for a transaction. We will examine the two methods for selling companies—the negotiated sale and the two-step auction—and discuss why one is more effective for the sale of an intangible company. We will also address the issue of confidentiality, always a concern in the sale of a company.

The events play out something like this. Preparing the descriptive memorandum requires about two or three weeks. This document describes the company in moderate detail. The investment banker typically drafts this document with input from the management team. The next step is to build a database of likely buyers. The number may range from 50 to 150 buyers depending on the market. The next task is to contact these companies regarding the acquisition opportunity. This part of the process can take from two to five months depending on the breadth of search.

The objective is to uncover several interested buyers who will want to investigate the company and eventually make offers. The buyers will usually present a letter of intent that summarizes the basic terms of the deal. If the seller accepts the terms, the buyer will begin its due diligence—an in-depth review of the company's business, financial statements, contracts, and legal documents. The final step involves the buyer's attorneys drafting the legal agreements that define the detailed terms of sale. At closing the documents are signed, the money is transferred, and the deal is done.

MAKE SURE THE SELLER UNDERSTANDS
THE PROCESS

It is important that the seller understand the process as clearly as possible prior to moving forward with the sale of company. I always encourage my clients to ask me as many questions as they feel are necessary in order to fully understand the process. What follows are a handful of basic questions that every seller should ask their investment banker. Remember that there are no right or wrong questions. The best questions are those that help the seller to understand and get comfortable with the transaction process. At the outset, almost everyone will have a slightly different idea about how the sale process works.

Questions sellers should ask about the process:

- What is the load on management? How much time is required of the management team? When do we get involved?
- How do you set a price range for the company?
- Do you plan to contact our competitors? If so, when?
- What and when should we tell our employees?
- How should we handle confidentiality?
- What is the transaction time line?
- What preparation is necessary for meetings with buyers?
- Should we give potential buyers our conservative forecast or our stretch forecast?

THE NEGOTIATED SALE

The negotiated sale is the most effective process for selling intangible companies when the purchase price is less than $30 million. In a negotiated sale, the investment banker contacts and negotiates with each company as if it were the only buyer. The banker provides each buyer with the information that it requests. The seller must be somewhat flexible and bend to the buyers' time and resource constraints.

This process may take place over varying time frames. A couple of buyers may respond right away and start the process rolling. Other buyers may respond later on. Typically, there will be two, three, or possibly as many as six companies who will respond with a high degree of interest. The goal is to get offers in at somewhat near the same time frame, but this is not always possible.

The best buyers for a small intangible company are usually not the big firms. A small acquisition of $5 million or $15 million will be much more important to a smaller buyer, one with revenues between $25 million and $175 million. These smaller firms are usually not experienced acquirers.

This is a summary of the negotiated sale approach:

1. Package the company. Identify and describe the company's strengths clearly and accurately, both in the descriptive memorandum and in phone calls, e-mails, and meetings.
2. Identify and contact all the potential buyers. Employ discipline and creativity in pursuing more than just the likely buyers.
3. Execute a disciplined process for following up and moving the buyers forward.
4. Negotiate by understanding the strategic implications of the acquisition for each buyer.
5. Endeavor to get multiple offers at the same point in time. Take the highest offer.

Package the Company

Putting your best foot forward is essential when selling a company. It is also extremely important to be as accurate as possible when describing the company, its products, its customers, and any other strengths. Sometimes it can be surprisingly difficult to describe a company clearly. This is particularly true for a company that offers a service rather than a product to its customers.

One of the investment banker's roles is to examine the company in light of the market. What strengths does the company have that acquirers are likely to be interested in? It is important to emphasize the seller's key strengths. A company's management is usually not objective in viewing its own products and services in the context of the market. As the investment banker moves forward with the process, he can provide valuable feedback to management about how the market views the company.

It is important to update the company's web site and ensure that it clearly and accurately describes the company's business. The web site is one of the first places a buyer will look to learn about a target. Most buyers will check out the company's web site before they will read the descriptive memorandum that describes the company. Many web sites are out-of-date or place the wrong emphasis on certain products or services. If the web site is not clear and accurate, the buyer may develop an incorrect view of the company's business. The web site is a buyer's first impression of the selling company. I always insist that the seller review and upgrade the content of its web site before we make contact with potential buyers.

One of my pet peeves in trying to learn about a company is going to their web site and finding out that they are "a global solutions provider whose solutions help their customers become more profitable through the application of software technology." This has absolutely no meaning. Every company is a now a global solutions provider. Many web sites have become so general and so bland that they are not at all helpful. I often start a conversation by asking the president to describe what his company does. He usually responds with, "Didn't you go to our web site?" My answer is, "Yes, that's why I am asking what your company does." But that is another book.

Draft the Descriptive Memorandum

The first step in the sale of a company is to draft a descriptive memorandum. This document summarizes most of the important information about the company. The descriptive memorandum may or may not contain confidential information. The issue of confidentiality is discussed later in this chapter.

The descriptive memorandum is designed to inform potential buyers about the seller's business. It includes all of the basic information about the company: its products and services, technology, markets, customers, and distribution channels. It summarizes the backgrounds of the management team and usually includes a summary of financial information. Generally, it is a good idea to include the history of the company so that the buyer has some understanding of how it got to where it is today.

In portraying the company's products and services it is critical to not only describe what the product does or what the service involves, but also to point out the specific benefit that the customer receives. It is important to explain why the customer cannot obtain these benefits through other means.

The memorandum is no place for vague descriptions and benefits as I have seen on many company web sites. I have been surprised at how many times buyers have an incorrect idea about the selling company's products or services. I thought the memorandum was perfectly clear but in retrospect it obviously was not. When I begin the sale of a company, I go to great lengths to make sure that I am describing it completely and accurately.

There are two general approaches to confidentiality when drafting the descriptive memorandum. The first, and one that I have found quite effective, is not to include confidential information in the descriptive memorandum. It describes the company and its business and includes sections describing the strengths and opportunities for the company. Confidential information, such as complete financial statements, can be provided to potential buyers later in the process and after a nondisclosure agreement has been signed. The advantage of this approach is that basic information can be communicated without the hassles associated with nondisclosure agreements.

With a higher level of confidentiality, all of the information in the descriptive memorandum is treated as confidential. In this instance, a potential buyer will not receive the descriptive memorandum until after it has signed a nondisclosure agreement. The drawback of this approach is that it slows the process down and makes it more cumbersome.

One of the aspects of the descriptive memorandum that I have found to be quite effective is to keep the document relatively short and easy to read. By short I mean 20 to 25 pages at the maximum. Easy to read means using 1.5 line spacing so that a buyer can easily review the document and gain a quick understanding of what the company does and why it is successful in its markets.

Sometimes the investment banker may draft two different versions of the descriptive memorandum. This is done when targeting buyers in two different markets. Each memorandum emphasizes different aspects of the seller's capabilities or technology and how the company's products or services can be targeted to those specific markets.

Identify and Contact Buyers

Once the memorandum is completed, the focus shifts to identifying and researching companies that might be good buyers. The investment banker will begin building a list of potential acquirers. The company often contributes to this list of buyers, suggesting companies that management is familiar with in the seller's markets. The investment banker identifies a wide range of buyers and assesses why each might be a good acquirer.

Buyers can come in many shapes and forms and it is important to recognize that the target may be a good fit for a variety of buyers. Creativity and imagination are helpful traits in keeping an open mind for likely buyers. Chapter 5 examines in more detail the process of identifying and contacting buyers; however, I review it briefly here to illustrate the sequence of the sale process.

The approach that I have found to be most effective is to cast a wide net, and then work diligently to cull the list so that you end up with a handful of well-qualified buyers. This very disciplined and rigorous process will succeed in any market space. Using this approach, I have a very high degree of confidence that all of the best buyers will have been contacted. No stone has been left unturned and we have not tried to "outthink" the market with preconceived ideas about who the best buyers are.

The search for buyers generally falls into three groups. The first group of buyers includes the obvious candidates and a handful of buyers in the core market. The second group of buyers is identified by digging into closely related markets. The third group is made up of buyers who are identified later in the process. These are probably the least obvious of the buyers and they are discovered by examining smaller niche markets that are on the periphery.

The process of identifying and contacting buyers continues for several months. We arrange conference calls and meetings to keep the process moving forward and we always attempt to get offers from multiple buyers so that the process becomes competitive.

Execute a Disciplined Process

Executing a disciplined process is essential for moving the transaction forward in a timely manner. When a buyer responds that it is interested, I will forward the descriptive memorandum. If the descriptive memorandum is confidential then I forward a nondisclosure agreement. After the buyer has reviewed the memorandum it will request additional information. Most buyers need to be prodded along in the process. Buyers typically have plenty to do and showing them an acquisition is just one more thing that they need to spend time on. Therefore, part of my role as an investment banker is to keep the process moving forward and make the acquisition a higher priority for the buyer.

The next step is arranging conference calls with the selling company. Typically, the first call is between the CEO of the buyer and the CEO of the seller. This call usually discusses general information about the seller as well as market issues. Who are your customers? How big is the market? Where do you see the growth in this market?

The second phone call takes place a week or two later. This call typically comes from the chief technology officer (CTO) of the buyer who will call the CTO of the seller to discuss issues concerning the technology. The next step in the process is usually a meeting at the offices of the selling company. If confidentiality is an issue, this meeting may take place off site.

This is a typical process for the sale of an intangible company. The process demands a high degree of discipline and thoroughness to make sure that it moves along at a timely pace and that all potential buyers are contacted.

The sale process is an imperfect one. Sometimes it can be messy. Occasionally a very good buyer will respond that they are interested late in the process. At this point, this buyer is well behind the time line of the other buyers. Now the timing is off and the investment banker has to juggle and improvise in order to get competitive offers within the same approximate time frame.

Prepare Financial Forecasts

When providing financial forecasts be sure that they are realistic and achievable. These should not be the financial forecasts from an old business plan that show the company growing from zero to $200 million in revenue in five years. The projections must be believable to the buyer. Projections should be based on historically accurate information combined with the revenue improvement and cost savings due to a particular buyer. In addition, be sure to state the assumptions that underlie the financial forecast.

Aggressive projections can bite back. In one transaction that I was involved in, the seller sent a prospective buyer a copy of the projected income statements for the next two years. The revenue projections were quite aggressive, targeting 25 percent growth per year. The buyer was interested and made a trip to meet with the company. In the meeting, the buyer remarked that the revenue growth was only half of the forecasted amount. Revenues may have been up 13 percent but they were 50 percent below plan. As a result, the buyer lost confidence in the seller and the transaction fell apart.

When selling an intangible company sometimes it is a good practice to prepare separate financial forecasts for each buyer. The reason why you should do this is that each buyer will have different strengths that the selling company can leverage when moving forward. One buyer may have excellent sales and distribution capabilities that the selling company can take advantage of. Another buyer may have an international presence that the selling company can exploit. Thus, the revenue forecast will vary from buyer to buyer depending on the synergies. The same is true for expenses. Operating expenses may be less if the company is acquired by one buyer than another buyer.

THE TYPICAL TIME FRAME FOR A DEAL

How long does it take to close a deal? Generally, six to seven months is a reasonable estimate of the required time to close the transaction. The time line can be a little shorter than that if buyers are responsive and are quick about making decisions and performing their due diligence. If there are problems, the deal can take longer, into the nine-month time frame.

One of the most frustrating problems in trying to move a deal forward is when one or two of the good buyers cannot respond in a timely manner. This happens because another issue is of a higher priority. For example, the company may be in the middle of another acquisition and its M&A team cannot devote time to this transaction. Even if the company has recently completed an acquisition, the company will not be able to consider another acquisition until the first one is digested. Sometimes the management team is distracted for other reasons. They might have just lost a major customer and are fighting to keep revenues up. In the case when a good buyer cannot move forward, the investment banker has to bite the bullet and move on. If a buyer cannot respond in a timely fashion, you have to move ahead without them. I have seen many CEOs become disappointed when this is the case but there is simply nothing that can be done about it.

At the other extreme, of course, there is no maximum time frame. In my experience, the longest a transaction took to close was 18 months. I also closed several transactions that took 15 months. In each case, there was an unusual event or a problem that upset the process and extended the time line. In a few situations the original buyer backed out at the last minute and the process had to be restarted. In another case, the seller lost a major customer that accounted for a third of its revenues. Events like these drive home the point about the importance of having multiple offers or at least one or two backup offers.

A good milestone in the time line occurs at the 10-week point. At this point I generally have a fairly good idea of who the best buyers are and how important the transaction is to them. By the end of 14 to 16 weeks the seller will have a very good idea of where the transaction stands. The seller will know which companies are interested in moving forward and will have an indication of the seriousness of their interest. The seller may even have received a letter of intent from one buyer.

What about doing a transaction quickly? How fast is a fast transaction? I have closed a couple of transactions in about 90 days. The time frame for the first transaction was exactly 90 days from the date I was retained to the date the seller received its cash. The second transaction took a few weeks longer. The lesson to learn from these transactions is that a deal can be concluded rapidly if it is absolutely necessary. In each of these transactions we did not achieve top dollar but the deal was concluded quickly and that was the shareholder's objective. Figure 3.1 shows a typical time line for the sale of an intangible company.

ANOTHER APPROACH: THE TWO-STEP AUCTION

The negotiated sale is particularly effective when selling companies for less than $30 million and when the value is strategic or intangible. The second method for selling companies is the two-step auction process, which is used in larger transactions, greater than $30 million in transaction size.

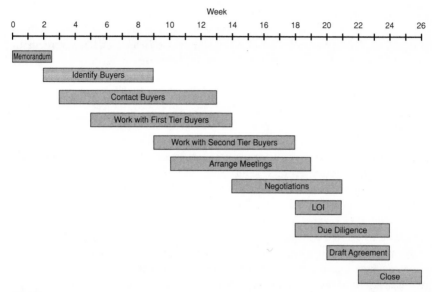

FIGURE 3.1 Typical Transaction Time Line

In the two-step auction process the investment bank sends information to probable buyers and asks for an indication of interest and a value range by a certain date. This method involves strict timing. Offers are required to be sent in by a specific date.

Once the preliminary offers are received, the investment bank selects the handful of buyers with the highest value ranges. Those companies proceed with due diligence in order to make final offers. At this point the selling company provides additional information to the group of good buyers.

A data room is utilized to facilitate this process. In earlier years the data room was a physical room (often in a hotel) crammed with boxes brimming with confidential documents and information about the selling company. The logistics were tricky because rival bidders wanted to keep their identities secret. Virtual data rooms are utilized now. Information can be accessed online and documents exchanged over the Internet. This is an easy way to give buyers access to all of the pertinent information regarding the seller.

A number of prospective buyers will be invited to enter the second round of bidding. These buyers will likely visit the company, tour the facilities, and meet with management. After the group of buyers has had time to review the due diligence information, they are asked to make a final bid. The investment bank sends a letter to the short list of buyers outlining the bidding procedures. A sample purchase agreement is usually included with the letter. Any changes to the purchase agreement are considered in the context of the bid. In other words, if a buyer wants to change the purchase terms, it will affect the attractiveness of its bid.

After the buyer is selected, the parties sign the purchase agreement and the closing takes place within a month or two. A two-step auction process typically takes between four and five months to complete.

There are a few variations on the auction theme. A modified auction solicits interest from a smaller group of buyers. Buyers are rated very high, high, medium, and low according to their perceived interest level. In another type of modified auction, only 10 to 15 companies are contacted.

The auction process turns off some buyers. An auction often makes buyers jump through hoops, so to speak, and buyers may feel that they are in danger of overpaying. It is not a perfect process; however, it can get a transaction completed in a very reasonable time frame.

The two-step auction process works well for large companies and for medium-sized companies with operating earnings greater than $3 million. In these situations the likely buyers are also large companies with dedicated acquisition teams. They can afford to spend the time and resources to evaluate a potential acquisition.

The auction process does not work well for transactions under $30 million in value. First of all, a buyer cannot make a realistic preliminary offer for a strategic acquisition. Unless the buyer is already very familiar with the seller, there is no way the buyer can assess the strategic value without an in-depth evaluation of the target. Secondly, the buyers for sub-30 transactions are small and midsized companies and do not have M&A teams or other devoted resources to respond to the time strictures of the auction process. The CEO is usually involved in any acquisition and his time is limited. I have tried the auction process on small transactions and it is simply not effective. It is difficult to get buyers to interrupt their businesses in order to give us a bid by a certain time deadline.

Investment bankers who try to run an auction process on small deals are trying to put a round peg into a square hole. The optimal price and terms are not achieved for the client. Do not assume that the process that works for large deals is also best for smaller deals. The negotiated sale is definitely more work than the two-step auction; however, it is the best way to complete a transaction at the highest price and the best terms.

WAR STORY: OFFERS IN BY FRIDAY

In this transaction the sale process was moving forward but not particularly fast. Our client was a software company that had yet to achieve profitability. It had developed software to resolve several issues in supply chain management and had made traction in the market with two major customers. The company had limited revenues and was burning cash each month. The venture capitalist had lost faith in management and wanted to sell the company.

We identified a handful of potential buyers but they were taking their time about moving forward. The venture capitalist decided she wanted to get things moving more quickly so she instructed me to get all of the offers in by a week from Friday. I had my doubts, but she was the client so I respected her wishes and proceeded to try to get offers in over the next week and a half.

I contacted each buyer and told them that we would like to receive their offers by a week from Friday. A week and a half went by and when Friday came around guess how many offers we received? Zero. Our client was not exactly what you might call "the prettiest girl at the dance." We could not command the attention of busy software companies and compel them to react to our time constraints.

The auction method works well for large profitable companies but it is not effective for sub-30 deals with limited profitability. The VC understood the process for selling a large company but mistakenly tried to impose that process on a smaller transaction.

THE RESTART

A restart is required when only one buyer has proceeded down the path towards closing and the deal goes awry. Usually this is because the buyer walked away at the last minute. There could be any number of explanations. The buyer could have gotten cold feet, it may have been unable to raise financing, or it may have experienced management changes. If the buyer is venture capital backed, the venture firm may not be supportive of the acquisition. There could be any number of reasons. If the transaction blows up late in the game the process must be restarted.

If there were multiple buyers early in the transaction time line then it is relatively straightforward to go back and try to negotiate a deal with one or more of these companies. If there were no other viable buyers then the sale process must be restarted. Sometimes this means delving into the market in a different way. It could also involve investigating related markets in greater depth to uncover new potential acquirers. If enough time has gone by and the market is fast-moving, a few of the smaller firms may have expanded fast enough to be viable acquirers. I have worked on a number of transactions in which I had to become extremely creative in exploring markets and uncovering new buyers.

It is always nice when deals go together smoothly and in a timely manner. Unfortunately, this is not always the reality when selling an intangible company. I have had to work on several restarts over the years. These deals required a significant amount of additional effort. The good news is that in each case a deal was successfully concluded and the shareholders were happy with the results, although they had to wait a little longer for their payout.

WAR STORY: A SUCCESSFUL RESTART

This deal went sideways the week before closing. The seller was Buttonware, one of the original PC software companies and their flagship product was *PC File*. As Windows began to gain broader acceptance, the founder (known as the father of shareware) wanted to retire. He had been at the game for a long time and his doctor advised that given his heart condition, retiring would be a good idea.

At the time there were only a handful of database companies in the market, none of which wanted to acquire Buttonware. So the search took on a more creative aspect. One of the companies that I uncovered was a young and successful antivirus software company called McAfee Associates. Why would an antivirus software company want to acquire a database company? John McAfee was a brilliant and creative man who thought that Buttonware's new Windows product, *Buttonfile*, would be an excellent product for the network administrators, who were McAfee's primary customers, to keep track of the various software programs that their companies owned.

The transaction moved smoothly towards closing. The due diligence was done, the documents were drafted and closing was set for one week away. McAfee Associates had recently hired a new CEO and one of his first decisions was to nix the Buttonware deal. It did not fit their new strategy, he said. So that was the end of that. I had to restart the process and try to find a good buyer for Buttonware. Eventually we closed a transaction with a Texas software company that owned a variety of software products and Buttonware's software would complement their offerings. The transaction eventually closed and Buttonware's founder got to retire. The time from start to finish—one year and three months. Sometimes stuff just happens and you have to deal with it.

HOW TO HANDLE CONFIDENTIALITY

Confidentiality is one of the key issues that must be addressed in the sale of any company. CEOs of companies are always concerned about confidentiality, sometimes overly so. A company should consider three aspects with respect to confidentiality. The first is confidentiality with respect to employees. A seller does not want its employees to leave or to become nervous or ineffective at their jobs. In addition, they want their employees to stay with the company and not be out seeking other employment.

The second aspect of confidentiality is with respect to customers. A selling company does not want to lose customers during the sale process. They also do not want to lose any potential new sales because of rumors about the company being sold.

The third aspect regarding confidentiality influences the decision on when and how much information to disclose to potential buyers. Another danger is that competitors may learn important information about the company. A nondisclosure agreement (NDA) can protect the company to some degree. The best way to keep truly confidential information from a potential buyer is to not disclose it to them until it is absolutely necessary.

The best way to handle confidentiality will differ from company to company and situation to situation. Confidentiality applies to a company's financial statements, technology, and trade secrets. Sometimes even the fact that the company is seeking to be acquired is confidential. There is a balance to be achieved between keeping the sale as confidential as possible and managing the sale process efficiently.

My typical recommendation is not to make the descriptive memorandum confidential. Most of the descriptive information about a company is not confidential anyway. Many potential buyers can be weeded out before confidential information truly needs to be disclosed.

In most of the transactions that I have completed, the NDA was not signed until after the buyer reviewed the descriptive memorandum and determined that it wanted to examine the acquisition in more depth. A serious buyer will certainly want to review the financial statements and detailed information about the technology and intellectual property. Both parties should sign a nondisclosure agreement at this stage so that proprietary information can be provided to the buyer.

Using a NDA too early in the process can create obstacles. The lawyers can get bogged down in the details of the NDA. We explore nondisclosure agreements in greater depth later in this chapter.

Communicating with Employees

The first decision that a company needs to make with respect to confidentiality is when to inform its employees. There are two schools of thought here. Some companies conduct the sale in a very open manner; others prefer complete secrecy until the deal is done. There are pros and cons for each approach. It is less disturbing to the company operations to maintain secrecy for as long as possible. However, employees should certainly be told about the sale before the due diligence period begins.

The best advice I can give a CEO is to make this decision based on the level of trust and the relationship that he or she has with the employees. Some CEOs will tell their full management teams early on in the process. Others will wait until much later in the process and then may confide in only a few individuals. It really depends on how close the CEO is to his people and the relationship he or she has with them. For most companies it is fairly clear which management people should be confided in early in the process.

Communicating with the Outside World

First, it is important to understand that after the transaction has been completed, both customers and employees will be better off. The company will be on stronger footing. It will have greater resources behind it and will be a more stable firm. The company will usually have greater access to capital. There will be less risk. This outcome benefits both employees and customers.

Informing customers is a judgment call on management's part. It is probably best to inform key customers, ones who account for a large percentage of the seller's revenues. Small customers do not need to be notified early on. However, should a customer hear a rumor and inquire about a sale, it is usually best to be truthful with the customer.

CEOs are often very concerned that prospective customers will get wind of the potential sale and therefore not purchase the company's products or services. Competitors may spread rumors in order to win the sale. This is one of the hazards of the sale process. Typically, the problem is not as bad as most CEOs believe. I think CEOs find the uncertainty of the situation more unsettling than the realistic prospect of customers leaving en masse. If the firm loses a few sales because of market rumors, the company will survive. The CEO needs to realize that in six months the company will have a new owner and it will be in a stronger position.

In one transaction that I was involved in management contacted a small group of key customers and told them early on of the company's plans for sale. Over the years management had worked closely with these customers to solve their software issues. They knew them well and a relationship of trust had been established. This was a good move on management's part. The good relationship between the seller and the customers paid off and the buyer developed a high degree of comfort that the customers would remain with the company.

An alternate way to handle the confidentiality issue is to position the transaction not as a sale but as a financing or corporate partnering transaction. A customer may ask management about the sale rumor. The simplest and most straightforward answer to the customer's question is to deflect it with a reference to financing or partnering such as, "Yes, we are looking for financing to fund our growth and one of the alternatives that we are considering is corporate partnering." The financing or corporate partnering angle simply gives the CEO a way to handle the question in case the subject comes up. In most cases when contacting buyers it is best to state that the company is seeking to be acquired.

If a CEO has strong feelings about the issue, I may proceed with a transaction by posturing it as a partnering situation. It is likely that a potential buyer will ask if the company would consider a sale. Some buyers may recognize immediately that any company that is seeking a corporate partnering transaction may also be open to selling. This tactic is advisable for the first communication that goes out to potential buyers, usually an e-mail or a letter. In a telephone communication it is less important to couch the sale in terms of a corporate partnering transaction. This tactic helps squelch rumors about a sale.

Competitors are the potential buyers that are most likely to spread rumors or cause trouble in the marketplace. So, it is best not to rock the boat until absolutely necessary. Competitors should usually be contacted later in the deal process. Sometimes the banker can wait as long as a month or two after contacting other buyers before contacting competitors.

Rumors always abound. Rightly or wrongly, rumors are constantly surfacing. Some are true and some are false. Rumors can proliferate even when a company has absolutely no intention of selling, so the best thing that management can do is be prepared when a rumor pops up and have an answer that addresses it.

Working with Full Confidentiality

If a company has major and legitimate concerns about confidentiality, the process can be handled on a fully confidential basis. With full confidentiality a potential buyer must sign a nondisclosure agreement before receiving any information about the selling company. Early communications describe the company only in general terms and the name of the seller is not disclosed. It is significantly more difficult to generate interest with such an approach because on the first contact potential buyers will have only a vague notion of what the company is. Moreover, the transaction is more unwieldy if there are strict confidentiality hoops to jump through. In the cases when full confidentiality is warranted the company and its investment bankers must simply put up with the inconvenience.

Why would a company be so concerned and insist upon full confidentiality? One of the main reasons for full confidentiality is to guard against employees leaving if they suspect the company is for sale. Most of the time full confidentiality is not a good way to go. It is too cumbersome and it slows the deal process down dramatically. It can add as much as four to eight weeks to the time line.

WAR STORY: WHEN FULL CONFIDENTIALITY IS IMPORTANT

At the time of this transaction, the industry situation was such that there was full employment in the software industry. A good software designer had no trouble getting a job and one that paid well. My client wanted to go to great lengths to keep his employees. He did not want to scare them or have them out looking for other jobs. The employees were the firm's primary asset. The company thought it would lose significant value if it lost some of its key engineers to competitors.

The firm was in a highly competitive market space and good software design engineers were difficult to find. The worry was that if competitors found out the company was for sale they would hire away the key software engineers. I recommended that the company inform key employees and put in place stay-put bonuses. A stay-put bonus rewards employees (usually with cash) for remaining with the company through the transaction period, usually six to nine months. However the president wanted to keep the sale information confidential for as long as he possibly could. No employees were notified and we went forward on a fully confidential basis.

In this situation full confidentiality kept the process confidential for a longer period of time. After several months the employees heard rumors and did ask management about the sale situation. The employees were a little miffed at not being confided in but it did keep the transaction confidential for a longer time.

Using Nondisclosure Agreements (NDAs)

Typically, the selling company utilizes an NDA provided by its attorney or investment banker. Although NDAs are standard agreements, there are always clauses that one buyer or another will want to change. Smaller buyers (with less than about $100 million in revenue) typically have no problem signing the seller's NDA as is. A larger company will always run it by their legal department and there will always be modifications. In many cases, a large buyer will want to use its own NDA, not the one provided by the seller.

This poses a problem because now the seller's attorney must review each NDA that is returned with changes or review the buyer's NDA. This slows the process down because two or three weeks might pass before an NDA is actually signed by both parties.

There are two types of NDAs: one-way and two-way. In a one-way NDA the buyer promises it will not disclose information about the selling company. In a two-way NDA, also called a mutual NDA, each party promises that it will not disclose confidential information of the other party. The mutual NDA is more apt to be needed when the purchaser will be using its stock as the acquisition currency. In this case the seller will want to see the buyer's financial statements and other information that outlines the growth prospects for the company. In essence the seller is becoming an investor in the buyer.

Most nondisclosure agreements state that the potential buyer will not disclose confidential information to others. It does not prevent them from using this information in-house. The primary worry regarding confidentiality is that the potential buyers will use this information internally, not that they will tell other parties. One way to solve this problem is simply not to disclose any information that could damage the company if it were in the hands of a buyer.

Some nondisclosure agreements include language that prevents this from being a problem. The NDA will state that the receiving party will not use any confidential materials to design, develop, provide, or market any product or service that would compete with any product or service of the disclosing party. In some instances this language may be too restrictive and the prospective purchaser may balk at signing the NDA. In my view this is a good paragraph. The greater danger is not that the prospective purchaser will disclose information to a third party, but rather that it will use this information internally to compete with the seller.

There are numerous stories from the early days of the PC software industry in which a young software company goes to visit a very large software company to discuss the sale of the company. The founders are so pleased that the large software company is interested in them that they disclose way too much information about their own technology. They tell the buyer's team almost everything about the software and its design parameters. The large software company says thank you very much and proceeds to develop its own software for that particular application. There is no reason to acquire the company because the small firm told the potential buyer how they designed everything. A good nondisclosure agreement will help prevent this situation from happening.

One way to guard against disclosing sensitive information to a buyer is to utilize a third-party company to review the software source code and other technology. The third party will examine the software and report on the quality of its design as well as other parameters. Large acquirers prefer using such a service because it helps protect them from lawsuits if the transaction does not come together.

The first portion of an NDA defines the meaning of confidential information. Confidential information typically includes financial information, customer lists, trade secrets, algorithms, software code, know-how, engineering, marketing plans and strategies, and other data. Confidential information does not include information already in the public domain or information already known by the prospective purchaser. The parties agree to protect all confidential information.

Most NDAs will limit the number of persons who will have access to the seller's confidential information. The NDA will specify that the potential buyer will make the confidential information available only to those of its employees, agents, and other representatives who have a need to know for the purpose of pursuing a business relationship between the parties. In other words the information will not be disseminated throughout the buyer's organization.

The NDA states that the prospective purchaser will not solicit the employment of people employed by the seller during the term of the agreement or for six months or sometimes as long as a year thereafter. The receiving party will agree to destroy or return all information to the disclosing party, either upon request or when the information is no longer needed. The term of the agreement is usually from one to three years following the receipt of confidential information.

Confidentiality is a key concern of any company that is seeking to be acquired. It is important that the appropriate level of confidentiality be determined and put in place. Nondisclosure agreements can protect the seller from most problems regarding confidentiality.

SUMMARY

Executing a disciplined process is the key to a successful sale of an intangible company and management should have a good understanding of the process at the outset. The negotiated sale is a more effective approach than the two-step auction when selling an intangible company, particularly those with a transaction size of less than $30 million. The small and midsized buyers do not have the in-house resources to respond to the strict time deadlines of an auction process.

The transaction time frame can be as short as three months or as long as a year and a half. A typical time frame is six months or maybe seven months at the most. Occasionally a transaction will encounter some serious obstacles and the process must be restarted.

How a company chooses to handle confidentiality is an important consideration for every transaction. The investment banker can review the alternatives for confidentiality to decide which approach is most appropriate for a specific situation. In addition, the company needs to make a decision about how it plans to communicate with its customers and its employees.

Now that we understand how the transaction process works let's review the most important issues about how to prepare a company for an eventual sale.

CHAPTER 4

Preparing a Company for Sale

Preparing a company for sale ahead of time can pay excellent dividends when the time comes to sell. Being prepared has two major benefits—the sale process progresses more smoothly and the price can be enhanced. Another reason to prepare early is in case the company receives an unsolicited offer to be acquired, not an uncommon occurrence for intangible companies.

In my opinion there is no difference between running a company well, with first-class execution, and running a company for the purpose of an eventual sale. A firm will create the maximum value by capitalizing on its market opportunities to the best of its ability. If a company's objective is to achieve liquidity, I do not believe that the firm should be run any differently. Generating revenues and serving customers will create the most value. There will always be several good buyers for any well-run company that is addressing a real market need and serving customers effectively.

If a company is thinking about selling, it should begin to prepare the company for the process a year ahead of time. Many owners wait until the last minute or do not prepare at all, and are often too far down the road in the sale process to effect any meaningful changes that will impact value. However, a number of issues can be addressed *prior* to a sale of the company that can improve the business's value.

Preparing a company for a sale triggers a number of questions:

- Where is the company exposed? What are the red flags?
- How can we increase profits and reduce the risks?
- What management decisions and practices should be reevaluated?
- What mistakes can be avoided when selling?
- What documents and other information should be prepared?
- How can you make due diligence less arduous?
- What areas of weakness need to be addressed?
- How do companies leave dollars on the table?

First of all, a company will not leave money on the table if it can do three things: (1) improve the profitability and operations of the business, (2) build confidence in the buyer by having its house in order throughout the sale process, and (3) reduce the risks associated with the business.

IMPROVE PROFITABILITY AND OPERATIONS

Addressing customer and market issues is one of the primary ways that a company can improve its profitability prior to a sale. First, diversify the customer base. If only a few customers account for a large portion of your revenues, it will reduce the company's value. Such a company is riskier than one with a diversified customer base. Second, keep your customers. There is nothing worse than losing customers during the sale process. A company that is thinking about selling must keep its customers at all costs.

Generally it is less expensive to improve the profitability of current customers than it is to attract new customers. Extend contracts and agreements for as long as possible. Give a price break to customers who sign up for a longer contract period. This ensures that customers will stay with the company over a longer term. It reduces the risk for the buyer and can enhance the valuation.

The company should also try to generate additional maintenance revenues. These are a less risky source of revenues. If some customers do not have maintenance agreements, it is a good idea to put some incentives in place to convert these customers.

Which marketing tasks create the most value? What marketing initiatives should you start, continue, or cancel? How should you weigh long-term versus short-term benefits? These are questions that will help guide your marketing budget and marketing plan.

Review your competitive situation. Make sure your view of the competition is current and accurate and that you understand exactly how you match up against competitors. A buyer will likely do its own competitive analysis and it should be consistent with your competitive assessment.

During the due diligence phase a buyer will want to examine all material customer contracts so it is a good idea to extend any contracts that should be extended. If certain customers have verbal agreements for certain preferences or services, it is good idea to put these agreements in writing.

Improving operations can involve a number of tactics. Putting in place better systems and procedures is an obvious one. Automating certain processes is another way to improve operations. Most companies will already know what tasks it needs to undertake to improve operations. The relative importance of these tasks may shift from time to time and budgetary influences will play a big part on which tasks the company can afford to implement. Good judgment is required to select those tasks that can be implemented prior to the sale process that will give the biggest return on investment.

GET YOUR HOUSE IN ORDER

Performing a review process will pay dividends. It is important to get your house in order, clean up loose ends, and prepare the company for the events and procedures of a company sale. Also, it is simply a very good way to run the company—organized, focused, and prepared.

The due diligence process can be an extremely time-consuming and sometimes painful process. The more prepared a company is ahead of time, the fewer surprises to the buyer there are, and the smoother the due diligence effort will be.

Getting the house in order includes addressing management and employee issues, intellectual property issues, administrative issues as well as a financial review that includes income forecasts. Let's examine each of these areas.

Management and Employee Issues

A strong management team makes a company much more attractive as an acquisition. Any company that plans to sell within a two-year time frame should make sure that it has a strong individual in each key management position such as vice president of sales, international sales, technology development, customer service, and any other key areas.

It is a good idea to review the terms of employment, benefit plans, and any other potential payments to employees in the case of a change of control. New employees should be required to sign noncompete agreements. Design incentives for management and key employees so they stay involved and motivated during the sale process.

Which people should stay on board after the sale? Buyers will usually ask the management of the selling company which employees are critical to keep. The transaction can give management an opportunity to deal with personnel issues. If there are any family members on the payroll it is a good idea to evaluate the need for their employment.

Intellectual Property Issues

One of the biggest problems that can derail the sale of an intangible company is poorly documented intellectual property. If the ownership is in question, the transaction will not take place. I have been down this road before and it is not a pleasant situation.

Make sure the company's intellectual property is properly documented with particular attention to ownership issues. It is critical that the ownership of all software and technology be clearly spelled out. It should be evident what software is owned and what software is licensed. Make sure that you have copies of all agreements. The buyer will want to review all of them during the due diligence phase. Prepare schedules of all patents, trademarks, and copyrights.

Software documentation is another important matter. The company should have a documented quality control system for such things as software design specifications, design reviews, risk analysis, code reviews, and so on.

Financial Review

Reviewing the financial condition can be a good exercise for the company. A company that plans to sell should get its accountants involved before the sale process begins. The company needs to be sure that its financial house is in order. And it needs an experienced accountant to tell them exactly what that entails. Use it as an opportunity to improve your internal controls and clean up your financial reporting.

A buyer will want to review profit and loss statements and balance sheets for the last three or four years. Are the financial statements in good enough shape? Make sure that your statements for the last four years are complete and accurate. How should you deal with questionable items? Is your capital structure a problem?

It is a good practice to have interim financial statements prepared throughout the year. A buyer will always want to review the most recent financial information on the company. If it has been nine months since the company's last official income statement, this can be a problem. It may take another month or two to prepare an interim statement. It makes a seller look bad when it cannot provide timely financial statements to a buyer. Put the procedures in place so that statements can be prepared on a monthly, or at least quarterly, basis.

Review your accounting policies. Sometimes companies have idiosyncratic ways of accounting for certain items. Make sure that you identify these areas and then switch to conventional accounting methods.

Show the profitability for each of your company's products. You should also be able to demonstrate profitability for each customer. If you do not already have this information, it is essential that you implement the necessary procedures. If you do identify any unprofitable customers, get rid of them.

They drag the margins down. Any overdue accounts receivable should be either collected or written off.

If the company has capitalized its software development costs, consider changing to the accounting practice of expensing software development costs. Expensing software costs is a more conservative approach and large amounts of capitalized software can be a red flag.

Make sure that the tax returns are complete, filed, and in order. If there are any significant differences between your tax returns and the company's financial statements, make sure that you can explain these differences.

Remove any personal assets from the company's books such as vacation homes or boats. It is also best to keep personal travel separate from the company's books. If there are any unusual shareholder loans it is a good idea to clean them up as well.

Review any potential off-balance sheet liabilities. Items such as environmental issues or deferred vacation pay can have a negative effect on the transaction. Make sure that you understand the potential liability of these issues. It is best not to surprise a potential buyer with any hidden liabilities.

Financial Projections   Projections for the profit and loss statement should be prepared for the next three years. These projections should be reasonable and achievable. Companies that project extremely optimistic revenues and profits get into trouble because they have difficulty achieving these projections once the deal has been completed. Another danger is that the buyer will simply not believe the projections. The seller must be realistic when making projections, otherwise they will come across as naïve and will lose credibility with the buyer. Balance sheet projections are less important for most intangible companies.

Do You Need an Audit?   Most of the time audited financial statements are not required in the sale of an intangible company. A small privately held buyer will rarely require audited statements. Reviewed statements are fine.

If the buyer is a publicly traded company or a large privately held company it may prefer audited statements. A privately held buyer that plans to go public in the next few years may require audited statements.

Remember that in small acquisitions the transaction is often structured as a sale of assets, not a sale of stock, so an audit would not likely be required. If a buyer does insist on audited statements, this can be accomplished later in the process. Audited statements are generally not worth the cost. Good clean records that have been reviewed by an accounting firm should be good enough in most instances.

Administrative Issues

Make sure that the company's web site is up-to-date and that it accurately describes the company's business. Buyers always check out a company's web site. Sometimes web sites are dated and place an incorrect emphasis on certain products and services. This can be confusing for the buyer. A few other tips:

- Make sure the board minutes are up-to-date and complete. It is easier to keep board minutes current as you go versus doing them later. This state of readiness often reflects the personality of the founder or CEO. Some are highly disciplined and organized all the way along. Others relish the chaos and can scramble when they need to.
- Company procedures and policies should be documented. Most companies have a number of processes that are not written down that should be. Documenting systems and procedures is a good discipline for any business.
- Make a list of all of the company's assets. It is a good idea to have statements and supporting schedules.
- Review all supplier contracts. Often it is best to extend contracts and agreements as long as possible.
- Make sure that the company is in compliance with all regulatory requirements.
- Get rid of all extraneous product lines and pet projects. Focus the company's efforts on the most profitable areas.
- If the company has any outstanding lawsuits or other legal issues, it is critical that these problems be resolved before beginning the sale process. Make sure any disputes between shareholders or management are resolved ahead of time.

Make sure the company's shareholder records are complete and accurate. In one transaction the outside accountant discovered in his pre-closing review that the company had never issued 20,000 shares of stock to one of the shareholders. The company had completed several rounds of financing over the years, and in this case one of the original shareholders had purchased additional shares in a later round of financing; however, the company had neglected to issue the shares. So the company issued the stock to the shareholder and it was not a problem. The point is that even though these are minor issues, it is better to discover them and resolve them earlier rather than later.

Review the terms of your building lease and make sure the lease is not about to expire. Also, do not sign a long-term lease. Depending on the buyer, this may create a liability. It is important to maintain flexibility. If the buyer plans to continue in the same space, a lease at a less-than-market rate is viewed positively. However if the buyer does not plan to continue in the space then a long-term lease is a liability. Unfortunately the company needs to address this issue for a specific buyer. Sometimes it is obvious what a likely buyer would want to do regarding the lease and the company can take steps accordingly.

Make sure that the company's office space and other building areas are clean, organized, and uncluttered. Founders tend to have personal quirks when it comes to organization; some are quite organized and some are totally disorganized. When a potential buyer walks through your office he will develop an opinion about the business based on how it looks. You want that opinion to be a favorable one.

WAR STORY: STOLEN MONEY ... AN INSIDE JOB

Kappa Corp. launched two new products one year that did not sell particularly well. The sales manager sold these programs to retailers as consignment although orders were written internally with standard terms. Thus, Kappa ended up taking back a majority of the goods. Other customers were sold items at drastically reduced prices that were not indicated on the purchase orders.

The sales manager generously extended the full return policy on all new orders. He found clever ways to circumvent the company's internal controls. He falsified expense reports and offered unapproved sales programs to inflate revenue numbers in order to achieve high commissions. This employee was fired, but Kappa was still dealing with the aftereffects when it came time to sell the company.

This situation needed to be cleaned up. With a good buyer in hand, I suggested that the company draft a written explanation of the situation. The company's financial statements needed to be explained because the margins on certain products were impacted negatively. The buyer would want to have an accurate picture of the gross margins for each product line. Management drafted a detailed explanation. Fortunately, the buyer understood the adjustments and the transaction closed on schedule.

(Continued)

Most companies will have some negative issues that must be communicated to the buyer. The lesson here is to confront these issues head on, be prepared for them, and be honest and upfront with the buyer.

REDUCE RISKS

The company must be aware of and have a realistic picture of the risks that it faces in its business. Examine the company's risk areas and think of ways to reduce those risks. For example:

- What are the company's market risks, management risks, technology risks, and financial risks?
- How could each of these risks have a negative impact on value?
- What risks can we proactively address?
- How can you minimize these risks for a buyer?

In one transaction that I was involved in the seller's major customer accounted for about 30 percent of its revenues. The buyer viewed this as a huge risk associated with the transaction. What if the client left? In this case the seller was smart. I strongly recommended that the seller stay close to this customer, inform them of the sale situation, and do whatever it could to keep the customer happy. The strategy worked. Early in the due diligence process the buyer met with this customer and was reassured that the customer would stay with the business. The customer realized that the buyer was a larger firm with greater resources that could do an even better job of meeting its needs.

Most CEOs and founders underestimate the degree of risk that surrounds their businesses. And this is generally a good thing. If entrepreneurs focused on the risks instead of the opportunities, they would never have started their companies in the first place. However, when it comes time to sell, having a realistic assessment of the risks will enable a seller to be prepared for the buyer's questions.

SELLING JUST TECHNOLOGY

Sometimes a company will want to sell off some of its technology, not the company. Why sell just technology? There are several reasons. The first is that the company is very young. It may have a few early adopter customers and minimal revenues but it cannot raise capital for growth. For some small companies its technology is its only real asset. The second reason is that a company may have several product lines or technologies. One product may experience strong market acceptance and the company is smart to shift its resources to focus solely on the successful product line. The company decides to spin off the other technology or product line.

It is important to differentiate between software and other kinds of technology. For the purposes of this discussion, technology will refer basically to software. Hardware technology often has a longer shelf life than software technology. Both are relatively short however.

Selling just technology is certainly possible but it is significantly more difficult than selling a company. There are usually no revenues associated with a technology, so it makes the sale more problematic. Not only will the buyer have to pay for the technology, they will have to invest capital to finish building out the product, and invest capital to bring the product or technology to market.

In the early days of personal computer software it was relatively easy to sell technology. The industry was exploding and technology was needed in almost every part of the software industry. Today's world is a different story. We have plenty of technology. In fact in many ways, we have too much technology. Of course there will never be too much excellent technology. The needs of the markets change so rapidly that new technology is continually required, especially software.

The biggest problem with selling just technology is that it has a very short half-life. In my view, after about 18 months any technology is extremely old. Often it is easier for companies to develop their own software than to purchase software or technology from another firm. An additional issue is that the acquisition of technology is a low priority for many companies. Plus there is always the "not invented here" problem.

In many cases the most likely buyers for technology are the company's major customers, assuming there are a few key customers who are using the technology. However, this can be a problem as well. In one transaction in which technology was the primary asset, two large software firms were clearly the best acquirers. The problem was that a year earlier the seller had licensed this technology to each of these two companies. The seller received a nice fee from each firm, but the companies had an unlimited license to the technology so there was absolutely no reason to acquire it.

On a related note, one type of company that is difficult to sell is a company that sells software tools. Over the years I have worked with a wide range of companies that had developed software tools. By tools I mean software that handles a specific task, such as software utilities. One example of a software tool is software that optimizes the performance of computer displays for optimum image quality, comfort, and productivity; it also detects and minimizes common sources of eyestrain.

Tools companies can be difficult to sell. Their customers are usually a handful of big companies who can use the tools effectively and profitably. However the tools are of lesser value to medium-sized and smaller companies. For small customers the price point must be lower in order for the tools to be cost effective. Software tools companies can rarely sell enough units of their products to be profitable and viable companies over the long run.

In my view, software tools companies should transform themselves into becoming service companies, using their tools to provide a service to their customers, rather than trying to sell the tools. It is a better business model and the customers do not really want to own the tools anyway, they just want a particular problem solved.

SUMMARY

A fast-growing firm will always have areas that are not perfect. The wise CEO spends the company's resources where they are the most productive—usually building sales and serving customers. Sometimes administrative issues can take a backseat. When preparing a company for sale, issues and surprises can pop up. Most of these are not critical issues but it is a good idea to handle them before the sale process gets too far down the road. Many times these are simple housekeeping issues. Establish sound systems, procedures, and accounting practices. They will pay dividends when the time comes for a sale of the company.

If a company plans to sell just technology, it must recognize that software technology has a very short half-life. The earlier a company reaches out to potential buyers, the better the chances of selling the technology.

Once a company is prepared, it can move forward with the process. The next chapter addresses the question of how to identify the best buyers. We talk about the most productive way to view a market and I introduce the concept of market maps. We will also discuss the best way to make contact with the buyers.

CHAPTER 5

Who are the Best Buyers?

Buyers of intangible companies come in all forms and sizes. At one end of the spectrum it could be a company with $5 billion in revenues that wants to acquire a $2 million company in order to obtain leading-edge technology. At the other end of the spectrum, a buyer can be as small as an $8 million company acquiring a $2 million company to gain new products and add customers. A more common occurrence is a company with $38 million in revenue that acquires a company with $7 million in revenue.

The best buyer may be a company that the seller knows well or it may be a company that the seller has never heard of. Sometimes the buyer is a larger player in the same market space and in other cases the buyer is a company from an adjacent market who will be using the acquisition as a means of market entry.

To some degree, all companies in a market are acquirers. Occasionally, a competitor might be the best buyer. Most companies are open to the idea of acquiring another firm that can bring needed technology, products, capabilities, customers, and other resources.

REASONS BUYERS BUY

Buyers have a number of motives for making acquisitions. They may use an acquisition as a way to gain new technology or new products and service capabilities. Acquisitions can be a good way to add customers or talent, such as an engineering or development team. An acquisition can provide a buyer with intellectual property, know-how, and patents. Acquisitions can also be an inexpensive and fast way to enter a market and capture market share, or add a brand name and a new geographic presence.

New and unique technologies are often created by smaller companies; however these firms frequently struggle in taking the technologies and the products that embody them to market. Small companies are pretty good at developing technology, but not so good at successfully selling the product or the service. Let's briefly review each of the asset categories that acquirers find attractive in making strategic acquisitions:

New Products and Services—More acquisitions are made to acquire new products and services than for any other reason. Buyers can sell the target's products and services through their existing sales channels.

New Technologies—Buyers use acquisitions as a way to capture newly developed technologies that they can incorporate into their own products. These products could be existing products or new products that the company is developing. Acquisitions to obtain technology are most common in the early phases of a market's development. In a late stage or consolidating market, acquisitions are rarely made to obtain technology.

   Most technologies can be used in a variety of ways. Technology developed for one market may be utilized in other markets. For example, one company that we sold had developed innovative software for caching data on a hard disk. The software organized the movement of data in a clever way and improved the effective speed of data transfer. As a result, it improved the speed and performance of a personal computer. It turns out that this technology and its algorithms also worked well for caching data on compact discs (CDs) and other storage media. We sold the company to a firm that manufactured CD drives. The manufacturer benefited because this software enhancement enabled its CD drives to transfer data at a faster rate than competitors' drives. This example is typical of many types of technology that can be used in different applications.

Additional Customers—Buyers always benefit by bringing additional customers onboard. In the consolidation phase of a market, customers are the primary reason that acquisitions are made.

Engineering and Development Teams—Talent is a key asset for most intangible companies. As buyers expand they discover that it is often difficult to hire enough good people. Acquisitions can be a great way to bring talented people on board.

Increased Capabilities—Capabilities include resources such as consulting talent, sales teams, or other service-oriented resources. These resources give the acquirer the ability to deliver new and additional services to its customers.

Distribution Channels—Acquisitions can enhance a buyer's distribution channels. We completed one transaction in which a European buyer acquired a U.S. company to add to its product line but more importantly to increase its distribution power in the United States.

Geographic Location—Acquisitions to obtain a geographic location or presence are not all that common with intangible companies; however in some cases this motive can drive an acquisition. We closed a transaction with an East Coast software company that acquired a West Coast software firm in order to provide better service to its West Coast clients. In another transaction a Canadian firm acquired a U. S. company to gain a foothold in the U. S. market. Generally, these are smaller-sized acquisitions.

Gain Mass—Smaller buyers make acquisitions to gain mass—to simply get larger. Usually this means adding revenues and customers. Even if the acquisition is not highly strategic it can be beneficial for a small buyer to grow in size and enjoy greater economies of scale. This may be an odd reason for making an acquisition; however it does happen from time to time. Large buyers rarely make acquisitions to gain mass. The motivation to make an acquisition to gain mass is probably most common among very small buyers, typically with revenues under $30 million.

The Price is Right—Sometimes a buyer will make an acquisition simply because the price is extremely attractive. It may not be a must-have acquisition but at a low price it is a good deal. The acquired assets are usually "nice to have" technology or a "nice to have" customer base; they are not critically important assets. These deals are very price sensitive. This type of acquisition is an inexpensive way for an acquirer to gather assets that are at least of moderate value.

We have sold a number of companies simply because the price was too good to pass up. Deals like this occur after an extensive search turns up no highly strategic buyers. The next move in selling the company is to approach the market in a completely different manner. We attempt to find buyers that could realize some benefit, even a modest benefit, by acquiring the seller's assets including customers, products, or technology for a very reasonable price.

Market Entry as Motive—Bigger buyers often use an acquisition as a way to gain a foothold in a niche market. As a result, these buyers are not located in the seller's primary market, but in an adjacent market. The buyers are using the acquisition to gain market entry—to enter a neighboring market, to gain new customers, and new technology. They will build on this acquisition to expand in that market sector. Over the years, I have closed quite a number of transactions with buyers that were situated in tangential markets.

About half the time in the sale of an intangible company, the buyer is from outside the seller's primary market space. It saves the acquirer development expense, but more importantly it saves time. It gives the buyer a foothold in that market, even if the buyer does not plan on using the seller's technology platform over the long term. An acquisition for market entry enables a buyer to enter a market earlier, often less expensively and usually with less risk. If the buyer were to develop similar technology in-house, there is always the risk of time delays and development problems, or that the technology may miss the mark with respect to solving the precise customer need.

CATEGORIES OF BUYERS

The best buyer is the company that can realize the maximum advantage from the assets of the selling company. It is the company that needs that particular technology or strategic asset the most. Many times the most likely buyers are companies that sell other products or services to the same group of customers. In this situation, after the acquisition has closed, the buyer can sell the acquired company's products and services to its own customers.

Sometimes buyers appear to be unlikely acquirers but they can turn out to be very good buyers. These are the non-obvious buyers. One set of very good but unlikely buyers includes companies in neighboring or adjacent markets. These companies are not participants in the core market of the seller. Unlikely buyers also include companies that can utilize the target's technology in a different application or in a different market segment. I discuss the concept of adjacent markets in more depth later in this chapter.

What about financial buyers and private equity firms? Are these entities good buyers for intangible companies? No, they are rarely good buyers. The sellers are generally not viable as stand-alone companies; they need to be part of larger firms that have complementary resources and products. Remember that these are strategic deals. The value is intangible, so these kinds of transactions do not make sense for private equity groups and other financial buyers.

One of the erroneous beliefs regarding mergers and acquisitions is that many CEOs think they know who the best buyers are ahead of time. "We know our space. We know all the good buyers in our market." What they do not realize is that 40 to 50 percent of all sub-30 technology acquisitions are sold to buyers that are not in the seller's primary market.

The universe of buyers can be broadly segmented into three general categories: small, midsized, and large.

- Small buyers—revenues between $25 million and $175 million.
- Midsized buyers—revenues between $175 million and $500 million.
- Large buyers—revenues greater than $500 million.

For a transaction that is less than $30 million in size the likely buyers will be the small buyers with revenues of less than $175 million. Transactions under $30 million are not significant for the larger buyers. For the sale of an intangible company between $30 million and $100 million the most likely buyers are the midsized buyers and occasionally the large companies. For a transaction greater than $100 million in size the large companies will be the best buyers.

Small Buyers

Small buyers are best for small acquisitions. A $5 million or $10 million acquisition is important to a small buyer. Sometimes the buyer itself may have revenues as little as $10 million or $15 million. Small companies want to become larger companies. Many small firms are on a rapid growth track and will make acquisitions to spur their growth. Acquisitions are almost always part of their strategic growth plans.

Small buyers are usually the most difficult ones to discover. Most of the time these companies are privately owned and, by definition, they are small so they are less visible and therefore more difficult to identify. As a result, the search component is more important in the sale of a company for less than $10 million than it is on larger deals. On a large transaction the good buyers are much more obvious; there is little risk that the investment banker will not identify all the good buyers. On a small deal there is a much greater risk that not all good buyers will be identified or contacted.

Smaller buyers may not be experienced or polished. They might never have completed an acquisition and may not be familiar with the acquisition process. They may ask many wrong questions and may not be sure how to proceed. For them there are many unknowns and probably some fears as well. Sometimes I will offer advice and counsel to the buyer even though formally I am representing the seller. Both parties need help in overcoming obstacles and reaching an agreement in order to successfully close a transaction.

The universe of small buyers with revenues less than $175 million is quite large. My estimate is that there are about 10,000 to 15,000 companies in this size range that are technology, software, and tech-services companies, and thus are potential buyers of small intangible companies. This is a rough estimate on my part and I present it to give the reader an idea of the order of magnitude of the number of technology, software, and tech-services companies.

Midsized Buyers

An acquisition is an excellent way for a midsized company with revenues from $175 million to $500 million to add capabilities and expand into new markets. A midsized buyer is different from a small buyer. In fact a midsized buyer acts a lot more like a big buyer. However, a midsized buyer will consider acquisitions as small as $10 million or $20 million if the acquisition achieves a strategic objective. It is unlikely that a midsized buyer will be interested in an acquisition with less than $10 million in revenue unless there is a critical strategic aspect.

A typical midsized buyer will have a small team of people on board that are experienced in the acquisition process. M&A may not be their full-time job but it is likely that they have some experience in completing transactions. Most midsized buyers have made an acquisition or even several acquisitions in the past. My estimate is that there are approximately 1,000 to 1,500 technology, software, and tech-service companies in the midsized range.

Large Buyers

Why aren't large buyers the best buyers? They have plenty of cash and most have a publicly traded stock. In every search effort we certainly do contact a number of large buyers. Big firms are easy to identify and it is important to be thorough. However, a sub-30 acquisition will rarely make an impact on a $1 billion company.

The one exception to this rule is when a small technology company has developed a unique technology that is critically important to the larger company. In one case I closed a transaction for slightly more than $2 million in which the buyer had revenues of $5.5 billion. The buyer had decided to enter a new market segment and it was amassing the capabilities to be a major player in that sector. Although quite small, this acquisition gave the buyer excellent technology and a small team of people who were experts in that market area. The buyer's plan was to build a $300 million division.

A large buyer will rarely be interested in an acquisition simply to add a few more customers. A venture capitalist queried me one time about one of his small portfolio companies, "Wouldn't a big company want to tuck in an additional $2 million or $3 million in revenue?" The answer is no, they would not. It does happen occasionally, but it is clearly the exception.

In another instance I was talking with a CEO of a fairly large firm about acquiring a small company. The primary asset of the selling company was its customer base and the revenue associated with them. The CEO told me that for $2 million in additional revenues they would be better off just hiring a couple of salesmen to bring in that same amount of revenues. He had a good point. If customers are the only significant asset, hiring additional salesmen is less bother than going through the acquisition process including the due diligence and legal work. This underscores why smaller buyers are the best buyers for sub-30 acquisitions.

One problem with selling a small company to a large company is that the buyer usually adheres to its normal due diligence procedures that are geared toward much larger acquisitions. As a result the due diligence process can take longer than it really should. By my estimate there are approximately 400 to 600 technology, software, and tech-service companies with revenues greater than $500 million.

The Same Buyer as Last Time

I have worked on quite a number of transactions in which the successful buyer was the same buyer who had considered acquiring the company a year or two earlier. In many cases the buyer actually made an offer. This situation is fairly common. The reason that the transaction did not go together two years prior is the obvious one—the parties could not agree on price. The buyer may have offered a price that was too low and then later realized that the strategic importance of the acquisition was great enough that a higher price was warranted. However, most of the time the seller simply wants a price that is too high. It is common for sellers to have unrealistically high price expectations.

The following are a few examples of transactions that were successfully completed with a buyer that had made an offer a year or two earlier:

Gamma Software Systems—This company was acquired by its German distributor. The parties had tried to complete a transaction two years earlier but could not reach an agreement on price. The founders were attempting to handle the negotiations themselves. After my firm got involved in the sale process, the buyer raised its offer and a deal was successfully concluded.

Beta Software Company—The two parties needed someone else to negotiate the deal. They had reached an impasse the year before. As an intermediary, I was in a better position to negotiate a transaction in which both parties could achieve their objectives. This was a good example of the benefit of a third party handling the negotiations.

Delta Technology—This was an excellent fit from the start; however the seller simply wanted more money than the buyer was willing to pay. Two years later the seller relaxed its price expectations and the parties reached an agreement and closed a transaction.

The list goes on. Sometimes the buyer raises its offer after it recognizes how important the technology and other assets really are. Sometimes the seller realizes its price expectations are too high. In other cases the seller's need for liquidity becomes more urgent. And sometimes a third party is needed to successfully drive the negotiations.

Competitors as Buyers

Contrary to what many people believe, competitors are rarely the best buyers. Unless it specifically needs the target's technology or products, there is very little that is of significant value to a competitor other than customers.

Even if the seller's technology is superior, it is highly unlikely that the acquiring company will replace its current technology with the seller's technology. The buyer prefers its own technology because they know it and understand it. I have done deals in which the seller's technology was newer and better designed than the buyer's technology. But the buyers did not want to switch to the target's technology. The buyer's employees and customers were trained and knowledgeable about their own technology. In addition, the cost of converting customers is very high. Any new technology that is expected to replace an older entrenched technology must be better by a large enough magnitude to offset the high costs of switching.

Many small technology companies lose sight of this fact. They think it is all about the technology. It is not. It is about solving the customers' problems. And if the customer's problem is solved adequately with older technology then that is just fine. Many CEOs of smaller technology companies become frustrated that the larger buyers do not want their nifty technology.

Occasionally a competitor will utilize an acquisition to fill a gap in its product line and this is a good motivation for an acquisition. However, competitors generally pay the least amount for an intangible company.

WAR STORY: A SAD TALE OF THE NON-STANDARD

One of my clients had developed excellent presentation software for consulting firms to communicate the results of their consulting assignments to their clients. The technology design was quite powerful and sophisticated. Unfortunately for the company, the market had matured and Microsoft PowerPoint had become the de facto standard. The company should have modified its presentation formats to comply with PowerPoint instead of trying to compete with it. (This is the old "ours is better" mindset.) The company's technology was superior but it could not compete with the growing acceptance of PowerPoint; it was bucking an uphill trend. The company's revenues had leveled off and it was difficult to interest a buyer in an acquisition of the company. This company should have tried to be acquired a few years earlier before a market standard had been determined.

Active Acquirers

There are a number of companies that I would call *active* acquirers. Generally these companies fall into the high end of the midsized group and the low end of the large buyers. Revenues range roughly from $250 million to $750 million.

These buyers have strict criteria and a well-thought out game plan. They have had many meetings and weekend retreats to hone their criteria. Their criteria are relatively rigid. There may be a minimum transaction size, typically $25 million. Some buyers insist on a minimum operating profit of $2 million to $3 million. These buyers typically have a comprehensive list of all the potential acquisition targets in their market spaces that meet their criteria.

One example is a software company that I have dealt with in respect to acquisitions. The company is publicly traded with about $250 million in revenue. The major shareholder is a private equity group that has aggressive goals for the company's growth. They are actively seeking acquisitions. The company has two primary criteria: (1) an acquisition must leverage the buyer's strong distribution and international sales capabilities, and (2) the target must be able to achieve $10 million in operating profits within about one year of the date of the acquisition.

The problem with such specific criteria is that it is so narrow that it severely limits the company's acquisition alternatives. This approach is not opportunistic. If they do acquire one of the companies on their list it is likely that it will be for a relatively high price. Companies with a strong growth imperative need to grow through acquisition, as well as organically, in order to achieve their growth targets. It may require more effort, but completing a couple of $10 million or $15 million acquisitions may be an excellent alternative.

IDENTIFYING THE RIGHT BUYERS

How do you find the buyers? How can you identify them? The key is to look for companies that touch on some aspect of the selling company: the same customer set, the same market area, solving the same type of problem, providing a similar or related service ... something that overlaps. This section illustrates the market-based approach for identifying buyers. I discuss the buyers on the edge, the non-obvious buyers, adjacent markets, and the occurrence of emerging buyers.

The Market-Based Approach

The approach that I have found to be most effective is the market-based approach. This method is successful because it initiates the search for good buyers from the perspective of the customer. It focuses on the need that is being addressed. The approach begins by asking a fundamental question: What problem does the technology or service solve for the customer? What customer needs are being met?

Customers just want their problems solved. They really do not care how the vendor gets the job done as long as their problems are solved. It could be with the latest and greatest technology or just with regular old technology. It is constructive to define a company by the benefits that it brings to its customers, not by the features of its technology. This question focusing on the customer's need encourages a useful perspective from which to begin addressing the market.

The second question that the market-based approach poses is: Which companies sell other products and services to this same set of customers? This is an excellent question because it leads one to look in areas that could be fruitful for identifying likely buyers. The third question in this approach is: Which potential buyers need to solve similar problems for their customers? This question shifts the focus to the benefits provided by the seller's product or service, regardless of the market.

Next, I delve into the industry, examining the market sectors that touch on the selling company's primary market. Even if innovative technology is the seller's singular asset, I still take a market-based approach. I do not delve into the technology in great depth. (I have utilized a technology-oriented approach multiple times and it is not fruitful for identifying good buyers.) Rather, I ask myself what problem the technology addresses and then seek companies with customers that need to solve a similar problem.

It is usually not necessary for the investment banker to scrutinize the technology in great depth. The buyer wants to hear about the technology from the seller's chief technology officer (CTO), not the investment banker. The investment banker can provide an overview, but a detailed discussion is not his bailiwick. When the deal progresses to the technical review stage, the buyer's CTO and several people from his team will have a phone conversation or a WebEx demonstration with the seller's CTO to review the technology.

Buyers on the Edge

Market spaces usually are gray around the edges. The boundaries are not distinct. Niche market opportunities are not always visible. They are not staring you in the face. No matter how well you know your market, it is always gray at the edges.

The term "buyers on the edge" refers to buyers in adjacent markets and other non-obvious buyers. These are a different set of buyers. The buyers are usually smaller; they are more diverse; and there are a greater number of these potential buyers.

Why search the edges of the market? Because that is where many of the best buyers are. And it is a good idea to suspend your industry knowledge. Industry knowledge can actually be limiting because one typically has preconceived ideas about which companies are good buyers and which are not.

The technology arena is an interesting one. Its main sectors include hardware, software, and tech-services. Hardware companies often acquire software companies. It is an excellent way for them to add value to their products and add higher-margin components. It enables them to offer their customers a broader range of products, services, and capabilities. A software company in one area may buy a software firm in another area. And either a software company or a hardware company may buy a services company.

Non-Obvious Buyers

Unlikely or non-obvious buyers can often be the best buyers. These are the buyers that are out of your market space who will use an acquisition for market entry. It is hard to know who these buyers are, what they want, and where they want to go with their businesses. The search for these non-obvious buyers is an exploration.

It is a good practice to consider tangential market sectors, not in a vague, general way, but purposefully, with a specific acquisition rationale in mind. Look outside of the seller's core market space. Look farther and wider. An acquisition is a window into niche market opportunities. Small technology companies are meeting a customer need. What is that need? Should the buyer be addressing those needs?

A good example of a non-obvious buyer is the acquisition of Microrim by the Canadian firm, Abacus Accounting Software. Microrim developed and marketed *R:BASE,* one of the first relational databases for personal computers. Abacus wanted Microrim's technology but they also wanted a U.S. presence. Abacus planned to use Microrim's database technology as the foundation for its new generation of accounting products. In this transaction, the buyer made the acquisition for opportunistic reasons. Abacus Accounting was not at all an obvious candidate to acquire Microrim.

Adjacent Markets

The best buyers are often found in adjacent markets. What is an adjacent market? An adjacent market is a market space that touches on or neighbors the primary market. For every market, there are usually about seven adjacent markets. Sometimes there are more and sometimes fewer, but seven seems to be the right number in most cases. For example, an e-mail direct marketing company will butt up against a number of markets: advertising agencies, customer relationship management (CRM) companies, marketing companies, marketing consulting companies, web site design firms, direct marketing services, and interactive ad agencies.

Buyers in adjacent markets use acquisitions as a means to enter new markets and to gain new technology and new customers. It saves development expense. More importantly it saves time. It gives them a foothold in a new market. Even if they do not plan on using the acquired technology platform over the long term, it is primarily an acquisition to gain market entry. A buyer can enter a market sooner and less expensively with a well-designed acquisition, and often with less risk. About half of the time, the buyer is from outside the seller's core market space.

FedEx's acquisition of Kinko's is a good example of adjacent markets. This acquisition was not an obvious fit. FedEx used the acquisition of Kinko's to gain market entry. There was a strategic angle that was perceptible after the fact, but before the transaction these two companies were in entirely different industries—one in the delivery business and the other in the copy business. However, they do sell to similar sets of customers. This is a good example of markets that appear unrelated but are actually adjacent.

"We know our space. We know the buyers in our market." That may be true, but sometimes the best buyers are not directly in a company's core market space. They are in the little spaces off to the side, the neighboring areas. Small deals can fit in more places and they require more creativity in searching the adjacent markets. Adjacent markets are fertile grounds for purchasers of intangible companies.

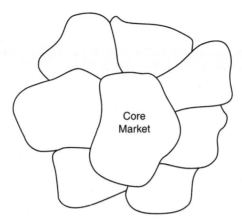

FIGURE 5.1   The Conceptual Market Map

Figure 5.1 depicts the concept of adjacent markets. The shapes representing various markets do not signify the size or importance of a specific market. They simply denote that there is a market nearby and it may overlap slightly with the core market.

Emerging Buyers

An emerging buyer is a company that has recently experienced strong growth and is now looking at acquisitions as a way to spur its growth further. The concept of the emerging buyers is related to that of adjacent markets. Emerging buyers are some of the best buyers and also the hardest buyers to find. The reason they are difficult to find is that they have not been there very long.

Emerging buyers are new companies that are growing rapidly. These buyers are in new emerging market spaces. They are unknown buyers. They were not here yesterday. Emerging buyers spring up rapidly. A few years earlier they were hardly noticed, hardly a player. They come out of nowhere overnight. They are not there and then they are there.

The emerging buyer is by definition in a new market sector and new markets are fluid and not well defined. The company is growing, usually fairly rapidly, and it wants to expand into the neighboring market which can be a good complement to its existing business and to its existing customers.

The distinctive fact about emerging markets is that they are up-and-coming. They are just budding and have not been there very long, so you do not know they are there. After a while, they become entrenched and you think, "Of course." If you look in hindsight or view it from the buyer's eyes, it often makes good sense.

Emerging buyers are the best bet in the under $30 million acquisition market. They can pay the most because they have capital and the acquisition will usually have more strategic importance to them than to other buyers. These companies are young and growing extremely fast. Speed is critical. They want to make the acquisition and build their company quickly.

Following are a few examples of emerging buyers:

- **Crocs, Inc.** invented a whole new category in the shoe market— lightweight, comfortable, and slip-resistant footwear. In this trans- action, Crocs acquired a small golf and adventure footwear com- pany. Crocs' market capitalization was $5.5 billion and revenues were $590 million at the time of the acquisition. Three years before Crocs' revenues were $14 million. Yes, $14 million! Crocs had experienced unbelievable growth. They were truly an emerging buyer. The company needed to continue its growth, and acquisitions were a key part of its strategy. Three years earlier the company was almost unheard of and now they are a major force in the footwear market.
- **Upsilon Corp.** was a small company in the Internet market research arena. It had been plugging along for a number of years. It must have done something right because it obtained $13 million in financing from three venture capital firms. Upsilon wanted to continue its rapid expan- sion, so it made three acquisitions including a small customer satisfac- tion research firm. Upsilon came out of nowhere. Prior to the venture funding the company was under the radar. Six months after this ac- quisition the company raised an additional $35 million to finance its remarkable growth.
- **Theta Consulting** was acquired by Blue Pumpkin Software. Blue Pump- kin was a rising star in the workforce-management software arena. This was an innovative and emerging software niche. The company was growing rapidly and the acquisition of Theta enabled it to offer addi- tional service capabilities to its customers. Blue Pumpkin was a lesser known buyer on the extreme edge of Theta's market space.

VIEWING A MARKET SPACE

Markets can be viewed in a number of ways. Most young markets are fragmented markets, which are always messy and may not always make perfect sense to the observer. Companies that were good buyers a year ago may no longer be good buyers or perhaps they were acquired. Small, rapidly growing, and well-financed firms may be the best buyers, but they usually are not very well known.

This section discusses how to view a market space. I introduce the concept of market maps in order to identify fertile areas for potential buyers.

Market Maps

Drawing a market map can be beneficial in helping to decide which market spaces and submarkets should be explored. It presents a clearer picture of the market, which is good in any case. It also helps in identifying niches for which we need to contact additional companies. Market maps can help answer the question—where have I not yet looked? It helps determine which sectors should be investigated in greater depth.

Picture the core market as a rectangular shape and then identify six or seven adjacent markets that touch on this core market. The approach leads to a more fruitful exploration of likely buyers. This method also helps in identifying and examining the tangential and fringe market sectors.

A graphic depiction of a market can be illustrated in several ways. The method that I have found to be effective in viewing a particular market is to represent the primary market space as an amorphous quadrangle or a blob. The amorphous aspect reminds me that market boundaries are fluid and not well defined.

A market map consists of a quadrangle for each market and quadrangles for each sub-market. Next to each quadrangle we list the companies that we have identified as part of that particular market sector. For example, a market sector for anti-spam software will be represented by a quadrangle that is inscribed by the words anti-spam software and next to it (in smaller type) we list the various companies that are part of this market. A variation on this theme is simply to denote the total number of companies in that market sector, rather than listing each company specifically.

Some quadrangles will have a lot of companies and other quadrangles will have only a few. The benefit of doing this exercise is that we can stand back and get a good picture of the markets. It is likely that one quadrangle may have only two or three companies listed. In this case it may make sense to drill down on this market sector in more depth and contact another five or six companies.

The market map also helps from a qualitative standpoint. If we have received good responses from companies in one particular quadrangle we will explore that sector in more depth because it is likely that there is a good reason companies in that niche are being responsive. A third benefit of the market map is that it spots areas where we have yet to identify adjacent

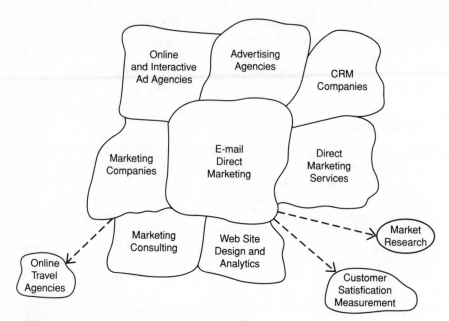

FIGURE 5.2   Market Map with Sector Names

markets. All markets have adjacent markets and we want to ensure that we do not overlook any in the search process.

It is important to note that the quadrangles depicting a market sector are not representative of the size of those market segments. They simply denote the existence of that particular sector.

The market map depicted in Figure 5.2 shows the primary market for e-mail direct marketing. It is surrounded by seven adjacent markets. It also includes three more distant market spaces. The reason that online travel agencies are included is that the selling company had a number of customers in the travel industry. This is a different way to slice the markets, but it can lead to non-obvious buyers. This diagram is a fluid representation of a fluid environment.

The market map is always a work in progress. It is not something that is drafted at the end of the transaction. As we move forward with the search to identify good buyers we list companies in each group by submarket sector. We build the initial market map after we have compiled a reasonable list of potential buyers. Figure 5.3 lists prospective buyers by market sector for the E-mail Direct Marketing space. These are companies that we either have contacted or plan to contact in the search process. If a particular sector has

E-Mail Direct Marketing

Alpha Email Marketing Co.
Beta Agency Email Marketing Co.
Gamma Agency Email Marketing Co.
Delta Agency Email Marketing Co.
Epsilon Agency Email Marketing Co.
Zeta Agency Email Marketing Co.
Eta Agency Email Marketing Co.
Theta Agency Email Marketing Co.
Iota Email Marketing Co.
Kappa Email Marketing Co.
Lambda Email Marketing Co.
Mu Email Marketing Co.
Nu Email Marketing Co.
Xi Email Marketing Co.
Omicron Email Marketing Co.
Pi Email Marketing Co.
Rho Email Marketing Co.

Internet/Interactive Ad Agencies

Alpha Interactive Co.
Beta Interactive Co.
Gamma Interactive Co.
Delta Interactive Co.
Epsilon Interactive Co.
Zeta Interactive Co.
Eta Interactive Co.

Marketing Companies

Alpha Marketing Co.
Beta Marketing Co.
Gamma Marketing Co.
Delta Marketing Co.
Epsilon Marketing Co.
Zeta Marketing Co.
Eta Marketing Co.

Advertising Agencies

Alpha Agency
Beta Agency
Gamma Agency
Delta Agency
Epsilon Agency
Zeta Agency
Eta Agency
Theta Agency
Iota Agency
Kappa Agency
Lambda Agency
Mu Agency
Nu Agency
Xi Agency
Omicron Agency
Pi Agency
Rho Agency

CRM Companies

Alpha CRM Co.
Beta CRM Co.
Gamma CRM Co.
Delta CRM Co.
Epsilon CRM Co.
Zeta CRM Co.
Eta CRM Co.
Theta CRM Co.
Iota CRM Co.

Direct Marketing Services

Alpha Direct Marketing Co.
Beta Direct Marketing Co.
Gamma Direct Marketing Co.
Delta Direct Marketing Co.
Epsilon Direct Marketing Co.
Zeta Direct Marketing Co.

Other

Alpha e-business performance
Beta Internet Consulting
Gamma Web Analytics

Marketing Consulting

Alpha Marketing Consulting, Inc.
Beta Marketing Consulting, Inc.
Gamma Marketing Consulting, Inc.
Delta Marketing Consulting, Inc.
Epsilon Marketing Consulting, Inc.

Marketing Research Companies

Alpha Market Research
Beta Market Research
Gamma Market Research
Delta Market Research
Epsilon Market Research
Zeta Market Research

Online Travel Agencies

Alpha Travel Agency
Beta Travel Agency
Gamma Travel Agency
Delta Travel Agency

Online/Digital Advertising

Alpha Online Co.
Beta Online Co.
Gamma Online Co.
Delta Online Co.
Epsilon Online Co.
Zeta Online Co.
Eta Online Co.
Theta Online Co.
Iota Online Co.
Kappa Online Co.
Lambda Online Co.
Mu Online Co.
Nu Online Co.

Customer Satisfaction Measurement

Alpha Measurement, Inc.

Web Design and Analytics

Alpha Design
Beta Design
Gamma Analytics
Delta Analytics

FIGURE 5.3 Annotated Market Map of the E-Mail Direct Marketing Space

only a few companies, it will be apparent that we need to research this sector in more depth.

Figure 5.4 depicts the market for predictive analytics (statistical software used for database marketing). The diagram illustrates the core market surrounded by nine adjacent markets and a few peripheral markets. The number in the bottom right corner of each quadrangle represents the number of companies in that particular market sector. This market map is a working document that helps guide the search process.

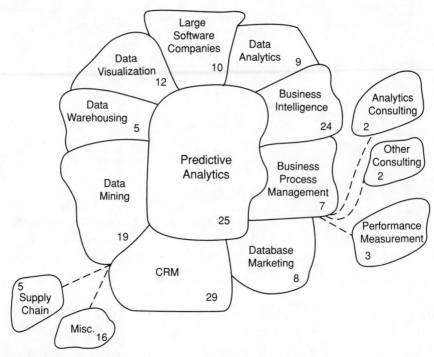

FIGURE 5.4   Market Map of the Predictive Analytics market with a count for
each market sector

Cast a Wide Net

Casting a wide net ensures that every good buyer will be contacted during
the search process. The larger the acquisition the fewer potential buyers
there are, both from a standpoint of fit and affordability. The smaller the
acquisition, the more potential buyers there are. We contact, on average,
about 125 companies per assignment. Sure, many are not interested and yes,
it is a lot of work, but that is what an investment banker is paid to do.
We cast a wide net and work diligently to narrow it down to a handful of
interested and qualified parties. With this method we can be confident that
we will have contacted all of the good potential buyers. In my experience,
almost half of the companies I have sold were to buyers that were outside
the primary market, so it makes sense to contact more than just the usual
suspects.

In addition to greater numbers, there is a wider range of buyers for
small acquisitions. When selling a large company with intangible value,

investment bankers generally contact 20 to 40 companies, maybe 50 at the most. In the sale of a small company, we generally contact between 100 and 150 companies on each assignment. This is not a shotgun approach but rather an investigation into wider markets and into adjacent markets.

We have found that it is worth the effort to contact every single company in a market space. Even those you think might not be interested. We even contact companies who may have said no to the acquisition a year or two earlier. Companies change. People move on. Markets change. Technologies change. Strategies change. We never presume to know the market.

Casting a wide net in the search for potential buyers turns up some unusual prospects. In a number of cases I have sold a company to a buyer that the seller's CEO was unaware of. It is significantly more work for the investment banker, but good things happen when you open a lot of doors.

WAR STORY: A WIDE SEARCH FINDS AN EMERGING BUYER

McAfee Associates was an emerging buyer. They were new on the scene and they had been experiencing great success and rapid growth with their antivirus software. I thought the company might be looking to expand through acquisition as well, so I contacted John McAfee about acquiring my client, a software firm. Maybe McAfee could utilize this software technology in some way. As it turns out, McAfee *was* interested. McAfee thought the software could be a useful application for the network administrators who were its principal corporate customers. Two years prior to this McAfee was unheard of. It was not an obvious buyer. A traditional search would never have uncovered them as a likely acquirer. This case is a classic example of the benefit of casting a wide net in order to identify the non-obvious and emerging buyers.

CONTACTING BUYERS

An Internet search can produce a fairly long list of companies in a short time frame. The selling company can be helpful in providing a list of who they think the likely buyers are. This is usually a good place to start. Other sources of likely buyers include members of the industry association if there is one. The bigger problem is qualifying the companies and making judgments about who truly might be a good buyer.

What is the best way to make contact with potential buyers? Who do we contact at the company? Identifying the right people is a straightforward task and typically it is not a problem. People usually are curious to know what company is for sale and we have found most buyers to be fairly responsive. For those who are not responsive, we simply keep contacting them until we get an answer.

The process of contacting potential buyers requires several months of effort. The first contact usually takes the form of an e-mail with a short description of the company and the key benefits it brings to its customers. E-mail is an effective communication tool because potential buyers can easily reply that they are interested in learning more or that they are not interested.

Contacting buyers is a bit of an art. Knowing how to speak with the CEO of a potential buyer regarding an acquisition is a vital part of the contact process. Phrasing is important, as is tone. In a very short phone call the CEO will be making a number of judgments about whether or not he and his team should spend time considering the acquisition. Does the company look like a tight fit? What is the company's reason for selling? Are price expectations realistic? Could this be a good opportunity? Might this be a waste of our time? If the CEO does not have a good feeling about the answers to these questions, he will be reluctant to spend his or his team's time looking into the acquisition.

Who Do We Contact?

What individual do we contact at a potential buyer? The CEO? The CFO? The in-house counsel? Perhaps the business development department? The answer depends on the size of the potential acquirer. The title of the person we contact at a potential buyer can vary widely depending on the size of the company. For smaller buyers, companies with revenues of $15 million to $125 million, the CEO is almost always the best contact. If he is difficult to reach, the chief financial officer (CFO) can be a good secondary contact. For companies with revenues greater than $175 million the in-house counsel can be a good secondary contact. For larger companies the business development group may be the best place to start. Each company is different and it can be fruitful to make contact with multiple people in the same company.

Having been in the merger and acquisition business for many years, I have developed and maintained a large database of technology, software, and tech-service companies. This information does have a short half-life but it is a good place to start. If I do not already know the CEO or the right contact person I will make a few telephone calls and find out the information I need. It is not particularly difficult to find the right people in an organization; but it does take some effort. With larger companies it can be more difficult. When contacting a large buyer, I always contact multiple people in the organization to make sure we get to the right decision makers.

Some midsized buyers will have a business development department that handles potential acquisitions. Business development people for midsized companies are a mixed bag. Occasionally they might be knowledgeable, but generally business development people are not particularly experienced. Another problem is that they rarely have any real decision-making authority. They are hired to save the CEO and CFO from spending too much time in the early stages of an acquisition.

Business development people tend to move around a lot; they do not stay in their jobs very long. They move up in the organization and across to other organizations. A large company may have a number of people in the business development department. I always attempt to find the most senior person on the business development team. It is also important to learn which person has the most power. My experience has been that the higher up in the organization a person is the more likely they are to understand the big picture and the more effective the negotiations will be.

Contacting Large Buyers

Companies with more than $500 million in revenues typically have M&A teams or strong business development departments that screen acquisitions. Sometimes it can be difficult to get traction with large firms because the business development people can become over burdened with too many things on their plate. If I am not getting the response that I require, I will contact other individuals in the organization to try to get the transaction moving forward. One of the best possible contacts is the vice president of sales for the appropriate division. The head of sales will have the best handle on the viability of selling the target's products through the buyer's sales channels. He is the management person who is closest to the market and to the customers. The buyer's CEO will eventually ask for his opinion about the projected sales and the viability of the acquisition.

A Deal Champion

Every buyer will have a deal champion for a particular transaction. This is the person that sees the value of the acquisition and attempts to persuade other people in the organization that the acquisition will create value for the buyer. For a small buyer, the deal champion is usually the CEO. For a large buyer there could be several deal champions that are in favor of a transaction.

In one transaction the selling company was based in Vienna, Austria. Likely buyers included a number of companies in the data mining and predictive analytics business including three very large companies—Microsoft, Google, and Oracle. Now you do not just approach companies like these and leave the process in their hands. It is important for the investment banker to drive the process and make sure that he or she is communicating with the appropriate person. It is easy to get bounced around or shuttled off to a junior person. You must stay on top of the deal. In this case I was aggressive in my approach; I made multiple contacts with each buyer and ended up connecting with the appropriate decision makers at all three companies.

In another example, I completed a transaction between a small technology company and a very large company. My initial contact in the business development group replied that the company was not interested. He was slow to respond to me, so while I waited for him to reply, I contacted several other people in the business development group and in different divisions of the company. It is a good thing I did because this company turned out to be an excellent buyer. One of my contacts became the deal champion and we successfully closed a transaction. Making multiple contacts at this large buyer proved to be very productive.

Continually Qualify

Qualifying the buyers continually is a key aspect of the process. You do not want to spend time with companies that are tire kickers. They can waste inordinate amounts time as well as encourage false expectations. We qualify each buyer to make sure they truly are a good buyer that can take advantage of the technology or other key assets. Qualifying the candidates is a continual process—a company may seem like a good buyer at first, but when we dig further we may find that they do not have the resources to make optimum use of the technology. Also, they may not have the financial wherewithal to complete the acquisition.

One of the biggest wastes of time is a buyer who is not qualified but is very interested in the acquisition. This does not occur very often but when it does you regret it immensely. So, I always keep a thought in the back of my mind asking the question—is this buyer truly serious and capable of closing the transaction?

The process is imperfect and sometimes the process can be messy. There are always surprises. Even though I attempt to contact a wide range of buyers and weed them out carefully so that I can obtain a few qualified buyers to make offers it does not always turn out this way. Sometimes the best buyers may be engaged with a larger acquisition. Sometimes a handful of good buyers are not discovered until later in the search process. All we can do in these cases is to manage the process the best we can. We also attempt to finesse the timing of the transaction—speeding up slow buyers in order to obtain multiple offers in about the same general time frame.

MARKETS ARE ALWAYS MOVING

The markets in which intangible companies operate are always in motion, in a state of flux. A good illustration of this concept is the market for software for municipal governments. These software applications automate many tasks that concern municipal governments such as building permits, planning, zoning, and utility billing. The municipal government software market is currently in transition. Small suppliers and vendors have made excellent progress replacing the older legacy software of their municipal government customers. Up until this point the bigger software vendors had not entered this market in a meaningful way. It is a messy market and is characterized by long sales cycles. Plus the revenue potential was not as great as other markets.

As any market grows in size, the larger software vendors will begin to take notice. Big firms are always on the lookout for new markets as long as the markets are big enough, or are becoming big enough, to merit their attention. The government software market was not particularly attractive to the larger players but as it increased in size the larger players began to take notice. Government agencies are becoming increasingly automated and are performing more of their activities online, such as issuing building permits.

An example of a bigger player beginning to move into this market is the acquisition of HTE, Inc. by SunGard Data Systems, Inc. in 2003 for $121 million. This was the first major move by a large company into this market. SunGard had revenues of $2 billion. HTE was one of the largest independent providers of IT solutions to local governments and had revenues of $70 million.

Now the bigger players are looking at this market as an attractive opportunity. This spells big trouble for the smaller vendors. This would be a good time for a smaller vendor to sell to a larger company that wants to break into this market. The smaller vendor can offer products, technology, customer base, expertise, and credibility in that market space. The remaining small vendors will eventually be squeezed as the large players enter the market. With greater sales capabilities and service and support resources, the large competitors will eventually win the battle for this market. The smaller players will have a tough time competing and at the current market inflection point they would be wise to consider selling.

THE PERILS OF POLARIZED MARKETS

Polarized markets can have a dramatic impact on the outcome and the price in the sale of an intangible company. A polarized market is one in which companies diverge toward the extremes, small companies at one end and large companies at the other end. This concept is significant because the price that a company commands will vary dramatically depending on the state of the market.

First let's take a look at a non-polarized market. A market that is not polarized will consist of companies in a variety of sizes. There will be a few large companies, a handful of midsized companies and a number of small companies. In some ways the state of the market parallels the market's stage of maturity. From the perspective of a seller, a non-polarized market is the best market because there are buyers of different sizes that provide the seller with a range of alternatives.

A polarized market on the other hand does not provide the selling company with a range of options. A polarized market will have three to five very large companies at one extreme and many small companies at the other extreme and no midsized companies. The small companies will usually be too small to make acquisitions and the big companies may be too large to be interested in a small acquisition. Midsized buyers are the best buyers for small acquisitions; however there are no midsized buyers in a polarized market.

When technology is the seller's key asset, the company will get the highest price if it sells to a buyer who truly needs that technology. In the early stages of development the market will not have become polarized yet and buyers will want to acquire the technology of an intangible company. As the market begins to mature and consolidate, a buyer will not be as interested in acquiring the technology because by then they will have their own technology. They will primarily want to make acquisitions to acquire additional customers. An acquisition based on acquiring customers will sell for a lower price than one motivated by capturing key technology. Chapter 7 examines in more detail the stage of the market and how it affects price.

Market State 1—Many Small Companies

A market in this state typically consists of many small companies and three or four big companies. Many small companies can mean as many as a hundred or more small firms. The quintessential example of such a market is the value-added reseller (VAR). A VAR is a company that adds value to a system and then resells it, such as off-the-shelf hardware combined with customized software to address the needs of a specific vertical market.

In one example, Rho Distribution Software had developed and marketed software to run the operations of distribution companies. A distribution company is a middleman between the manufacturer and the retailers. The distributor usually has a warehouse with inventory and it provides products to a certain geographic region. A beer distributor is a good example.

The distribution software market was totally polarized. There were four large national firms and several hundred small companies (VARs) dispersed across the United States. The large firms did not want to acquire new technology because they had their own technology. Plus, they did not particularly care about adding a few more customers. So the large companies were not viable buyers. The small companies were too small to afford an acquisition. And there were no midsized firms in this market. As a result there were no good buyers to acquire Rho Distribution Software, so the company opted to continue building its business and was not acquired.

Occasionally two small firms may merge. A small buyer will not have enough cash to finance the acquisition so it will almost always be structured as a stock transaction. The buyer will want the revenues and the customers but probably not the technology. Rarely will an acquisition of this type be completed for an attractive price.

Market State 2—All Big Companies

When the market consists of only a handful of very large companies this is a sign of a mature market. This is a tough market when selling an intangible company for less than $30 million. The large companies have their own technology and large customer bases. A big company may be interested in acquiring the customers of a $20 million company, but it will not be interested in acquiring the customers of a company with less than $10 million in value; it is just too small.

The only motive a large company might have to acquire a small company in this market stage is to add additional customers and possibly to enter a new geographic area. A related reason is if the small company has a strong presence in a specific vertical niche market. Such an acquisition could help the large buyer develop a foothold in that niche so that they can build upon it. A company that seeks liquidity should pay close attention to the state of the market and sell before the market reaches this polarized state and consists of only a few large players.

Market State 3—A Few Midsized Buyers

This is the market state that is the most fruitful for acquisitions. Midsized buyers make the best buyers for sub-30 intangible companies. They want to become large companies and one of the best ways to accomplish this objective is through acquisitions. Midsized companies usually have adequate cash for acquisitions. They may also have a publicly traded stock that is a good acquisition currency. Acquisitions are almost always an important part of their strategic plans. Many midsized firms have previously made acquisitions and are familiar with the process. A sub-30 company that is thinking about selling should keep a watchful eye on the market and sell when there are still a handful of good midsized buyers.

In another case, a software firm sought to be acquired by a larger company with greater sales and marketing resources. As in the previous example, the big buyers were not interested in the technology or in the customer base which were the seller's primary assets. Fortunately, in this market there were a handful of midsized companies, one of which was an excellent buyer and a transaction was successfully concluded. The buyer did not want the target's technology but it did find value in the small set of good customers and in the seller's position in its vertical niche market.

SUMMARY

Viewing the markets in an innovative way can lead to the discovery of not just the normal buyers but the unexpected buyers, the non-obvious buyers. As we have noted, buyers can come in a variety of shapes and sizes including small, medium, and large. And each size of company will have different eccentricities and preferences about how it selects and completes acquisitions.

Mapping the markets is an interesting and effective device for viewing the market space and it ensures that no areas are overlooked in the search for buyers. At the core of the market-based approach is understanding the customer need that the product or service addresses.

In some cases, the best buyer may be an emerging company that is growing rapidly and seeks acquisitions to continue its growth. If the markets are polarized, the search for a good buyer will likely be more difficult. Occasionally a buyer will come back into the picture after making an offer a year or two earlier and will successfully acquire the target.

Buyers can be publicly traded companies or privately held companies and there are advantages and disadvantages to each. The next chapter examines the pros and cons associated with these two types of ownership.

CHAPTER 6

Public or Private—
Pros and Cons

The buyer of an intangible company may be publicly traded or privately held. If the selling company is being acquired for cash, then it is irrelevant whether the buyer is public or private. However, the shareholders of many intangible companies prefer to receive the stock of the buying company. There are tax advantages and there is the opportunity for appreciation in the value of the stock. In this case the shareholders will want to carefully consider the advantages and disadvantages of the buyer's ownership status before making a decision.

Selling to a publicly traded company can give the selling shareholders liquidity in a short time frame. Selling to a privately held company does not provide immediate liquidity, but it can give the selling shareholders significant upside potential. If a privately held buyer later goes public or is acquired at a higher price, the selling shareholders could realize appreciation in the value of their shares.

This chapter reviews the pros and cons of selling to a publicly traded company and to a privately held company.

WHAT TO CONSIDER WHEN SELLING TO A PUBLIC COMPANY

Many entrepreneurs build companies with the goal of eventually achieving liquidity by either taking the company public, selling the company, or merging with another firm. Selling to a publicly traded company offers a number of advantages, including liquidity for shareholders, tax benefits, the potential for stock appreciation, and access to resources such as capital, management, and distribution capabilities. Generally, the public market values shares at a higher price than does a private buyer.

Companies go public for several reasons, but first and foremost is liquidity for the owners' shares. Access to capital to support the company's growth is an important consideration as well. A publicly traded stock gives the company an advantage over a private company when using stock to make acquisitions. In addition, employee stock options, which are helpful for attracting and retaining key employees, have more relevance when the company's stock is publicly traded.

In order to be a candidate for a public offering, a company generally needs to achieve annual revenues of at least $25 million, have a record of high growth, a defensible market position, and a management team with a proven track record. The benefits of being a public company generally increase, and the drawbacks decrease, to the extent that the company grows its revenues, earnings, and market capitalization over time.

A company that is thinking about selling should consider both large and small public companies as buyers. A large public company will usually have less risk but a small public company may grow faster and potentially experience greater price appreciation.

The rest of this section outlines some of the key opportunities and challenges of selling to or merging with a public company. I use the terms sell and merge interchangeably. It may be more accurate to identify a transaction as a merger when the buyer and seller are of similar size; however the terms are equivalent for most purposes.

Advantages of Merging with a Public Company

Selling to or merging with a public company may achieve many of an owner's goals, including:

Liquidity. Shareholders of the privately held seller exchange their shares for shares in the public company. They may eventually sell all or a portion of those shares in the stock market.

Access to Capital. The public company typically can raise capital on favorable terms to sustain its growth, usually through a secondary public offering. The improved debt-to-equity ratio may enable the firm to borrow additional funds as well.

Access to Resources. The public firm is generally well staffed with management talent, has qualified marketing and sales personnel, and technical talent. Additionally, public companies usually have established sales and distribution channels and may have complementary technologies and product lines.

Fulfill Strategic Reasons. Many of the reasons for selling may be strategic (i.e., product fit, economies of scale, market synergies, or simply survival in the market). Market synergies can result from pursuing either the (a) same markets, or (b) complementary new markets. The acquisition of the business intelligence company, Business Objects, by SAP, the enterprise software company, gave SAP new capabilities to bring to its clients. The acquisition also helped SAP in its competitive battle with Oracle who acquired Hyperion earlier that same year.

Tax Advantages. An exchange of shares is almost always a tax-free exchange for the selling company. Usually this is not a taxable event. The sellers pay no taxes on the stock received but they do pay taxes when they eventually sell the stock. The sellers' tax basis remains the same. The selling shareholders have the flexibility of being able to sell their shares whenever they choose (after the restricted period for control persons). Stock can also be gifted to children, usually resulting in a lower tax bracket when the shares are eventually sold.

Drawbacks to Merging with a Public Company

If a seller receives stock in the sale of his company, he is marrying his fortunes with those of the acquiring company. The potential exists for the stock to increase in value—or decrease in value.

Drawbacks may include:

Potential Lack of Immediate Liquidity. The shares of a small public company with a market capitalization of less than $100 million may not be very liquid. Market capitalization is the number of shares outstanding multiplied by the stock price. It may not be possible to sell a large block of stock in the market simply because there may be very few buyers. Selling a large number of shares in the market can also push the share price down significantly.

Restricted Stock. The public company may wish to use unregistered or restricted stock in the acquisition. The buyer issues restricted stock because it does not want the seller to dump these share on the market for a period of time. Restricted stock can only be sold after six months subject to certain volume limitations and can be sold without restriction after one year. This requirement was relaxed in 2008, reducing the holding periods from one year and two years respectively. If a selling shareholder becomes a 10 percent shareholder of the acquiring public company, that shareholder is subject to volume limitations and SEC reporting requirements on transactions in the acquiring company's stock. The seller is taking a risk that the shares will not fall in value over this period.

If the shares of stock are not restricted, the buyer may insist upon a "lockup agreement" that prohibits the sellers from selling their shares in the market for a period of time, often as long as a year and possibly longer for a portion of the shares. The buyer requests a lockup because it does not want the seller to sell the shares and possibly hurt the stock price.

Suffering from Market Volatility. The public company could suffer a substantial decline in its stock price due to economic events that occur well after the merger. The dot com bubble of 2000 left a landscape littered with companies and shareholders who sold their companies for stock in public companies and the stock proceeded to plummet in value. It is important to remember that price is only half of the equation. Risk is the other half. The seller should have a clear understanding about the amount of market risk involved.

Business Risk. The company's core business could decline or management could take actions that adversely affect the company. The net result is that the stock price could fall. Business risk is always a concern. Sellers who are seeking to reduce their overall risk need to be cognizant of the buyer's business risk.

Market Perception. The stock market may respond negatively to the merger. This was the case in Macrovision's acquisition of Gemstar. The day the merger was announced Macrovision's stock price fell 25 percent. The market may believe the purchase price was too high, the strategic fit was inappropriate, or that the synergies cannot be realized. The merger could result in a lower share price for everyone.

Transparency. Public companies have greater transparency than they used to. If the seller takes a key management position with the buyer, he may be exposed in a way that he may not want. The Sarbanes-Oxley Act raised the standards of corporate transparency and accountability and these standards include sanctions to assure compliance.

Market and Stock Issues to Consider

The selling shareholders should consider several market and stock issues when merging with a public company. Sellers should understand the degree of liquidity that the buyer's stock has in the market. The sellers should also consider whether to negotiate the price for a fixed dollar amount or a fixed number of shares.

Liquidity of the Market   Are enough shares traded to establish a real market? Are the shares actively traded? What is the daily trading volume—just a few hundred shares or many thousands? Some smaller public companies have very little trading activity which makes it difficult to sell even a moderate number of shares without driving the price down.

The number of shares in the hands of the public that are available for trading is called *float*. (As opposed to shares in the hands of founders and management that are restricted.) Find out what the float is. If only a limited number of shares are available to trade, it will be difficult to liquidate stock. If a founder sold his company for $8 million in stock and later decides to sell the shares in the market, he may find it difficult to sell that many shares without pushing the price of the stock down significantly.

What is the potential for appreciation? Is the outlook bright for the future financial performance of the acquiring company? Do your homework—check out the stock and its upside potential. If you had received cash instead of stock, would you purchase a large quantity of the company's stock? Review stock analysts' reports. Ask the company which analysts follow the company and get copies of recent reports from their brokerage firms.

Fixed Number of Shares or Fixed Dollar Amount   Consider whether your objectives will be met best by getting paid in stock or cash. In an exchange of stock, there are three basic transaction structures:

1. **Fixed Number of Shares.** The buyer exchanges a fixed number of shares for all of the seller's stock. There is a risk that the stock price could fall after the merger announcement. This may not be a problem in the long run, but it is not a good short-term development for shareholders who want to liquidate soon.
2. **Minimum Cash Equivalent.** The buyer guarantees the sellers a minimum share price and makes up the difference in cash. For example, Gamma Corp. assured Delta Corp. shareholders a minimum price of $36 per share and will make up the difference in cash if Gamma's stock price falls prior to the deal closing.
3. **Fixed Dollar Amount with a Flexible Number of Shares.** The buyer makes up any difference in the agreed price with additional shares of the buyer's stock.

The price of the buyer's stock is typically determined as the average of the last 20 days of trading. This is the common practice; however the stock price can be established in any way that the parties agree.

Company owners who are evaluating their exit strategies should consider a merger with a public company. The advantages of liquidity, tax benefits, and access to capital and resources make it an alternative worth considering.

WHAT TO CONSIDER WHEN SELLING TO A PRIVATE COMPANY

Selling to a larger private company will usually reduce the shareholders' level of risk. The seller may be significantly better off owning the buyer's shares of stock than its own shares of stock. There may be a greater chance that the buyer (presumably a larger company) will go public or be acquired.

When selling to a private company it is important that the seller have a similar vision for the company's growth. Unless the transaction is a cash deal, the seller will become part of the buyer's business and may be involved with it for many years. The seller needs to be sure that it agrees with the long-term growth plan for the business and the management teams must be on the same wavelength.

Another aspect regarding selling to a privately held company is that the seller relinquishes control. It is no longer in command of its destiny. There is a reduction of risk but also a reduction in control. The seller must now follow the philosophy and direction of the acquiring company.

Sometimes management will stay on board and sometimes it will not. The addition of the few good managers might be one of the reasons the buyer is interested in the acquisition. Other times there may be duplication in management and the buyer will not want to employ the entire management team.

The obvious disadvantage of selling to a private company is that its stock is not liquid. The shareholders will have to wait for a future liquidity event in order to get cash for their shares. Occasionally this can pay off nicely because the value of the stock can rise, sometimes dramatically. Of course the opposite is also true. The value of the stock can fall and sometimes fall precipitously.

What other issues should a seller consider if it is thinking about trading its shares for shares of a privately held buyer? What is the value of the buyer's stock? (Remember that the relevant question is not the value of the stock, but the percentage of the buyer that the seller will own after the transaction.) How likely is the buyer to be acquired down the road? Sometimes the seller can negotiate a buyback provision that enables its shareholders to sell their shares back to the buyer at some point in the future.

Should You Take This Stock?

One of the foremost questions when considering whether to take the stock of a private company is—what are the prospects for liquidity down the road? Is there a good chance that this company will be acquired in the near future or possibly go public?

The buyer may have a strong opinion about the value of its stock. The buyer's value may be determined by the valuation on the last round of venture financing. The buyer typically will want to use this value because most of the time it is a fairly high value.

It is important to differentiate between the true company value and the valuation as of the last round of financing. A company may conclude a round of financing with a pre-money valuation of $40 million. If several venture capital firms invest $15 million then the post-money valuation is $55 million. The value of the company itself has not increased but now the company has an extra $15 million dollars in its bank account so the value is $55 million.

The post-money valuation of $55 million does not mean that this is the market value of the company. In other words, it does not mean the company could be sold for $55 million. Usually it would be sold for less. The pre-money and post-money numbers are simply after effects of the quintessential question which is: "What percentage will the company give up for $15 million?" In the example above $15 million is buying 27 percent of the company ($15/55 = 27\%$). All that matters to the venture capital firm and to the founders and other shareholders is what percentage they will own. The valuation is calculated by simply dividing the $15 million by 0.27. This is not a "valuation" in the true sense of market value. It is a valuation used in the parlance of financing, an important distinction.

The reason this is important in the current discussion is that the buyer is likely to insist upon using the valuation from a recent financing because it gives them a higher value for their stock. Generally it is best to agree with the buyer on the value of its company (usually because it is an uphill battle to do otherwise). A smart seller will employ the same metrics to calculate the value of its own company. For example if the buyer asserts that its value from a recent financing is 3 times revenues then the seller should also declare that its value is 3 times revenues. In reality, the buyer will be a larger and probably more profitable company and therefore less risky, so that its multiple of revenues will be greater than that of the seller. So, maybe the seller can insist that its value is 2 times revenues. (I do not buy into the revenue multiple as a means of valuation, but I will certainly use it in negotiations if it helps my position.) Remember that the valuation question is inconsequential in actual fact. The only relevant question is: "What percent of the buying company will the seller own after the transaction?"

If the buyer is a small company or similar in size to the seller, it can be difficult to establish a value for the buyer's stock. One of the overriding points to remember in this case is that the shareholders of the seller will most likely be better off owning shares of the buyer's stock than their own stock. Why? Because the combined companies will be significantly larger than the seller and thus less risky. Also, the combined entity will have a greater chance of succeeding in the marketplace and as a result the shareholders will be better off.

How to Value the Buyer's Stock   If the buyer is a fairly large company there may be comparable market data that can provide a basis for its value. If several public companies compete in the same market, the price-earnings ratios of these firms can be a good indicator of value for the buyer. Price-to-sales ratios can also be used but to a lesser degree.

If the parties cannot agree on the buyer's valuation and if the buyer is a large enough company (with earnings before interest and taxes of more than $3 million), it may be sensible to engage a valuation expert to determine the value of the buyer's stock. The cost of a valuation can range from $10,000 to $35,000. Such a valuation may or may not hold any credibility with the buyer but it could help the seller to better understand the basis for the valuation.

In one transaction that I was involved with, the buyer was a privately held company and it planned to go public or be acquired in the near future, probably within the next two or three years. The company had experienced significant growth and good profitability so it was an excellent candidate to be acquired. The firm's revenues were about $20 million so it was of a size that would be attractive to a number of buyers.

Several firms in the industry had recently been acquired for 2 to 2.5 times revenues. In one transaction that was quite visible the price calculated to be 4 times revenues. Most of these companies were privately held so no information was available regarding their profitability. The multiples of revenues were all the information we had. Remember, multiples of revenues are not an accurate way to value a company. In this situation it was all we had, so it was better than nothing. With revenues of $20 million, using a multiple of revenue does hold some validity. In this instance the companies were reasonably comparable and the range of revenue multiples was relatively narrow.

In this case I estimated the value of the buyer's stock to be between 2.5 and 3 times revenues. It was at the high end of the range because of its rapid growth and solid profitability. The buyer acquired my client for a specific number of shares of stock. Since the selling shareholders would become shareholders in the buyer, I asked the buyer for copies of its financial statements which it readily provided. This rough value calculation gave us a reasonable idea of the value of the shares that the buyer was exchanging for the seller's shares. If the buyer was acquired at even a reasonable value the seller's shareholders would achieve an acceptable return on their original investment. There were several other buyers in the picture; however this buyer had much more upside potential. This turned out to be a good call because two years later the buyer was acquired for $150 million. The shareholders of the seller achieved an attractive return.

WAR STORY: WHAT IS A PRIVATE COMPANY'S STOCK WORTH?

The sale of Kappa Consulting to Omicron Software used a valuation of $180 million for Omicron's stock. This was the valuation in Omicron's most recent round of venture capital financing a little over a year prior. No, it was not grounded in reality but Omicron's management was happy with that number. They were also in the driver's seat on this deal since they were the only good buyer in the picture. So, we agreed to that valuation.

The nice thing about this transaction was that there was very little bickering over valuations. Omicron was pleased because it was making an acquisition with its high-priced stock so that took pressure off the price discussion. Since this was a generous valuation it allowed the price for Kappa Consulting to be higher than what it might have been otherwise. Omicron Software offered $9 million for Kappa Consulting. The shareholders were pleased with this figure and the parties agreed on the deal. Do not forget that the only thing that really mattered was the percentage of ownership that Kappa Consulting shareholders had in Omicron Software after the close of the transaction.

Selling the Stock Back

If the seller does not want to hold the buyer's stock for a long period of time there are a couple of alternatives. The first is to sell the company with payment in the form of a note from the buyer. A standard promissory note will have a term of three to five years with a moderate interest rate, typically at the prime rate, or maybe one or two percentage points over prime.

A second creative solution is to make an agreement that the buyer will buy back the seller's shares over a period of time. For example, let's say the transaction currency was $6 million worth of the buyer's stock, say 600,000 shares. The seller would eventually like to achieve liquidity for these shares. The parties could agree to a buyback structure whereby the buyer agrees to purchase the shares back from the seller over a period of years. The buyer will purchase these shares at a predetermined price or perhaps at a stated multiple of profits or cash flow.

The structure might look something like this. In the first year no shares are purchased. In each of the next four years the buyer will purchase 150,000 shares of stock from the seller at $10 per share. These types of structures are entirely negotiable. The share price could be a flat $10 per share or it could increase based on the profits of the buyer or based on some other metric. A buyback option makes sense when the buyer is a large enough company that it has sufficient cash flow to afford to purchase the shares in the future.

SUMMARY

If the selling shareholders are not completing a cash transaction, they should consider the pros and cons of accepting stock from a public company or a private company. The advantage of selling to a public company is that the shares of stock will be liquid at some point relatively soon depending on the restricted period. A key issue to consider is the liquidity of the market. Are there many shares or only a small number of shares being traded in the market? A thin market has few buyers and sellers and selling a large number of shares could push the price down dramatically. Volatility is another issue to consider; some stocks are more volatile than others.

Although not offering immediate liquidity, selling to a private company may give the shareholders a chance for greater price appreciation. Individual investors sometimes prefer a stock transaction over a cash transaction because the shares can still increase in value. The buyer's stock may be a very good investment.

The next chapter reviews the concept of value, one of the more elusive and interesting notions surrounding the sale of an intangible company. We take a look at a variety of types of value including how time can add a strategic component to value. We also review the three traditional approaches for determining value. The chapter concludes with an examination of how a buyer will determine price and how market timing impacts price.

CHAPTER 7

The Concept of Value

There are more myths, misinformation, and misunderstandings about value than any other topic in the merger and acquisition field. It is difficult for people to truly grasp the concept that the value of an intangible company is whatever a buyer is willing to pay. Most people believe that companies have intrinsic value, that value falls within a narrow range, and that multiples of revenues are worthwhile. This is simply not true for intangible companies.

The main point is this: value is solely a function of the market, not of some internal measure. The value of an intangible company is like the value of Elvis' guitar: the value is simply how much a buyer is willing to pay. There is no one single correct price, such as, the latest multiple of revenue times the firm's revenue. Value can range dramatically depending on who the buyer is and the strategic importance of the acquisition to that buyer.

Let's review our objective: to sell the company for the highest price. How do we do this? We go out to the market and contact all of the best buyers and ask them to make offers. We negotiate intelligently and attempt to get competitive bids so that we can truly get the best offers from the buyers. Then we select the buyer that offers the best price and best terms.

A number of factors affect the value of the company in addition to its historical earnings and potential future income. The company's market position and market share are important. The relationship with its customers and the company's ability to execute will impact value. The talent of its management team and its development team also affect value. The relative value of these strengths will vary in importance from buyer to buyer.

In this chapter I examine what the concept of value really means. I also review the traditional methods of valuing a company and how a buyer will determine the price that it is willing to pay. I discuss the tipping point in a market and how market timing has a dramatic impact on achieving the optimum price.

VALUE IS NOT NECESSARY

If I trade my skateboard for your bicycle and we are both happy with the trade, then it is a successful transaction. No determination of value was necessary. The market for an intangible company is similar to a barter economy. If a farmer trades three goats and two pigs for two cows with another farmer, no valuation is necessary.

Management often spends way too much energy upfront fretting over the question of valuation. Sometimes management thinks it must determine a minimum acceptable price upfront. This is not possible when selling an intangible company. The price, the real price, is determined by the market and not by any other means. I suggest to sellers that they not worry so much about the valuation right now but rather that we go out to the market, contact all the good buyers, get offers, and negotiate the best price that we can and then accept the highest offer.

People do not like uncertainty. They will gravitate to a measurement. Even if it is a wrong measurement, at least they have an answer. People are uncomfortable with uncertainty and the quest for an upfront value underscores this point.

REVIEWING THE MYTHS

Myths were addressed in Chapter 2. We will review a few of them here because they are critical when considering the concept of value.

   Intrinsic Value. In our earlier discussion regarding the concept of intrinsic and extrinsic value, I pointed out that the value of an intangible company is extrinsic; it depends on the market, on the buyer. By definition there is no intrinsic value in an intangible company.

   A Narrow Value Range. The myth of a narrow value range is a subtle one. It is important to understand that the range of value can be quite wide. A seller may receive offers of $3 million, $6 million, or $11 million for the same company. The variations in price reflect the fact that different buyers will find different levels of strategic value.

   Revenue Multiples. In the section on myths we also discussed the problems associated with revenue multiples and why they are poor indicators of value. Multiples of revenues are bogus for four reasons. First, because the range of multiples is too wide to be useful. Second, because comparisons using the multiple are simply not valid. Just because one company sold for a certain multiple of revenue does not mean that another company will sell for that same multiple, even if the companies are similar. Third, revenue multiples do not consider cost structures, management talent, pricing, profitability, or growth. And fourth is the problem of narrow markets; there are only a limited number of strategic buyers who can benefit from the seller's key assets. These buyers care only about the strategic fit with their company, not some revenue multiple.

WHAT IS A MARKET?

Value exists in the context of a market. This begs an obvious question: What is a market? A market is a group of buyers and sellers who come together to buy or sell something. If the market is comprised of many buyers and many sellers then this is a liquid market. A good example is the stock market. There are many buyers and many sellers for most of the stocks traded on the exchanges or over-the-counter. The more buyers and sellers, the more liquid the market is. Liquidity is important because it enables one to buy or sell shares without driving the price up or down significantly.

The market for shares of a small public company is not as liquid as for shares of a large public company. If an investor wants to buy or sell shares of a small public company it will cost him more because there are fewer buyers and sellers. The spread between the bid and asked prices is greater. In addition, the sale of a large number of shares will push the price down, sometimes significantly.

For a small privately held company whose value is intangible there is no market of buyers. Since intangible companies are acquired by strategic buyers, there may be at most four or six companies in the world that are truly good buyers. This is not enough buyers to represent a real market.

TYPES OF VALUE

In order to better understand intangible value, let's first discuss *financial value*, which is a more widely understood concept. Financial value is value based on expected future cash flows. In essence the buyer is purchasing a stream of cash flow in the future. The historical earnings can often be a good predictor of future earnings.

For a public company, market capitalization is the simplest measure of a company's financial value. Market capitalization is the current stock price multiplied by the number of outstanding shares. Market capitalization, or market cap, ignores debt however, and for companies with substantial debt this can change the picture dramatically. In most cases, enterprise value is a more accurate measure of value.

Enterprise value is defined as a company's market capitalization plus any outstanding debt and less cash in the bank. This may seem counterintuitive at first but the cash reduces the cost of the acquisition. The simple rationale is that if one acquires a company for $100 million and the company has $25 million in cash, the real cost of the acquisition is only $75 million.

Baseline value is the minimum financial value of a company. The baseline value can be calculated using the discounted cash flow method. This valuation method projects future cash flows and discounts them according to the level of risk. I will explore this topic in more depth later in this chapter.

Most owners of smaller technology companies would not want to sell the company for the baseline value. They typically want a higher price, one based on the company's *strategic value*. Strategic value is the value to one particular buyer. Strategic value will vary from buyer to buyer depending on the degree to which a buyer can capitalize on the technology or other assets of the selling company.

The term synergy has been dramatically overused in the merger and acquisition business. I hesitate to use the term but sometimes there actually are synergies between the buyer and the seller. Synergies can include increased revenues, cost savings, process improvements, tax advantages, and other benefits. Increased revenues may result from cross-selling the target's products through the buyer's distribution channels or vice versa. Later in this chapter we will review an actual example of how one buyer calculated *synergy value*.

THE TIME PREMIUM

Time adds a strategic component to value. Intangible transactions often include a time premium. When a company acquires a target, the target's products are available to sell now versus later if the buyer were to develop its own products. This is why a time premium is appropriate. The time premium can be substantial, sometimes 100 percent or 200 percent more than the value of the technology itself. That is because it is an essential addition to the buyer's product line.

One of the reasons that buyers acquire intangible companies is because they need a particular technology and sometimes they need it in a hurry. Let's take the hypothetical example of Theta Software Company. Theta has developed software that does a better job of managing and integrating wireless devices. Theta has a team of five developers and it has taken them three years to develop and test the software. The software is fully operational and is being used by five large customers and now Theta is rolling out the product to the broad market.

Make versus Buy

A buyer that needs this technology could develop it in-house or they could acquire Theta. This is the old make versus buy question. What would be the cost of developing it in-house? It took Theta 15 man-years to develop the technology. Let's assume that this technology is of high importance to the buyer. The buyer figures it could develop the technology in 15 man-years as well. Since they need it right away, the buyer could hire 15 software developers and finish the technology in one year.

However in developing the technology in one year versus the three years that Theta required probably means that not as many development tasks could be performed in parallel, so it might take the buyer an extra six months to develop the technology. Add another six months to fully test the technology.

Acquiring existing technology that has been fully tested and debugged can save the buyer a significant amount of time and enable it to get to market sooner. When a market is moving rapidly, time can be a very important factor and a buyer will likely take this into account when determining the price that it is willing to pay for technology.

So the total time required for the buyer to develop the technology so that it is ready for market is two years. 15 man-years over a two-year time period totals 30 man-years. All 15 developers would probably not be needed for the testing phase so let's call it 25 man-years.

At a cost of $200,000 per developer per man-year that means the total cost to the buyer would be $5 million. (This cost represents the fully burdened cost. In accounting parlance, fully burdened cost includes salary, benefits, employment taxes, and related overhead expenses.) So, the buyer could spend $5 million over a two-year period and own technology that is equivalent to Theta's.

But I Want it *Now*

The buyer wants the technology right *now*, not in two years, so it is willing to pay a premium to acquire the technology right away. How much of a premium? The answer to that question depends on the opportunities that the buyer faces in the market. Perhaps the buyer could sell the technology immediately to its customer base and generate sales of $8 million the first year with a $1.5 million contribution margin. (The contribution margin equals revenues minus the variable costs.) The second year the buyer estimates that it could sell $12 million worth with a contribution margin of $2.5 million. The total contribution margin for the first two years is $4 million.

Another way to view this figure is to describe it as a time premium. In other words, the value of Theta's technology to the buyer is $5 million (development cost) plus $4 million (the time premium), or $9 million in total. This analysis from the buyer's point of view illustrates that the buyer is better off if it can acquire Theta Software at a price of less than $9 million. At a price greater than $9 million the buyer is better off developing the technology itself.

There is a lot of room to negotiate between the value to the buyer and what it cost Theta to develop this technology. Theta is a smaller company than the buyer but even if it paid the same $200,000 per man-year the total cost to develop the technology would be about $3 million. If Theta is happy with a $1 million profit it might be willing to sell its technology for $4 million. So therein lies the room to make a deal. Theta would accept a price of $4 million or greater and the buyer would be willing to pay up to $9 million. This is why selling intangible companies is quite interesting. There is simply no right number for value.

TRADITIONAL VALUATION METHODS

There are three primary methods for valuing a company. Each of these methods approaches value from a different angle. The approach that makes the most sense depends on the specifics of the company and the situation. Even though valuations do not usually apply to the sale of an intangible company, understanding the basis for value can be beneficial. Occasionally in negotiating a transaction the other party may rely on or embrace one of these valuation methods so it is a good idea to understand the various valuation approaches.

A baseline valuation can be helpful to a company that is thinking about being acquired. The baseline value will not be as great as the strategic value for most intangible companies, but it is a place to start. The valuation methods described below can be helpful in determining the baseline value for an intangible company.

Determining the value of a business is more of an art than it is a science. A spreadsheet is an extremely useful tool in a valuation. However, the assumptions that lie behind the numbers are more important than the numbers. Adjusting the assumptions that underlie a forecast can have a more dramatic impact on the valuation than simply changing the forecast.

In the long run, a company's value will be measured by its earnings. The software industry is still relatively young and many companies have yet to achieve profitability. One day even Google will be valued according to its earnings.

The traditional methods for determining value include:

- Market Approach
- Asset Approach
- Income Approach

The Market Approach

The Market Approach is usually the best method to value a company. The only problem with this approach is that it is often difficult to find companies that are truly comparable. It is also difficult to find information on private companies and private transactions. Comparing large companies is fairly straightforward. It is not difficult to identify good comparables for companies with revenues between $200 million and $800 million. However it is a different matter when trying to identify a public company that is comparable to an intangible company with $15 million in revenue.

The Market Approach uses multiples of earnings of similar companies in the same industry to calculate value. This is typically the best way to measure value. However, in fast-moving industries such as technology and software, very few companies are similar enough for comparisons to be valid.

A valuation must use similar companies that are truly comparable. In one instance I was an expert witness in a valuation case regarding a small stock brokerage firm with eight employees. The expert witness for the other side had done a valuation that was based on comparing this brokerage firm to Oppenheimer & Co., the large New York investment bank. This made no sense at all. Apparently, he regretted this comparison because when he was being deposed by the lawyer, beads of sweat literally fell from his forehead onto the yellow tablet in front of him. That was interesting.

For publicly traded companies the firm's value is determined by the stock market and it is reflected in the price of the company's stock. The Price Earnings (P/E) ratio is the stock price divided by the company's earnings per share. It is a simple and straightforward valuation metric. In the public market, stock prices have averaged about 15 times earnings over the last 80 years. High growth companies have price earnings ratios greater than that and lower growth companies have price earnings ratios less than that. For example, if a company has a P/E ratio of 20 and it earns profits after tax of 5.0 percent this imputes a multiple of revenues of 1.0. ($20 \times .05 = 1.0$). The average Fortune 500 stock trades at 0.9 times revenues. The numbers make sense. The median net profit as a percentage of revenues for the Fortune 500 was 5.8 percent in 2007, which was a good year. In earlier years the median was 4.8 percent.

For privately held companies the most widely used metric for calculating the value is the multiple of operating profits. Operating profits are defined as earnings before interest and taxes, or EBIT. This multiple is preferred over the multiple of net profits because companies can pay different amounts in interest and taxes depending on a wide range of variables. The multiple of EBIT takes interest and taxes out of the equation. A company that is acquired through an all cash transaction will have no debt and no interest expense. Another company acquired with debt will have significant interest expense. Depending on the way a company is financed, interest expense can be relatively high or minimal, so it makes sense to view the value irrespective of the company's financing structure.

What really matters most is cash flow. In recent years EBITDA has come into vogue as a representation for cash flow. EBITDA adds back depreciation and amortization to operating profits. For many years private equity firms have used the valuation metric of 5 or 6 times EBIT to determine the value of a company. A company's depreciation expense is generally a good approximation of its capital expenditures. However EBITDA does not include capital expenditures. Capital expenditures are necessary expenditures; capital equipment needs to be replaced every so often. By not including capital expenditures cash flow is overstated. Thus, the value can also be overstated. An astute buyer will eventually discover this in the due diligence process and will reduce the price accordingly.

A more accurate measure for cash flow is the term "free cash flow." Free cash flow is defined as net income plus depreciation minus capital expenditures minus changes in working capital. The reason depreciation and amortization are added back to income is because they are strictly accounting conventions; cash is not affected. Free cash flow is defined as:

Net income + Depreciation and amortization − Capital expenditures
− Changes in working capital = Free cash flow

Working capital is defined as current assets minus current liabilities. The change in working capital equals the working capital at the end of the period minus the working capital at the beginning of that period. The time period is typically one year but it can be any period that one wants to analyze. The concept is that as a company experiences growth it will require more working capital. So, some of the profits must be reinvested in the business and this reduces the cash flow available to the shareholders. Free cash flow is a widely accepted measure of the amount of cash that a business produces. The multiple of free cash flow is an excellent tool for valuing the company.

The Asset Approach: Replacement Cost

The Asset Approach entails adding up the market value of all the company's assets: accounts receivable, finished goods inventory, raw materials inventory, equipment, buildings, and so on. This valuation method is rarely applicable to intangible companies. Most intangible firms, by definition, have little in the way of tangible assets. Inventories may not be significant. Accounts receivable are always a good and relatively liquid asset.

The primary asset of a software or technology company is its intellectual property. It is extremely difficult to place a value on software. It may have required many man-years to develop, but the value of that software depends on what a buyer is willing to pay for it.

Another way to think of the asset approach is replacement cost. How much would it cost a company to develop similar technology themselves? Replacement cost is often the minimum value for any company. If one adds up the values of the assets the total will not come very close to the true value of the firm. The company's strategic value is usually much greater than the total of its assets.

The Income Approach: Discounted Cash Flow

The Discounted Cash Flow (DCF) method projects future profits or cash flows and then discounts them by a percentage that reflects the certainty of achieving those earnings. This stream of cash flows is discounted to the present using a theory called net present value. The idea is that a dollar received today is more valuable than a dollar received a year from now.

The chief difficulty that people have with this method is understanding the meaning of the discount rate. The discount rate is not the rate of inflation. It is a measure of the risk that the company can achieve the projected earnings. The discount rate is also the required return on capital. In other words, what return do investors require or expect in order to make the company an attractive investment? Another way to view the discount rate is as the company's cost of capital.

Let's take this phrase "required return on capital" and examine it a little more closely. An investor has different opportunities from which to choose to invest his dollars. The investor can invest in the stock market and expect to earn a return of between 10 and 11 percent over the long term. (The average real return over the last 50 years is 10.3 percent.) And if we were to select just one stock, for example IBM, we would find that it has provided investors with a total return, including price appreciation and dividends, of 10.7 percent per year for the last 10 years.

The required return on capital for the investor then becomes the company's cost of capital. Let me restate it a different way. The cost to the company for obtaining capital is equal to the return that the investor seeks for his capital. If investors seek a return of 25 percent for an investment in company Alpha because of its risk characteristics, then Alpha's cost of capital is 25 percent.

A technology company, especially a smaller technology company, has greater business risk than IBM so it must return more than 11 percent to its investors. The required return to investors for a firm with less than $20 million in revenue will usually be from 20 to 25 percent, and higher if the company has a limited history or significant business risk. Business risk includes product risk, technology risk, financial risk, market risk, and so on.

An intuitive way to understand the discount rate is to ask a simple question. Would you rather invest $20,000 in IBM stock or in the privately held XYZ Software stock? If I had a choice between earning 11 percent on IBM stock or 20 percent in a small software company, I would choose IBM every time—it is significantly less risky. In order for XYZ Software to be attractive enough to the investor, the expected rate of return should be greater than 20 percent. For start-up and small companies with minimal revenues and a short history, the required return on capital should be 35 percent, or as high as 45 percent. These companies are risky and the discount rate must reflect this risk.

Valuation theory dictates that the discount rate be calculated, or built up, by starting with the risk-free rate and then adding additional amounts for equity risk, size risk, and company specific risk. The risk-free rate is the rate that an investor could earn on 20-year treasury bonds. The equity premium reflects the fact that stocks are riskier than government bonds. The size premium reflects the fact that small companies are riskier than large companies. Company specific risk is a judgment on the analyst's part that adjusts for a variety of risk factors such as management, market characteristics, financial structure, and so on. This is an example of the discount rate calculation:

Risk-free rate (20-year treasury bonds)	4.5%
Equity risk premium	8.0%
Size risk premium	4.4%
Company specific risk	4.0%
Total discount rate	**20.9%**

These figures for equity risk and size risk result from a number of financial studies that have been completed to determine the correct values for these risks. These percentages are fairly consistent among valuation professionals. Technically, the 20-year treasury rate is the yield for a 30-year bond with 20 years left until maturity.

The appropriate discount rate is determined by the judgment of the analyst performing the valuation. The more experience the person has the better his or her judgment will be in understanding the risk nature of the business and therefore the appropriate discount rate.

I have seen many valuations using the discounted cash flow method in which the discount rate was way too low, unrealistically low. Just to restate the point again—using a discount rate of 11 percent implies that the company has the same risk characteristics as IBM. This is rarely the case for a sub-30 company and therefore the valuation will be radically overstated.

The second mistake that people typically make when using discounted cash flow is projecting revenues and profits at unreasonably high levels. The discounted cash flow model is a good one because it is simple, straightforward, and easy to calculate on a spreadsheet. However the only way this model makes sense is if the projections are reasonable. And by reasonable I mean very reasonable. Revenue growth must be reasonable. Gross margins must be reasonable, cost of sales must be reasonable, and administrative expenses must be reasonable.

As a business grows, its gross margins typically decline; they do not increase. I cannot tell you how many valuation models I have seen in which the gross margins were projected to increase over time. This is totally unrealistic. The gross margin percentage must be reasonable and based on historical results. As a business grows its costs of sales also grow. Administrative costs increase as well. Tax rates typically go up as businesses increase in size. So to make this point again, the projections, all the projections, must be reasonable.

An illustration of the discounted cash flow calculation is shown in Table 7.1. Cash flows are projected for five years. The model assumes that the cash flow will be the same every year after year five. The terminal value is calculated by dividing the cash flow in year five by the discount rate. In this example it is 2.3 million divided by 22 percent. Another way to think about terminal value is to assume that the company will be sold at the end of year five for $10.5 million.

TABLE 7.1 Example of Discounted Cash Flow Calculation

($ in millions)	Year 1	Year 2	Year 3	Year 4	Year 5	Terminal Value
Cash Flow	1.4	1.6	1.8	2.0	2.3	10.5
Discount Rate	22%					
Net Present Value	$8.1 million					

If the company is projected to continue growing after year five, the analyst can simply extend the projections for several additional years. Another way to factor in growth is to calculate the terminal value by subtracting the growth rate from the discount rate and then divide the year five cash flow by that number. This is a way to account for the company's growth over the long term.

Note that the cash flow is after-tax cash flow, not pretax. This is another misuse of the discounted cash flow model. I have heard many sellers say, "But we do not pay any taxes. We are an S-Corp. (or an LLC)." Yes, but the company that acquires your firm *does* pay taxes and what they care about is their after-tax cash flow. Remember, the point that we are addressing here is the value of the company to another party.

The discounted cash flow method is a good way to compute a baseline value for a company as long as the projections are reasonable. The drawback of the discounted cash flow approach is that the assumptions are subjective. The more rapidly the business is growing the more difficult it is to accurately forecast the profits. It does force one to make reasonable assumptions about future performance, so it is a good exercise. If the projections are reasonable, very reasonable, then the model can be helpful. In addition, the discount factor must be accurate. It is very tempting to increase the valuation by simply decreasing the discount rate. I have seen a number of valuations using this model with the discount rate of as low as 7 or 10 percent. This is absurd and it makes for a valuation that is ridiculously high.

The discounted cash flow method is a good model for establishing a baseline value for a business. This is the value based on its financial performance on a stand-alone basis. The baseline value must be built upon reasonable assumptions, not pie in the sky. And the discount rate must reflect the true risk of the business.

Many intangible companies have revenue that is comprised of two parts: new sales and recurring revenues. Recurring revenues include support, renewals, and maintenance revenues. Recurring revenues have a greater degree of certainty, and thus less risk, than do new sales. Sometimes it is helpful to calculate the value of these two components separately since they have different levels of risk.

WAR STORY: WHEN DCF IS APPROPRIATE

This example illustrates a situation in which the discounted cash flow model was appropriate to determine the value of a company. In this case I was engaged to determine the value of two companies. The first was a software company with revenues of about $8 million. It had a sister company with many of the same shareholders and a handful of outside investors. The sister company was originally set up to handle the sales and marketing for several of the main company's products. The sister company was much smaller and was not profitable. The main company had to contribute cash every year to keep the sister company afloat.

Over time management realized it made no sense to have two separate companies. Given the fact that there were outside investors in the sister company, management realized it needed an independent, third-party valuation in order to acquire the sister company. The sister company had revenues of $1 million and had never generated a profit; however it had made good inroads in the market. The brand name in this vertical market was fairly recognizable. So there was value there. The only way to approximate value in this case was to use the discounted cash flow model. I projected three different scenarios to model the company's growth in revenues and profits. These scenarios included Conservative Growth, Most Likely Growth, and Aggressive Growth. Using three scenarios makes good sense when valuing a company that has a limited history. The models produced three different valuations and I used my judgment to weight them as I felt appropriate. I also used my judgment from many years of selling technology companies as a cross-check on the final valuation.

In this case the discounted cash flow method produced a very reasonable rationale for the valuation. The sister company was successfully acquired by the main company.

RULES OF THUMB FOR DETERMINING VALUE

Looking for a simple answer? Sorry, there really are not any rules of thumb that are of any merit. Revenue multiples calculated after the fact are rarely applicable to other transactions. Only in industries where companies have similar cost structures and operating characteristics do revenue multiples make sense. Everyone likes rules of thumb because they make life easier. But by making life easy, they make life inaccurate.

There is one rule of thumb that is of some practical use. Most companies with revenues of less than $20 million are worth between 4 and 6 times cash flow. This may be a useful rule to calculate a company's baseline value. It is a metric that is often used by financial buyers. The only problem with this rule of thumb is that it does not ascribe a very high value to a company with intangible value. Company owners are not particularly happy with the value calculated by this rule because it is much lower than the strategic value. The value to a strategic buyer will usually be substantially more than the value calculated with this rule of thumb.

When to Use Professional Valuations

First of all, is a valuation really necessary? What do you do with the number that is derived from the valuation? Do you put a price tag on the company? Do you decline to sell it if that value is not realized?

Most professional valuations are requested to determine a company's fair market value. The definition of fair market value is the price at which a property would change hands between a willing buyer and a willing seller, neither being under any compulsion to buy or to sell, and both having reasonable knowledge of the relevant facts. This definition was handed down by the United States Supreme Court (in the Cartwright case) and is relevant to tax law, marital dissolution, and other situations.

If operating profit (EBIT) is less than $2 million, my recommendation is that the company not obtain a professional valuation. It will not be accurate enough to be helpful. When a company is small, the valuation range from the low valuation to the high valuation can be such a wide range as not to be helpful at all. The information value is minimal at best. Plus, for small companies, a small change in expenses can have a dramatic impact on profitability. For example, if the two founders give themselves a nice bonus profits may be cut in half.

Another issue with determining the value of small companies is the degree of certainty. For the valuation of a small company the degree of certainty can be quite wide. I may determine that the value of a company is $5.3 million, with a range of $3.2 million to $7.2 million. This range is my best estimate after considering all the factors; however, the range is extremely wide. In the valuation of another company I may determine that the value is also $5.3 million but the range is from $4.8 to $5.8 million, a much narrower range. Thus, it has a much higher degree of certainty.

For larger companies, with operating profits greater than $2 million, a valuation may be helpful. The comparable companies in a market approach are more likely to be truly good comparables. Usually these valuations are reasonably accurate if they correctly assess the risks of the business. Plus, the concepts addressed in the valuation may be useful in the negotiations. For a strategic sale, however, a valuation is not usually relevant.

Sometimes a professional valuation is required. The earlier case of the firm acquiring its sister company is a good example. An arms-length valuation was necessary because the firms had overlapping shareholders. In a divorce if one party owns shares of a privately held company a valuation may be necessary. Other situations in which valuations are required include tax situations, lawsuits, estate tax and gift planning, shareholder buyouts, and financial recapitalizations. Employee stock ownership plans (ESOPs) are also required to have a valuation performed on an annual basis.

Valuations Can Be a Problem

Sometimes valuations can be a problem. They can set expectations unreasonably high for the seller. Putting a high price tag on a company can scare away some buyers, particularly if the price is unrealistically high.

In the sale of one company, before I was brought on board, the CEO had engaged a valuation firm to determine the value of the company. The valuation utilized a number of inflated assumptions and the projections were extremely optimistic. In addition the cash flow analysis failed to include future capital expenditures so the cash flows were overstated. As a result the company's valuation was inflated. It made the CEO feel very good about his company; however, as I moved forward with the sale I realized that the CEO had unrealistic expectations regarding price. As a result the sale process was a difficult one. The valuation actually did the owner a disservice.

WAR STORY: IS A VALUATION NECESSARY AHEAD OF TIME?

In meeting with the CEO we discussed the process for selling the company in some depth. When the discussion shifted to valuation he wanted to know what the value was and discussed at some length why he thought the value should be $10 million to $15 million. I had to interrupt him to ask an important question. I asked him what he would do or not do, what he would decide or not decide, if he had a number for value before we began the process. Would he not sell the company? Would he just take the first offer if it was higher than the valuation number?

The reason I brought this up is because if he wants to sell for the highest price we must go out to the market and generate offers. If he determines a value upfront of say $10 million and then goes out to the market and gets offers of $5 million, $7 million, and $8 million, will

(Continued)

he not sell the company? Who said the $10 million number was the right number in the first place?

If the owners truly want to sell the company the best course of action is to reach out to the market, run a disciplined process, negotiate intelligently, and take the highest offer, no matter what the "valuation" is ahead of time.

Managing Seller Expectations

Trying to sell a company that expects an unrealistically high price is almost always a complete waste of time. Sellers can be greedy. And the market is not stupid.

It can work the other way too, however. I have been involved in a number of situations in which the price that we received was far higher than the expectations of the seller. This is certainly a nice situation. This result occurs by running a disciplined and smart process, by contacting a wide range of buyers, and getting interested parties to the table at the same point in time. A well-run process can ensure the best price. Whether or not it is an exceptionally high price depends of course, on the market and how much a particular buyer is willing to pay for the company.

WAR STORY: UNREALISTIC FOUNDERS

This software company had three founders who had been running their software business for a number of years. The firm had achieved a reasonable degree of success, so the founders decided to sell the company. I brought in several good buyers who were willing to acquire the company. These buyers presented offers in the range of $4.5 million. The founders wanted a price of $6 million. Divide $6 million by three founders and you get $2 million each—a magic number. The founders simply could not bring themselves to sell for an amount that would net less than $2 million per partner. The company had established a good track record of earnings; however the earnings and growth potential were not strong enough to support a value of $6 million. The market would determine the company's strategic value.

The founders also had an emotional attachment to their business. The chief technical officer was particularly extreme in his view. He repeatedly told me that their technology was superior to all their competitors' software. I had clearly communicated the technology's strengths to each potential buyer, making sure that they were aware of the software's capabilities and exceptional design features.

The price offered was a fair one. I explained my rationale to the founders but they would have none of it. The seller certainly has the right to reject any offer. The founders had been working for a number of years, they were ready for a change and their reason for selling was a good one, but their expectations were unrealistic and they never did sell the company.

HOW A BUYER DETERMINES PRICE

How a buyer determines price depends on the degree to which the buyer can capitalize on the components of value. It is important to differentiate between price and value. Value is what the acquisition is worth to the buyer. Price is the amount the buyer pays. As long as the price is less than the value, the buyer should be willing to make a deal.

The buyer will view value in the context of its own company. They see value solely through their own eyes, as they should. How a buyer determines price depends on the context of the situation. The buyer will determine the price of a stand-alone division differently than it will for a product line that will be integrated into the buyer's company.

Understanding the buyer's thinking process is a key part of negotiating a transaction. The buyer is not just going to pay 1.5 times revenue because that is the revenue multiple du jour. The buyer will study the company intensely. They will have many internal meetings. They will do multiple spreadsheet analyses. They will examine cross-selling opportunities and evaluate the potential for selling the target's products through their own distribution channels. They will review each line item multiple times. And they will discount the projections for reasonableness. Many buyers will have a target number for return on capital and any acquisition must achieve that hurdle rate.

On a number of transactions I have been on the buyer's side of the acquisition discussions. I have helped acquirers rationally analyze how much they should pay for an acquisition. They did not just say well I guess 1.3 times revenues is the right number because that is what XYZ sold for. It is irrelevant. What is relevant is what the buyer believes it can earn on the assets and capabilities of the selling company.

How Does the Buyer View Value?

How does the buyer view value? The buyer can determine value internally or externally. Externally means with reference to other companies and other buyers. Internally means based on their own analysis of what the company and its assets are worth to them. Sometimes a transaction takes on both aspects of value determination. A buyer may analyze the target and conclude that they can pay a maximum price of $11 million and still achieve their desired return. They may enter a bidding contest with other buyers, using an external measure of value, bidding up to a maximum of $11 million. Most of the time companies utilize the internal measure of value without regard to other buyers. One of the reasons for this is that most intangible transactions do not utilize the auction sale process.

The buyer will end up with two numbers—the low number and the high number. The high number is the maximum price they can pay for the acquisition and still achieve their required return on capital. The low number is simply their lowest offer, hopefully without insulting the seller.

The following questions are an example of one particular buyer's acquisition thought process. In this case, Tau Technology Corp. was seriously considering the acquisition of Sigma Software. These questions should give the reader a good idea of the kind of analysis that Tau Technology undertook in order to determine what price it should offer for Sigma Software. The buyer's acquisition team developed its initial set of questions:

1. What is the long-term market potential for the company? Is the business sustainable at the current profit levels? Can we grow the business significantly?
2. What are the real operating profits? Will increased penetration into the market result in incremental profitability?
3. What are the components of the fixed costs and variable costs?
4. What are the financial projections for the remainder of this year and for next year?
5. What is the profitability of each product line?
6. How profitable is each customer?

7. What is the company's market share? How is the company's market specifically defined?
8. What is the real potential for cross-selling products?

Examining an acquisition target is an iterative process. The buyer asks what it thinks are the important questions. Some answers will be easy to obtain and some will be more difficult. Then the buyer's team will come up with additional questions and repeat the process.

There are two components to the buyer's evaluation of price with respect to the acquisition of an intangible company. The first is to calculate the projected cash flows for five years (or longer) and determine the financial value of these cash flows. The second component is the buyer's exploration of the strategic benefits of the acquisition. This aspect is more qualitative than quantitative in nature, however eventually the buyer will need to establish a numerical value, or a range of values, for the strategic benefits.

Calculating the Baseline Financial Value

In this case the buyer performed fairly detailed financial modeling. They projected a low estimate, a high estimate, and a best guess for the income statement projections. The model assumed that there was an 80 to 90 percent probability that the projected numbers would fall between the low estimate and the high estimate. This is a good way for a buyer to delve into the income statement rather than just generate a point estimate for next year's number. It is a good practice to bracket each number with the low and high estimate.

Table 7.2 outlines a typical scenario showing how a buyer might evaluate a potential acquisition.

- List in two columns the seller's most recent income statement and the seller's projections for the current year.
- In the next three columns insert the buyer's estimate for the base year (the 12 months following the acquisition date). Column headings are Optimistic Estimate, Pessimistic Estimate, and Best Guess. (For readability, I omit some of the detail.)
- For each expense item estimate a number for the appropriate column. The far right column includes comments and the rationale for the entry.

After the base year forecast has been completed the next step is to project cash flows for the next five years using the best guess scenario as the first year. Projections for the next four years build on these figures given the assumptions about the company's growth.

TABLE 7.2 Buyer's Income Statement Projections (thousands of dollars)

	Actual Last Fiscal Year	Projected Current Year	Year 1: Optimistic Estimate	Year 1: Pessimistic Estimate	Year 1: Best Guess	Description
Revenue	*5,858*	*6,200*	*6,700*	*6,000*	*6,400*	Based on trends, discussions—few synergies
Cost of sales:						
Materials	541	583			625	Increased annually from 4.3% to 6.2%; more to come
Labor	910	953			1,033	Range 16.2% to 17.4% last 4 yrs
Shipping	465	490			500	Avg. $485k last 3 yrs; $490 projected
Total cost of sales	*1,916*	*2,026*	*2,108*	*2,195*	*2,158*	
Gross profit	*3,942*	*4,170*	*4,592*	*3,805*	*4,242*	Compares to margins of $4.3 projected this yr; $4.1m actual
(As a % of sales)	*67.3%*	*67.3%*	*68.43%*	*63.4%*	*66.3%*	Range 65.2% to 67.8% last 4 years
Expenses:						
Advertising	2	12			15	$12 this yr; little in prior years
Marketing	11	24			55	Avg $23 last 2 yrs; CEO desires addl $30k-ish annually to drive sales
G&A Salaries	1,543	1,545			1,725	+50 Ops Mgr; +20k for CEO + prod. manager + 2 new sales reps
Benefits	335	357			390	
Outside services	86	220			160	Assumes annual audit; some legal/professional ongoing

						Notes
Building rent	226	248			255	
Equipment leases	78	79			85	
Supplies	65	63			70	
Telephone	89	92			95	
Other admin expenses	85	105			75	
Travel	201	269			313	+$25 (CEO/Sales Mgr T&E and relationship maximization)
Total Expenses	*2,721*	*3,014*	*2,974*	*6,692*	*3,238*	Assumes buyer provides working capital as part of purchase price
Pretax income	**1,223**	**1,160**	**1,618**	**113**	**1,004**	
Income taxes	416	394	550	38	341	Assumes 34% rate
Profit after tax	*807*	*766*	*1,068*	*75*	*663*	
Add depreciation	(85)	(85)	(85)	(85)	(85)	
Less capital expenditures	30	35	35	65	50	
Less additional working capital required	40	50	55	85	65	
Net Cash Flow	*822*	*766*	*1,063*	*10*	*633*	Avg $70k last 6 yrs (avg $30k last 3 yrs)

After the cash flow projections were completed the buyer calculated the value of these cash streams using the Discounted Cash Flow Method. In this case the five-year projected cash flows were discounted at 20 percent and the value was calculated to be $3.7 million. This discount rate reflected the fact that this business was not particularly risky and a large portion of its revenues were recurring revenues from existing customers. This is the baseline financial value and the buyer assumed that the target company would operate as a stand-alone entity. This number represents the value before any expected synergies were considered.

Synergy Value

The target company's financial value ranged from a low value of $3.3 million to a high value of $3.9 million with a point estimate of $3.7 million. However there were a number of other capabilities and opportunities that were synergistic with the buyer's business.

The buyer examined the synergies one by one, estimating the revenue generated from each activity as well as its profit contribution. The buyer then discounted the profit contribution in order to represent a more conservative estimate. A typical synergy item may have been discounted by 50 to 80 percent. This is a large discount but it protected the buyer from being overly optimistic and overpaying.

One synergy item was selling one of the target's products through the buyer's market channels. (The cross-selling actually worked both ways, selling the buyer's products to the target's customers and the target's products to the buyer's customers.) This is how the buyer determined the value of cross-selling one product to its own customer base:

Number of buyer's customers that could be prospects for the target's product	1,300
Number of these that already are customers of the target	250
Number of buyer's customers that could use product	1,050
Percent that will convert to the target's product	25%
Number that will convert to the target's product	263
Average revenue per customer	$10,000
Total potential revenue	$2,630,000
Contribution margin of 40% (= revenue - cost of sales)	$1,050,000
Tax rate	35%
Annual benefit (after-tax net income)	$682,000
Net present value (at 20%) of annual benefit	$3,200,000
Discount (estimate by buyer's management)	80%

(This discount is due to target's capacity issues and availability of sales people's time to make "warm calls.")

Value of cross selling target's product to buyer's customers: $640,000

This example shows how the buyer's management team examined the potential of selling one of the target's products to its own customers. Management estimated that the synergy value for this cross-selling opportunity was $640,000. This is the amount that the buyer was willing to pay the seller for that particular synergy.

In this acquisition management made estimates for 10 other areas of potential synergy. These synergies included items such as merging web resources, utilizing unused advertising space, generating tax benefits, offering additional services to current customers, charging for a currently free service, and selling the buyer's products to the target's customer base. The buyer calculated values ranging from $40,000 to $320,000 for each synergy. The total value of the synergies totaled $1.48 million.

Total Acquisition Value

To arrive at the total acquisition value, the buyer added the total value of the synergies to the base financial value of the target. The base financial value of $3.7 million plus $1.5 million in synergy value produced a total value of $5.2 million. This buyer was willing to make the acquisition for any price up to $5.2 million.

A different buyer may have calculated very different numbers for the synergies or may have identified entirely different synergies altogether. In this case the target was an excellent fit and the buyer and seller benefited from a number of complementary products and distribution channels.

WAR STORY: REAL SYNERGIES IN SALES AND DISTRIBUTION

Delta Designs had revenues of about $7 million but the company was having difficulty getting to the next level of growth. It needed additional capital to grow or to be acquired by a firm with greater distribution power. One of the buyers for Delta Designs, Inc. was Epsilon Corp.

(Continued)

Epsilon had revenues of $95 million and could be an excellent fit. It had distribution and sales channels that could dramatically help Delta get its products to the market. In representing the seller, I projected income statements for the next 12 months and adjusted a number of items on the forecast to reflect synergies specific to this buyer.

1. Sales growth was projected at a higher rate—25 percent per year. Epsilon had several key retail channels that Delta Designs could take advantage of. Additionally, sales will improve because of better relationships with sales reps. Epsilon simply had more clout than Delta did.
2. Customer returns were expected to be reduced significantly because of the Epsilon retailer relationships.
3. Gross profit was expected to improve from 35 to 42 percent over a four- or five-year period. Delta Designs could also increase its international sales through Epsilon's distribution system. By selling direct, Delta could increase its international margins by 30 percent.
4. Delta Designs could reduce warehousing costs substantially.
5. By reducing redundant personnel, Delta could save approximately $100,000 per year.
6. Delta Designs could eliminate the factoring of receivables and reduce its outstanding bank line. Annual savings were estimated to be $250,000.
7. Shipping costs will be reduced because of a higher volume discount.

These numbers were real figures, not pie in the sky. The projections reflected the actual benefits that Delta could realize by being part of Epsilon's organization.

The Price/Value Overlap

From the seller's perspective there is no maximum price of course, but there is a minimum price. The minimum price that a seller will accept is one that is slightly greater than what the seller regards as the value of continuing to run the business as it currently exists. The seller will reject any price less than what it perceives to be the minimum price.

If the offer is too low the seller may be better off continuing to operate the company as it is and building additional value or generating cash. The company may produce enough cash that its present value is greater than the minimum price. Discounted cash flow analysis can be helpful to the seller in making this determination.

Hurdle Rate

Many buyers have an internal return on investment or hurdle rate that any new project or acquisition must achieve. Another issue that impacts the price decision is the company's cost of capital. The cost of capital is usually calculated as a weighted average of the cost of the company's debt (after-tax interest cost) and equity capital. A company may have a hurdle rate of 17 percent which means that any new investment or acquisition must be forecast to achieve a return of 17 percent or greater.

Total Cost of Acquisition

One of the major differences between how a buyer and a seller view the price or the cost of an acquisition is the concept of total cost of the acquisition. The seller typically thinks of the cost of the transaction in terms of the amount of money that it will receive. A buyer on the other hand will view the cost of the acquisition as the total of all costs related to completing the transaction. These costs include the acquisition itself, legal and accounting fees, investment banking fees, integration costs, plus any additional working capital that must be contributed and any other costs that are required to make the acquisition happen. The buyer will factor in all the costs surrounding the acquisition. The concept of total cost of acquisition is a good one and the buyer is wise to consider any acquisition in these terms.

Five Resulting Situations

After an acquisition has been completed there are several alternative states that describe how the company will be integrated into the buyer. This resulting state will influence how the buyer determines value. The selling company can be:

- A stand-alone company
- A division of the buyer
- Integrated into the buyer's company
- An additional product line or two
- Technology integrated into the buyer's products

A Stand-alone Company The value of an acquisition that will remain as a stand-alone company is a function of the profits that the target will generate in the future. The buyer will make its own assessment of the company's future revenues and profits. These may be similar or quite different from the revenue and profit projections prepared by the management of the seller.

There are likely to be areas where the acquisition can produce greater revenues and higher profits because of the tie-ins with the new parent company. These tie-ins may include access to existing customers of the parent company and cross-selling opportunities with some of the parent's products.

A Division of the Buyer   If the acquisition is to be a division of the buying company, the calculation for return on investment is a little bit more difficult because the acquisition's cash flow will be mingled with the parent company's cash flow. Many of the overhead expenses will be paid for by the parent company. Items such as insurance, accounting services, and legal services will likely be paid for by the parent.

An Integrated Unit   If the acquisition will be an integrated unit of the buyer, the buyer will most likely view value in terms of contribution margin. Contribution margin is defined as revenues minus the variable costs.

An Additional Product Line or Technology   The buyer will view the value of a product line in terms of its contribution margin as well. However, the value of a product line or a technology may also be viewed in strategic terms which are more qualitative than quantitative. The acquisition of a product line or technology may also have a competitive aspect—acquiring a product line to keep up with or head off a competitor.

The appropriate comparable is how much it would cost the buyer to develop the technology or products in-house. We investigated this topic earlier in this chapter and concluded that the value is the amount of time and effort required to develop the same technology or product plus a time premium because the buyer can sell it now versus later.

Another way to think about this kind of value is to borrow a term from the energy industry called "avoided cost." Avoided cost is the total amount that the buyer would have spent to develop the technology or the product line in-house. Sellers should consider this concept when negotiating and try to understand how a buyer will view the value of their product lines or technology.

Recognizing Risk

How a buyer views value, and therefore price, must consider future profits but also the risk associated with those profits. One of the problems that I see in the merger and acquisition business is that sellers underestimate the risk associated with the acquisition of their company. It is important for the seller to recognize these risks and to understand how these risks will impact a buyer.

In the process of determining what price to offer, a buyer will typically go through an analysis to assess the risks involved in the acquisition. Risk encompasses a number of areas: market risk, financial risk, management risk, technology risk, and product risk. In each situation some risks will outweigh the others and there are usually one or two types of risk that will be of paramount importance to the buyer.

Each risk category will include several specific types of risk. Let's take market risk for example. The specific risks that make up market risk include current competitors, future competitors, and pricing. There may be additional market risks depending on the situation. The smart buyer will examine and quantify three possibilities for each risk: minimal risk, moderate risk, and high risk. The buyer should examine each of these with respect to *current* competitors as well as with respect to *future* competitors:

- Minimal risk—competitors pose little threat.
- Moderate risk—competitors are somewhat active in trying to win business.
- High risk—competitors are very active or expected to be quite active in this market.

It is important for the buyer to accurately understand the risks and not be overly optimistic. Excessive optimism on the buyer's part is sometimes displayed in aggressive profit projections but more so in underestimating or not correctly recognizing the current and future risks.

OPTIMUM PRICE VS. MARKET STAGE

Recognizing the pre-tipping point of a market space is critical if a company wants to sell for the optimum price. Why is this important? Because market timing is the primary driver of price when selling a company. Whether it is a high price, medium price, or low price, the market timing has more influence than any other factor.

The market may be on a different time schedule than your company's growth curve. If a company waits to sell until its revenues have peaked, there may be little growth left in the company. The company has maxed out. Buyers will realize this and will not pay top dollar. Paying attention to the reality of the market is not only a good survival skill; it is the primary requisite for realizing the optimum price.

The best time to sell is when the big companies decide to move into a market. That is when they are willing to pay top dollar. Large companies need to acquire technology, market knowledge, and expertise in a hurry. They want to acquire the technology, rather than develop their own technology in order to make a speedy market entry. They also need to acquire a company that has a team of people who understand the market, the customers, and the customers' issues.

Large companies are rarely early movers into new markets. Big companies want to go into big markets, not small markets. New markets are almost always small markets. So, until a market has clearly demonstrated that it will be big, the large companies sit on the sidelines and wait until they are sure that the market will be significant. Once these larger companies do decide to move, the pre-tipping point is at hand. Now the clock begins to tick and the tipping point is not far behind.

How to Recognize the Pre-Tipping Point

Why the pre-tipping point? Because if you wait for the tipping point, it will be too late. The biggest exit mistake that technology companies make is that they decide to sell too late in the game. They want to sell when the company has peaked. The problem is that this is usually unrelated to market timing. This is an internal focus and an internal focus rarely leads to the highest price. Many technology executives ignore market timing. The highest value is achieved by looking externally and capitalizing on the optimal market situation.

Market Stages

The life cycle of a market consists of several stages that are typically illustrated by a graph showing industry revenues over time. These stages are introduction, growth, maturity, and decline. A similar graph can illustrate the best time to sell. However, instead of the vertical axis representing total revenues, it represents the relative selling price of acquisitions. It is critical for a selling company to view the market stages from this viewpoint—from the perspective of how much a buyer is likely to pay. The stages break out like this:

1. Early development
2. Growing nicely
3. The light bulb goes on
4. The slide
5. Consolidation

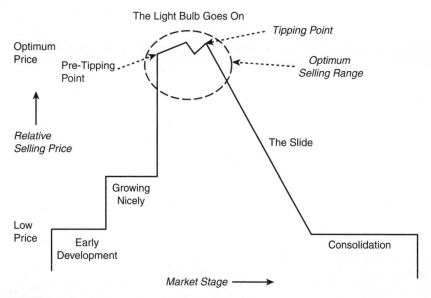

FIGURE 7.1   Selling price vs. market stage

Figure 7.1 charts the selling price against the stage of the market. The selling price is denoted in relative terms, not specific dollar amounts. The diagram shows the pre-tipping point when the first large company makes an acquisition in this market space (at the top). The tipping point follows shortly thereafter when one or two other market players are acquired. This time frame is the optimum selling range, when sellers will achieve the best price.

Early Development   In the early development stage a number of smaller companies are developing technologies and scrambling to get customers. The market is disorganized and in flux. It is unclear which technologies will become the standards. Since the market is new, there are not any medium-sized companies in that specific market. The large acquirers do not yet know if this market will be a significant market. If a buyer is willing to make an acquisition at all, it will be for a moderate price at best. Medium-sized buyers are the only buyers at this stage because a small acquisition of less than $20 million will be meaningful to them. These buyers are situated on the edge of the market or in an adjacent market, not in the core market.

Growing Nicely   Small companies are expanding from $5 million in revenue to $20 million in revenue. At this stage an intelligent buyer will pay a reasonably good price for technology and people who have a familiarity with the market. However, most large buyers will not make acquisitions at this stage. They will wait until it is proven that the market is large before moving in.

One of the problems with the growing nicely stage is that most small companies prefer to continue building on their own rather than be acquired. They think the timing is premature. Most entrepreneurs are quite independent and the idea of selling early is anathema. Discrepancies can arise between the goals of the entrepreneur and the objectives of the shareholders. The company must be clear what its goals are—to build a business and stay independent (sometimes at all costs) or to build a business and sell at the optimal time.

If a company is growing nicely, it usually wants to continue down this path. The entrepreneur and his team are doing well and having fun. They have overcome hurdles and obstacles. It feels good to be growing nicely. They want to continue enjoying the ride. The last thing they want to do is to sell. They view selling as "game over." If they were to consider selling, it would be after just one more good quarter of revenue, one more new product release, one more industry trade show, and so on. There is always something.

An ironic situation can occur at this point. A second-tier company may not be growing quite as nicely as the company described above. It may be having difficulty making headway in the market so it decides to sell to a larger company on the periphery of the market. Now the second-tier player has access to greater financial resources and the sales and distribution capabilities to make major inroads. Its technology may not be the best, but with strong sales and marketing power it can be a potent force in the market.

The Light Bulb Goes On   At the light bulb stage the large companies finally get it. They recognize that the market will be substantial in size. They make acquisitions and are willing to pay top dollar. Acquisitions are the best way to grab a foothold in a short time period. Competitive pressures dictate that they participate in this market, so they follow each other into the market. They do not want to be left out. Even a company on the edge of the market who is not a major player may make an acquisition in order to procure software or technology that can be part of their overall product solution.

The apex of the graph represents the point in time when the first large company makes an acquisition to enter the core market. This is the pre-tipping point. A second company will soon follow with another acquisition. Companies are realizing that this will be an emerging and vital market.

Sometimes a third company joins the fray. Rarely, however, will there be more than three big players making acquisitions at this stage. Sometimes a major player will make several acquisitions. The first medium-sized company to sell often obtains the best price—the first seller advantage.

The Slide   The slide begins after the tipping point, after the large players have moved in. Standards are beginning to solidify and companies with non-standard technologies will lose out. The only reason an acquisition would be made during the slide phase is if a large company chose to acquire a medium-size company in order to add mass and potentially shore up some of its product offerings. In this phase the big companies are firming up U.S. operations and possibly moving into a few foreign markets. The acquisition of an overseas company is about the only good possibility in this stage. The large companies have already made their acquisitions and any remaining smaller players must settle for a smaller piece of pie.

Consolidation   In the consolidation phase buyers will make acquisitions only to add customers. The price will not be a high one. Buyers do not need to acquire technology or engineering teams because they already have their own teams and technology. Even if a smaller company has truly better software or technology, the costs of switching are too high to make an acquisition attractive or worthwhile. A buyer may seek to acquire a company in a new geographic location. Another possible acquisition is a firm with a strong foothold in one or two vertical markets. However, the majority of acquisitions made in the consolidation phase are motivated by a desire to add to the customer base.

Mapping the Movement of the Market

Market movement maps are an excellent way to visually represent the state of the market and the movement of that market. There are three states: the present state, the movement, and the future state. What can we learn from looking at these diagrams?

The Present   This market movement map (Figure 7.2) depicts the present market situation, typically consisting of a handful of small players. The technology is not cast in concrete; no standards have been set. There are no big companies because the market is too new and too small for them. However, there are a few big companies in adjacent markets that are keeping an eye on the pace of growth in the core market.

Many company executives have a myopic viewpoint, focusing only on their core market. Their viewpoint is black and white—a buyer is regarded

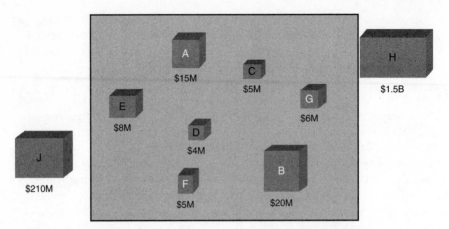

Dollars are company revenues. Total market size is $63 million.

FIGURE 7.2   Market Movement Map: The Present

as either in their market or not in their market. However, the gray edges of the market and the adjacent markets can be fertile areas for good acquirers.

Movement   The Market Movement Map (Figure 7.3) is a dynamic map illustrating the movement of companies into the market, making acquisitions, as well as companies moving away from the core. This is where the market begins to morph. Some companies are moving in, some are making acquisitions, and some are doing both. A big company in an adjacent market is making an acquisition. A smaller firm is moving toward the edge of the market, deciding to focus on a particular vertical niche rather than cater to the market as a whole.

Many companies do not see this picture very clearly. The management teams are busy running their companies and have their heads down, focused on developing technology and selling product. Their focus is often operational, trying to "peddle faster," rather than thinking about the broader strategic picture.

Medium-sized companies rarely make acquisitions during this morphing phase. The likely target companies are their competitors and they may not particularly like them. They think their own technology is superior so why would they acquire another company?

Market bitterness may also play a role. A company may have lost sales to a competitor or heard remarks at a trade show that the competitor was badmouthing them. These reasons may seem petty but they can inhibit a growing company from seeking an acquisition. So, they choose to grow

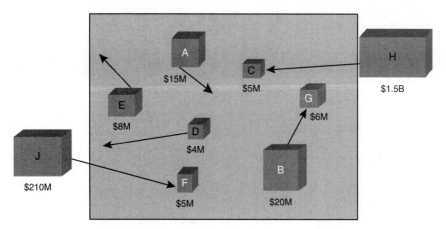

FIGURE 7.3   Market Movement Map: Movement

only organically. The downside is that a bigger company in an adjacent market can acquire a small player and very rapidly gain a strong market position, sometimes eclipsing the medium-sized company that was doing fairly well in the market originally. The lesson here is that when the market begins to morph, when the big players begin to move, a medium-sized firm needs to take action and make an acquisition in order to grab a bigger piece of the market. A smaller company should seek to acquire or to be acquired or it will be left to languish.

The Future   The Future Market Map (Figure 7.4) looks almost exactly the same for most market sectors. There will be one or two market leaders and one third-place company. If a fourth or fifth company exists, it will be small and will not be particularly profitable.

There are a few other observations to make from the market movement maps. Notice that Company A does not make an acquisition. It grows from $15 million to $20 million, which is respectable, but now it is a third-place player. Company H and Company B have grown through acquisition and have eclipsed Company A. Notice that this market has tripled in size from $60 million to $180 million in total revenues and it is still growing. What started out as an insignificant market is now a very respectable market.

Recognizing the Pre-Tipping Point

The first major sign that the pre-tipping point has been reached is when one of the large companies makes an acquisition in the core market space. Large

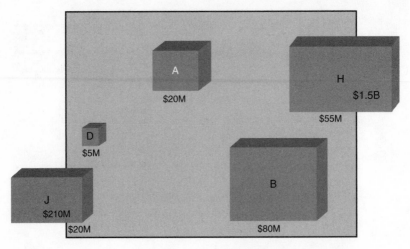

Total Market Size: $180 million

FIGURE 7.4   Market Movement Map: The Future

is a relative term—it could be a $1 billion revenue company or it could be a $200 million revenue company. It depends on the market, the size of the market, and the relative size of the companies in that market.

When a second large company makes an acquisition in the space, it is time to get moving. The tipping point is near at hand. The time period between the first acquisition and the second acquisition could be short, within six months or maybe a little longer, up to 18 months. But rarely is the second acquisition any farther down the road than that.

A good example of the pre-tipping point is the online advertising industry. Google bought DoubleClick for $3.2 billion. A month later Microsoft acquired aQuantive Inc. (which owns Avenue A and Razorfish) for $6 billion. This deal was disclosed less than 24 hours after WPP Group's $649 million acquisition of 24/7 Real Media. In the time span of less than two months the three major players have made three acquisitions. The tipping point is clearly at hand.

Another clue is when a large company develops technology internally in order to enter a new market space. If this is the case, articles and news releases will report about the company's move into the market sector. For example, Microsoft developed its own software for its music player, Zune.

A large company may contact a smaller company out of the blue about acquiring the company. The target should not dismiss the idea too readily. It may be the right market time. If a big company has acquired, or is acquiring, one of the target's competitors, it may be wise to be proactive and explore a sale to another large competitor.

If a company wants to sell for the optimum price, the best thing it can do is pay attention to the stage of the market. This goes against the instincts of many technology people who are overly focused on their own technologies. The stage of the market is the primary driver for realizing the optimum price for the sale of an intangible company.

SUMMARY

The concept of value is an intriguing one, particularly for companies whose value is intangible. In this chapter we explored different types of value—financial value, enterprise value, baseline value, and synergy value. We also examined the time premium aspect of value and looked at the situation in which a company is considering either acquiring or developing its own technology—the old *make versus buy* question.

This chapter reviewed the three traditional valuation methods. Understanding these approaches is important, not because they correctly value an intangible company, but because they may arise in negotiations. If the other party in a negotiation alludes to one of these valuation methodologies, then it pays to be conversant in them.

We examined the issue of how a buyer determines price in order to give potential sellers an idea of how the other party thinks. A key point is that value does not exist in a vacuum but in the context of the buyer's business. How the selling company will be integrated into the buyer's company also influences how the buyer views the acquisition's value.

Risk is the other side of the price/value coin. The better the seller comprehends its own risks, the better job it can do in explaining or mitigating these risks for the buyer.

Market timing is the primary factor that affects price in the sale of an intangible company. The seller will obtain the best price when a large buyer decides to enter a particular market sector. The tipping point occurs when three large companies have made acquisitions; after this point it is unlikely that a selling company will get a premium price. The technology markets are dynamic and fluid. It is critical for a selling company to understand the movements in the market and to sell when the timing is optimal.

Now that you are comfortable with the concept of value, let's turn to the poker game of negotiations. In the next chapter we take a look at the negotiating process, including some effective negotiating strategies. We discuss game theory, the opening gambit, and knowing your opponent. I include a few rules and tactics as well. The chapter reviews some negotiating mistakes and I underscore the importance of always having alternatives.

CHAPTER 8

The Poker Game of Negotiations

Negotiating the sale of an intangible company is really a high stakes poker game. Negotiating is much more like poker than a problem-solving analytical exercise. The strategic nature of intangible deals makes the negotiating aspect all the more important. There are no right answers. There are no true comparative value multiples. At the end of the day, the price you get is the price you negotiate.

Like poker, the cornerstone of negotiations is reading and understanding people. Knowing people and their motivations helps immensely in playing the negotiation game. Negotiators and poker players need to know when an opponent is bluffing and when they are not. Poker is also a game of making good decisions; as is selling an intangible company. Poker is about adjusting to the game that you are involved in. The same is true for negotiations.

An interview with the reigning U.S. women's poker champion caught my attention. She learned the game and how to calculate odds at a very young age from her father. She can calculate the odds extremely quickly. As a result, while the other players are busy calculating the odds she is reading the people. She says that the secret to her success is that she "plays the people. I do not play the cards." The best poker players are the best at reading people. The less skillful players are not as adept at reading people.

I play poker with two different groups of friends. One group is a bunch of software engineers who are extremely smart. These guys have exceptionally high IQs. The group's humor revolves around silly puns and variations on puns. The conversations are quite interesting though. We talk a lot about science. It seems everyone reads scientific journals of some sort or another. In one game the conversation drifted to the speed of light and how it affects certain scientific phenomena—truly good stuff. However if I raise the bet by 50 cents everyone will fold faster than you can say 'particle accelerator.' These guys can calculate the odds, but they cannot read the faces. They think it is all about the cards. I always win money—and it is easy money.

My other poker group consists of a handful of business people. These guys are managers and CEOs. They are very experienced in dealing with people. Of course, the CFO is the worst player in the group. The humor can be bawdy—a combination of coarse jokes and witty put-downs of fellow players. Sometimes the jokes are funny. No, the guys cannot calculate the odds, but they are first-rate at psychology. These guys can bluff and they are not afraid to call one of my bluffs. It is difficult to win money with this group. When I do win money I am pleased; it is money well earned.

Like poker, if there is one quality that helps one achieve success in negotiating it is understanding people. Success in negotiating the sale of a company is not about understanding the technology in depth or about having superior market knowledge; it is about knowing how to play the poker game of negotiations.

Many intangible companies sell before they have established a record of earnings and value normally depends on earnings. How do you negotiate when you are unsure of your company's value? How do you set a price? Negotiating the sale of a company whose significant assets are intangible is different from most other negotiating situations. It requires an understanding of the market situation and in-depth knowledge of the other party combined with skillful posturing.

In this chapter I will examine some of the negotiating strategies that are effective in selling intangible companies. I will look at different ways to understand the opponent and his objectives. Game theory can provide some insights on how to work with a tough opponent. I discuss a few rules, tactics, and communication dynamics that can make negotiations more successful. I also point out some common negotiating mistakes.

THE NEGOTIATING PROCESS

It is important to get the order of the negotiation activities correct. The first order of business is to agree on the big points, the broad issues. Then try to reach agreement on the middle issues and last work out the details. I have noticed that many tech CEOs will jump right to the details early on in discussions. This is a big mistake because it creates more unresolved issues before the more important issues have been agreed upon.

In the sale of an intangible company, negotiating does not start when the parties "sit down at the table." It is not an event that begins when the parties discuss the final price and terms. Negotiations begin at the very first contact with the other party.

Buyers will tell me things along the way. I am gathering information and learning what is important to them. Sometimes subtle psychological information will help me make judgments about how to interact with them and give clues to their level of seriousness. Most people are relatively transparent, as they are in poker, even if they do not think they are. It is the rare buyer that can conceal much in its communications. This is where an experienced negotiator can really add value. He will notice things or sense things that a less experienced person will simply not be aware of.

Let me give you an example. After a few telephone calls I finally connected with the president of a company that I thought would be an excellent buyer for my client. The buyer knew of my client and after some brief introductory comments the president commented, "This is very good timing for us. We are planning to make some acquisitions and we are just finalizing a round of financing to use for acquisitions." From my position, this was great information to know.

Equally as important as his words was the tone of the CEO's voice. I could tell that he was intrigued by this acquisition opportunity. Later on I would remember this. Without hearing those words I would not have had the same depth of understanding of the potential buyer's situation. This information would prove to be quite valuable in later negotiations. If I had a choice between asking a higher number for price versus a lower number, I would choose the higher number. Little things like this can make a big difference on the ultimate price of the transaction.

GOOD NEGOTIATING STRATEGIES

What strategy is best for negotiating when value is intangible? Generally, the most effective negotiating strategy is one with high, but realistic, expectations that include small concessions. The savvy negotiator should have a realistic sense of what can be accomplished. He chooses from a range of strategies and tactics to fit the situation. Knowing what is realistic is only achieved through experience. Different stages of the negotiation typically require different strategies.

Negotiations are dynamic situations—the tone and balance can change dramatically throughout the discussions. The perception of value can change as well. It is not advisable to prescribe a set strategy before negotiations begin.

A few fundamental points are worth mentioning:

- Examine the company and understand its strengths. Learn as much as possible about the other party—its strengths and weaknesses, its market segments, and its customers. Understand how the seller's technology and intangible assets are important to the buyer.

- Keep the focus on areas of mutual interests. Emphasize the common ground. Asking for too much could sour the atmosphere.
- Try to break a large problem into a number of smaller issues that can be more easily negotiated.
- Anticipate concessions and plan a few in advance. A no-concessions strategy is dangerous, since concessions are usually expected. Do not compromise too early, but have a few in your bag. A smart negotiator compromises by giving up something, in order to get something in return. For example, ask for a promissory note early on and eventually concede to a royalty payment.
- Do not be afraid to introduce a few trial proposals. The other party's response can be very illuminating about their preferences and assumptions.
- The corollary to asking good questions is keen listening. Listen for things that give clues to the other party's assumptions. Skillful listening is an important talent of successful negotiators.
- Determine the shareholders' indifference curve ahead of time. In other words, think about what combinations of price and terms shareholders would be indifferent to. Would they accept $8 million cash and $7 million in stock, or $4 million cash and $15 million stock? This is not about the total amount of the payment, but about the relative preference for different types of payment.
- Treat every buyer and every person with respect. Do not put them off. Do not jerk them around. Stay true to your word. It will pay dividends later.

Every transaction contains uncertainties. Each party will have a different perception of those uncertainties and have a different attitude toward risk. A skilled negotiator will recognize these differences and use them to achieve a joint solution.

KNOW YOUR OPPONENT

In every negotiation one of my objectives is to gain an in-depth understanding of the buyer and its strategic direction. Asking general casual questions can be a highly effective means to gather information for negotiation. For example: What do you see as the benefits of coupling this technology with your existing products? Polite probing can uncover all kinds of clues that give insight to the other party's mindset and what they might be willing to pay.

Try to learn as much as possible about the other party. Learn about their specific market. Who are their customers? Why do their customers buy from them? If possible, tour their facility and meet as many managers and employees as you can—you will learn more than you might think.

Probe to understand why the buyer is interested in your company. Understand how the acquisition will affect the buyer. What is the seller's key strategic value to them? How can the buyer transform the target's intellectual assets into earnings? How do they see the seller complementing their strengths? Quantify it as much as possible. What is the buyer's framework for evaluation? Their view will often be different from yours.

Learn how critical the technology is for the buyer's business. I try to uncover what the technology would enable the buyer to accomplish, what new products they could develop, what range of revenues they could generate, what the competitive advantages are, and if possible, how soon the payback period would be.

What would it cost for the buyer to develop the seller's technology on its own? Consider the total cost to design, build, debug, and test the software application (or other intangible asset) themselves. Then add a time premium for the value of having the technology today versus two or three years from now if the buyer developed the technology itself. Buyers pay attractive premiums to have immediate access to technology and to avoid the time and cost of developing it themselves.

Try to understand how the buyer views value. Ask them how they arrived at their price. It is much easier to sway someone using their own reasoning and assumptions than it is to convince them that your reasoning is correct. Show the buyer how it can pay for the acquisition in several ways. How soon can it earn back the purchase price? Perhaps maintenance revenues for the first several years will pay for half the acquisition cost.

Do not forget the competitive aspect—by acquiring your company, the buyer keeps the company out of the hands of a competitor. Determine what their alternatives are to completing a transaction with you.

UTILIZE GAME THEORY

Game theory is the study of competitive interaction. By thinking in terms of game theory, one learns to think several moves ahead and tries to anticipate the actions and reactions of their competitor. Game theory studies how people try to outsmart one another. In game theory you look at problems from two perspectives—both yours and the other party's. It is human nature to focus only on your position. Game theory stresses the importance of focusing on the other party's needs and competitive actions.

The other party will try to discover what your alternatives are, for example to sell to another buyer, to continue in business, or possibly to raise capital for growth. They will likely offer a price slightly higher than what they perceive as your best alternative.

How do you get the best price? The best price is obtained by demonstrating the strategic benefit that will have the maximum financial impact for the buyer. It must be reasonable and believable, not fantasy. In the end, the price depends on the buyer's perception of the impact of the acquisition on their business. That is why it is critical to understand how they perceive this impact.

WAR STORY: THE $4 MILLION DOLLAR RETORT

During these negotiations, I walked out of the buyer's conference room after a long and intense negotiating session. As I walked down the hall I noticed the VP of Sales sitting in his office with the door open. I poked my head in and said, "This is a great deal for you. You guys can pay for this acquisition in two years." He immediately replied, "Heck, we can pay for it in the first year." As I continued down the hall I knew that we had them.

This was a golden moment. He should never have told me that. I realized that I could ask almost any price and they would accept it. Had he not made that statement I probably would not have asked for the absolute top price. I would have requested a price that was about 15 percent lower, or several million dollars. I am convinced that this one sentence cost the buyer $4 million dollars.

THE OPENING GAMBIT—SETTING A PRICE

Who should make the first offer? It is commonly believed that being the first to mention price puts that party at a disadvantage. This is not as big a disadvantage as is generally thought. Most of the time there is an expectation that the party who initiates the discussions should be the first to mention price.

The two dangers in setting price are, of course, setting the price too low or setting it too high. If you set the price too low, the negative is obvious—you do not get as much for the company. What about setting the price too high? What is the danger in that? Maybe setting a high price is a good way to get the most for the company. Actually, it does not work that way. This is an unsophisticated view and an unproductive one. In setting the price too high, it sends a very clear signal that the seller is unrealistic or simply does not know what they are doing. The company runs a significant risk, and a very real risk, that the buyers will not give attention to the deal. It is a red flag that suggests that working on the transaction could be a complete waste of the buyer's time.

In selling an intangible company there really is no way to set a specific price. Nor is there any real advantage in doing so. Many CEOs think that you must set a price; that it is simply the way it is done. How can you sell something without setting a price?

It is the rare transaction in which I have set any kind of price. How do you know what is too high? Well, you do not. There really is no way to know. So what should you do? The answer is to not set a price. The approach that I have often used is to go ahead and suggest a price range, but not a specific price. Sure, I am dancing a bit, but that is the fun part, that is the poker game. How I respond changes from situation to situation.

It sounds like I am giving them an answer to the price question, but what I am really doing is asking the buyer to make an offer. For example: We hope to get somewhere in the $8 million to $10 million range. Or, I may offer two alternatives, not just one. For instance, I might ask for $7 million all cash or $3 million in cash and $6 million in stock. Do not be afraid to ask for top dollar as long as it is still in the ballpark of reasonableness.

Sometimes the buyers want to know a ballpark price in order to decide if they should spend the time to consider the deal and to discover if the seller is realistic or not. So I give a range, but it is always a wide range, such as, "The seller is hoping to get $12 million, but we are not stuck on that number. We are asking you to make an offer that reflects what it is worth to you." Or perhaps something like, "the venture capital backers have invested $8 million and the shareholders are hoping to get their money back." Most of the time buyers are not really expecting a definitive price. But they think they should ask, and of course, there is no harm in asking.

Telling a potential buyer that the expected price is in the $6 million to $9 million range really means $6 million, right? Some people think if you put forward a range of $6 million to $9 million then a buyer will simply offer $6 million even if the business is worth more to them. If a buyer assumes this and offers you $6 million, they will lose the deal to another buyer who offers $7 million. This underscores the importance of reaching out to more than one buyer.

With more than one buyer in the picture, the initially stated price is irrelevant when the first buyer makes an offer because its bid becomes the operative price. The response may be, "we appreciate your earlier offer of

$6 million; however, we have received another offer for $7.2 million. Would you like to increase your offer?"

Actually, if the seller states that it is seeking a price between $6 million and $9 million, this is such a wide range that it is not a real price that all. However the buyer will always ask what the price is. With this type of response, the seller has answered the price question and has not put itself at any disadvantage.

The advantage of initiating the price discussion is that it gets the price issue on the table and it is now the other party's turn to respond. You can learn a lot about the other side's thinking by how they respond. There is also the anchoring phenomenon—subsequent discussions tend to center around this initial value, which can work in your favor.

What about the case when there is truly only one good buyer? If the negotiator for the seller clearly understands the strategic benefits to the buyer, he will decline a low offer and continue to negotiate for a better price. This is why understanding value from the viewpoint of the buyer is critical.

COMMUNICATION DYNAMICS

People communicate on a number of different levels in every conversation. There are variations in pitch, tone, cadence, and intensity. There is always a subtext. People are emotional and it is difficult for them not to let the emotions come through in a conversation.

Nonverbal communication is a very important part of communication. Some studies say greater than 50 percent. Even on the telephone, pitch, cadence, rhythm, and tempo all give signals. Is the guy relaxed? Is he in a hurry? Is he stressed? Does he mean what he says? Is this an important point or a minor point to him?

The best negotiators are experts at listening. They pick up on the nuances. These nuances are important because they give insight on how to weigh the importance of various statements that are made by the other party.

Every communication should be designed to achieve an objective—to put forth a point or a message, to convey the strength of a position, or to understand the strength of the other party's position. A communication may be initiated to find something out, to elicit a response, or to understand gradations in meaning. Sometimes I ask questions, not because I care about the answer, but because I simply want to see how the other side will respond or react.

NEGOTIATIONS DO NOT HAVE TO BE LOGICAL

One of the most important concepts that I have ever learned about negotiations is that negotiations do not have to be logical. Are you kidding me, you must be thinking. Of course they are logical. How else could one negotiate?

By not being logical I do not mean being emotional per se, although using emotional replies is also an effective tactic. By not being logical I mean that arguments do not need to follow logically, conclusions do not need to be in order, and responses can be random.

Being illogical can be an effective ploy to throw someone off their game. It throws the other side off balance. Understanding this concept can also help you recognize when the other party is not being logical.

I majored in mathematics in college and I am generally a highly logical person. I often do a logic diagram in my head when I am negotiating with someone. Most of the time technology people are also highly logical.

Occasionally when negotiating a deal in a non-technology industry I would notice if someone's logic is flawed. Initially my reaction was to try to show them the inconsistency in their logic. This approach was never very effective. If the person was logical they would have responded logically in the first place. It is not like their response was, "oh yeah, thank you very much for pointing out the flaw in my logic. Now I see your point, you're right. Let's do it your way."

On the contrary, I did not make much progress at all. Eventually I did learn an effective technique and that was to try to discover how the other person thinks; how does their mind work? And then I could use their own reasoning to turn them around to the point of view that I wanted to achieve.

Along a similar line, be aware of emotion in both your and the other party's arguments. Never underestimate the power of emotion in negotiations. A good emotional argument will beat a logical argument almost every time.

NEGOTIATING RULES AND TACTICS

Negotiating requires interpersonal finesse. Using finesse requires understanding what kind of person you are dealing with and people have many different personalities. One of the keys to effective negotiations is knowing the kind of person you are interacting with and working within the context of his or her personality.

1. Take your ego out of the equation. It is much easier to work this way. Nothing upsets you. Nothing gets your dander up. They just cannot get to you.
2. Use the buyer's point of view. Try to use their language and their value constructs. How do they view value? How do they regard the seller's strengths? Seek to understand everything from their point of view.
3. Reverse it. Use their own logic against them. If a multiple of profits or revenues is good for their side, the same multiple is also good for your side. If the buyer values its company at 6 times cash flow, then use 6 times cash flow for the seller's value, or 10 times earnings, or whatever the metric is.
4. Pay close attention to the timing in a transaction. When did they return a phone call or reply to an e-mail? Did they respond immediately or did they wait a few days? These details give important clues to a party's level of interest.
5. Debrief after every meeting. If a management person calls or meets with the other party, call and discuss it afterwards. What did he say, how did he say it? What was his attitude? Did he mention anything about the XYZ issue? What was the tone of the conversation?
6. Have patience. Patience is truly a virtue in the negotiating process. It has been my experience that technology people are not the most patient people. They want to respond immediately to any question or inquiry. Patience is a key deal skill.

Do Not Let the Buyer Set the Agenda

In any negotiation it is important not to let the other side control the agenda. Technology people are extremely linear in their thought processes. This trait makes it easy for a buyer to control the negotiating agenda and thus put the seller in a weaker position.

A buyer may continually ask for information on a variety of matters. Many tech CEOs will reflexively give the buyer all the information it requests without questioning whether it is appropriate to share the information at that point in time. For example one buyer wanted to interview a number of the seller's customers very early in the process. This was totally inappropriate. The buyer may have had ulterior motives or maybe they were just inexperienced. In any case, I advised the seller that I should have a conversation with the buyer to resolve this situation.

In the sale of most intangible companies the buyer is usually a larger company and the seller a smaller company. There is a tendency for the CEO of the smaller seller to simply do whatever the buyer says. In one transaction the buyer asked the seller not to have his investment banker call them, so the CEO insisted that I not contact that buyer. In this case the CEO simply did whatever the buyer wanted.

In another transaction the deal was running into some obstacles so I suggested that I join a scheduled conference call. My client, the seller, called the head of the deal team for the buyer (a very large company) and asked if it was okay if I joined the conference call. What was he thinking? Is it okay if my advisor joins the call? The CEO was overly concerned with doing whatever the buyer wanted and he lost track of the concept that his financial adviser could help solve deal problems.

A seller can be very responsive and provide all the information that a buyer requests, however the seller should handle it in a way that protects his interests. It is not in the seller's interest to let the buyer set the agenda.

Solve Both Sides

There is never just one problem to solve; there are always two problems to solve. The same problem viewed from two perspectives is really two problems, and they could have two different solutions. Each side has its own opinion of the problem, its own view.

A negotiator must solve the issues for both sides or no deal will be transacted. The other side must work out its own problems, but a skilled negotiator will assist in solving the other party's problem to the degree that he can. Because no deal will happen until all the problems are solved. Of course, first the negotiator must know that a problem exists. The negotiator must pay keen attention to the other side, recognizing its concerns and issues as well as those of his client. Solving a problem is much easier if the negotiator clearly understands the problem as well as how each side views the problem.

No Assumptions, No Box

If I look back over my years of negotiating transactions and ask myself what abilities are the most important I would say two things. First is to make absolutely no assumptions about any aspect of the transaction. The savvy negotiator will make no assumptions about price, no assumptions about structure, no assumptions about the timing, and no assumptions about the people on either side—absolutely no assumptions. A good negotiator has no preconceived ideas. There are no givens.

The second ability is to be totally creative when trying to solve any of the issues surrounding the transaction. A creative negotiator will seek unconventional methods when working out deal issues. The key to this skill is to truly think outside the box, but thinking outside the box does not just pertain to coming up with solutions to the problem. More importantly, thinking outside the box pertains to how one views the problem. Viewing the problem in creative ways is the key to developing creative solutions. Notice the plural; I did not say to view the problem in a creative way, but in creative ways. There are many ways to perceive any problem. The more imaginative ways a negotiator views a deal problem, the more solutions he will uncover.

COMMON NEGOTIATING MISTAKES

Inexperienced negotiators make a number of common mistakes. First they tend to focus only on their side of the situation; they do not fully understand the other party's point of view. They are poor listeners and they cling to their assumptions.

Another serious mistake is letting a large problem engulf and mire the discussions. With creativity and an open mind, a big problem can often be broken down into smaller issues that can be solved more easily.

Not thinking creatively about the deal structure is another mistake that occurs too often with rookie negotiators. Many transactions settle on deal structures that are inefficient. In other words, a different structure could have been implemented that would have been preferred by both parties and made both parties better off.

Never Use E-Mail to Negotiate

Never ever use e-mail to negotiate. Ever. There is absolutely no immediate feedback. You cannot hear their reaction. You cannot hear the tone of the other person's voice. You cannot perceive their confidence or their lack of confidence. You cannot ask an immediate follow-up question. You cannot tell how they *feel* about the issue.

Many technology CEOs prefer e-mail as a communication medium. They can think about their response ahead of time. They can reply when the time suits them. In my opinion, most technology CEOs, especially the younger ones, vastly prefer e-mail and they will use it during negotiations, usually to their own detriment. Never negotiate or send deal terms via email. And just because the buyer asks a question by e-mail does not mean the seller must reply by e-mail.

The telephone is a much richer communication medium. The telephone offers immediate feedback and includes the tone and color of conversation. If you are on the telephone, you always receive some sort of feedback. Feedback is critical; you will always learn something.

I have been absolutely amazed over the years by how much I could learn about a person by simply talking with them on the telephone. A huge amount of information is conveyed. Plus, there is always that little chitchat at the beginning of the conversation. Maybe the guy is a golfer or a skier or a pilot and you can build instant rapport. Negotiating by telephone is far superior and more of an art than negotiating by e-mail.

Blind Spots in Negotiating

Technology people generally are not effective negotiators because they underemphasize the people, emotional, and subjective issues and they overemphasize the technology and engineering issues. In addition, they can be what one might call "tone deaf" to the nuances of communication dynamics.

CEOs can have blind spots when working a deal. Many of the technology people have a common blind spot—they are extremely literal and they take everything at face value.

Unseasoned negotiators often have unrealistic expectations for price and terms. Such expectations can lead the negotiator down the wrong path and make the person unwilling to compromise when he is actually negotiating from a position of weakness. Understanding the relative positions of strength and weakness for each party in a negotiation is critical to achieve the best outcome.

In one transaction that I was involved in, we ended up with only one good buyer. An exhaustive search had turned up several buyers but they were unwilling to pay a price that the company was comfortable with. So it looked like only one buyer would pay a reasonable price. One of the venture capitalists on the board wanted to play hardball in negotiations with the buyer. He suggested that we tell the buyer that we had a better offer and that they had better counter with a higher number than their previous offer. Well, this is just foolish. I did not negotiate the deal that way because if the buyer had said no deal, as it likely would have, then we would be stuck without a buyer. It is simply not worth it to try to get an extra 5 or 10 percent and risk blowing up the deal when you only have one viable buyer.

WAR STORY: NEGOTIATING HORSEPOWER?

In this case, after I had brought several good buyers to the table, the founder told me that he did not need my help for negotiating. The

(Continued)

founder commented that "We have a lot of negotiating horsepower on our board of directors—several attorneys, two CEOs, and a venture capitalist." This is the myth of negotiating horsepower. It is certainly good that the company had experienced people on its board of directors. However the negotiating begins the first time a buyer makes contact with the seller. It does not begin later in the game when the parties are trying to pin down the price. It is continuous and ongoing.

The nuances and body language that one learns about the other players along the way are very important clues in discerning how to reply to a particular party. It has nothing to do with horsepower. This founder's comment drove the point home that he did not understand the process. Eventually the founder inserted himself completely in the negotiations. He did not want my involvement; he wanted to negotiate the transaction himself.

I spoke to the founder a few years later and discovered that the business had not done particularly well. He was not happy running the company and did not get along with or respect the buyer. The most surprising point, however, was that the buyer had reduced its price at the last minute during the negotiations. The structure also included a significant earnout portion and the seller never performed well enough to achieve the earnout bonus.

Six months after that conversation I learned that the founder had left the company. This was a bad deal all around, including for the buyer. Sure, the buyer got a cheap price, but he did not earn the respect of the founder and ended up with an investment that was mediocre at best. There are two lessons to learn from this case. First, a founder or CEO should not negotiate the sale of his own company, regardless of the "negotiating horsepower" on its board. And second, it is critical to have one or two additional buyers in case the primary buyer bows out or reduces its price at the last minute.

MANAGING AND GENERATING ALTERNATIVES

Alternatives are a key part of any negotiation. They are imperative for helping a company negotiate from a position of strength. It is important for a seller to recognize the alternatives that it does have and to generate additional alternatives. The company must also manage these alternatives during the negotiating process.

Any company that is considering a sale should always have a backup plan. Always. Manufacture an alternative if you need to, but always have one. Alternatives are particularly important when you are negotiating with only one buyer. Sellers can get preoccupied with the negotiations and forget the importance of generating alternatives. In addition, many companies do not realize that they have alternatives, good alternatives.

The best alternative is a competing buyer. A company always has two additional alternatives: (1) raising capital to expand the company, and (2) continuing to run the company as it is.

This first alternative may be a stretch for some companies but the buyer does not know that. You may have raised capital to get this far so there's no reason you couldn't raise additional capital to continue building the business. Even if a company's investors or venture capital firms may have said they will not invest additional capital, the other side does not know this. Investors put up more money all the time.

The second alternative is to continue running the business as it is. This may be a slower growth path, but the risk level is lower too. The company and its shareholders may prefer this alternative to selling at an unattractive price. This alternative may not be particularly appealing to the shareholders but it is a feasible alternative. Staying the course is always a company's fallback position.

Sometimes there may be another buyer in the picture, but not a particularly good buyer. In many transactions I have had conversations with potential buyers in which they said they would be interested in acquiring my client but only at a low price, "keep us in mind as a last resort." Okay, now the company has a backup offer. The other buyers do not have to know that this backup offer is extremely low. Remember, negotiating is a poker game. Even a mediocre buyer can be an effective alternative.

In one transaction I leveraged the interest of a mediocre buyer to increase the transaction price. In this deal we had three potential buyers. One buyer responded very quickly and made a preliminary offer, although it was not a particularly attractive offer. We went back and forth a little bit to see if we could improve the offer, but it was clear that this buyer was not going to increase its offer by a meaningful amount.

A second buyer replied that it was interested in the acquisition, but it was slow in moving forward with the process. I researched this buyer and had discussions with my client about how this buyer could utilize the seller's core technology in order to get an idea about how much they might be willing to pay. The CEO and I came to the conclusion that this second buyer would not be able to capitalize on the seller's assets as much as other buyers could, so we put them on the back burner and did not expect a high offer from them.

As I proceeded with a disciplined search effort, I uncovered a third buyer. This buyer moved steadily through the process and eventually offered a reasonable price. Because we had at least one backup offer, I let this slip in conversations with this third buyer. I negotiated with this buyer and eventually improved the price by 15 percent. Even though we really had only one viable buyer, I leveraged the mediocre buyer to increase the price. There is a significant benefit to having a backup buyer even if the offer is low. It enables the negotiator to truthfully state that the seller already has an offer on the table.

Generate Alternatives

Generating alternatives is a critical part of the sale strategy. It can be a significant amount of work to generate alternatives but it is well worth the effort. The best way to generate alternatives is to contact a wide range of potential buyers, including the non-obvious buyers. There is simply no substitute for additional buyers. If we contact 100 to 125 potential buyers in a search, it almost guarantees that there will be alternative buyers. Sure, the majority of these companies do not turn out to be good buyers; however in the process we have uncovered a small set of companies that are good buyers.

One of the biggest mistakes that a CEO makes when selling his own company is not generating enough alternatives. He thinks he knows the market and who the good buyers are. This is hubris and overconfidence. Most CEOs are too busy to spend the time to generate additional alternatives.

Generating alternatives is one of the tasks that the investment banker gets paid to do—to comb the market for all potential buyers. By doing so, the investment banker makes sure that all potential buyers are contacted and that the seller has alternatives. It is a significant amount of work but it is the right thing for the client.

Manage your Alternatives

The effective negotiator will manage the alternatives as well. If these alternatives include other buyers, that is great. But manage them. Get them to the table at the same time. It does little good to have their offers come in over different time frames—months or even weeks apart. Make sure each buyer is aware of your alternatives. Drop a hint or two, or tell them straight up that you have alternatives.

The savvy negotiator is prepared; he is ahead of the game. Do not just respond to someone else's game, control the game. And generating and managing your alternatives is the best way to control the negotiating game.

WAR STORY: OPTION MONEY

In this transaction the buyer was attempting to acquire two companies within the same general time period. The transaction with my client had run into some problems and I called the founder of the other selling company to get some clarification about the buyer. I had developed a rapport with the founder and he informed me that the buyer had paid him $800,000 for the option to purchase his company within six months at a set price. When I called him the option was just about to expire. It appeared as if the buyer could not come up with the cash to complete the transaction.

I called the founder again after the option had expired and found out that the buyer had paid him an additional $400,000 to extend the option for another four months while the buyer attempted to raise capital. The buyer never could come up with enough cash and the deal expired. So the buyer did not acquire the company and the seller walked away with $1.2 million. The transaction process was slowed down dramatically; however the founder decided not to sell the company. The founder continued to grow the business and he plans to sell it sometime in the future, but he is $1.2 million richer.

Corporate Partnering—Not a Viable Alternative

Sometimes in discussions regarding the sale of a company, management will state that what it really wants is a corporate partnering deal. Their reasoning is that the corporate partner will invest cash in the company and allow management to stay in control and continue growing the business. Management prefers this type of arrangement compared to a sale of the company because they really do not want to sell the company. They just want a big brother to put up additional cash. This is not realistic; nor is it a feasible alternative.

Large companies do undertake corporate partnering arrangements; mid-sized and small companies do not. A company like Cisco or Intel will partner with a small firm occasionally and invest $25 million in the company. For a large company, a corporate partnering transaction is tantamount to providing venture capital financing. A large company has enough cash to easily finance these partnering deals. It is a type of outsourced research and development.

Companies with revenues of less than $500 million, however, seldom enter into these types of transactions. These companies do not have any extra cash for projects like this. For them the situation is black and white. If the technology is critical, they want to own it outright, not be a corporate partner. If it is not critical technology, then they do not want to waste their time with it. Corporate partnering is not a viable alternative for a company that is thinking about selling.

SUMMARY: IS NEGOTIATING AN ART?

Is negotiating really an art? Absolutely it is. If there is any part of the sale process that stands out it is negotiations. Nothing is more challenging than negotiations. The only way to develop these skills is through experience, dealing with many different types of people in many different situations.

What is the art of the deal? What does that really mean? These are examples of some questions that suggest negotiating is an art:

- How will you know if the other side is willing to go higher in price?
- How can you tell if the other side is bluffing?
- How do you know if a certain request is reasonable or not?
- Does the buyer mean what he says about how he views value?
- Will the buyer be annoyed if we slow the process down?
- What is the likelihood that the buyer will walk away if we ask for $1 million more in the purchase price?
- If we ask for these additional terms will the buyer lower the price?
- What is the right amount to raise our price?

There are no easy answers to questions such as these. A spreadsheet model will not give you the answers and you cannot look them up on the Internet. The only way to know is to go with your instincts taking into consideration everything you have learned about the other party along the way.

Negotiating the sale of a company with intangible value is a challenge. The savvy negotiator studies his opponent closely and he understands the market dynamics for the seller's technology and other key assets. The final determination of price will depend on the bargaining skills of the two contenders. The price you get is the price you negotiate.

In the next chapter we examine the more interesting challenges and opportunities that arise in selling an intangible company. Transaction obstacles can include a host of issues including people problems, financial issues, intellectual property concerns, and many more. Shareholder problems can also spoil a deal. We examine the reasons that a company may not achieve a successful outcome. And on the optimistic side, we review how a company should respond to an unsolicited offer to acquire the company.

CHAPTER 9

The Challenges and Opportunities of Selling

Problems crop up in every transaction. In fact a typical transaction will have a number of problems, not just one. And they all have to be solved before the deal gets done. There are problems with people and problems with customers. There are financial obstacles. There are issues regarding technology and intellectual property. One of the biggest problem areas is shareholders and management. And sometimes a deal is going great from the seller's side and then a problem occurs on the buyer's side.

Sometimes companies are not sold, even after a long and thorough sale process. It is not simply that no buyer was willing to pay an attractive price, although that is a common theme. Other problems crop up that can kill a transaction and this chapter reviews these issues.

On the brighter side, occasionally a company will receive an unsolicited offer to be acquired. This is a fortunate situation. It is crucial that the seller think through its options and respond in the best manner to make the most of the situation.

ROADBLOCKS, OBSTACLES, AND DEAL KILLERS

Almost every deal blows up at least once. After the CEOs shake hands there is only a 60 percent chance of successfully closing the transaction. Many things can happen along the way. It is best of course if you can foresee issues and head them off before they become problems, but this is not always possible. Sometimes you just have to deal with the issues as they are.

What kind of things can happen? The seller could lose a large customer. The technology may have become obsolete. Hidden liabilities can be an unwelcome surprise. Problems concerning the ownership of the company's intellectual property or litigation problems can arise. Shareholder issues may crop up that can kill the deal.

Obstacles and problems fall under a number of categories. These include people problems, customer issues, financial obstacles, product problems, intellectual property questions, and shareholder issues.

People Problems

Employees can quit. This issue is always a major concern of CEOs when the transaction process begins. In one transaction that I was involved with, the chief technical officer quit in the middle of the deal process. No blame should be placed on him. He had been a loyal employee for many years and had stuck with the company through thick and thin. Finally he was offered a position at a firm owned by one of his good friends. He simply could not pass up the opportunity. He remained on the board of directors and was helpful during the transaction process. There was no question, however, that his absence hurt the deal and reduced the price that the company received. He was a major asset. Even though the technical team was a good one, he was the primary architect.

Personality conflicts can occur between any of the various parties involved in the transaction. The buyer may have a personality conflict with the chief technology officer of the seller. A founder of the selling company may have issues with the buyer's CEO.

The sale of one U.S. company to another U.S. firm provides a good example of the odd and unpredictable issues that can crop up. One of the founders of the selling company was from Australia and he lived there. For a variety of reasons, the buyer did not want to have just one employee located in Australia. So the buyer requested that the Australian founder be terminated and then immediately rehired as a consultant.

Conceptually this is fine; however Australia has some employment laws that caused a problem. If an employee is terminated in Australia he or she must be paid a termination benefit, somewhat similar to a retirement account that builds up over the years. In this case the founder had been with the company for 12 years so the amount was not insignificant. The seller was required to make a sizable cash payment to the employee even though the employee was still with the company. The seller thought this was unfair because it resulted from the buyer's preference regarding the employee in Australia. The parties eventually worked it out; however, this is an example of just one more bump along the road to closing.

Unfortunately, sometimes someone can die during the course of a transaction. It may seem strange to mention this; however, I have been involved in a number of transactions in which someone died during the process. It could be a relative of the CEO, the founder's parent, maybe one of the buyer's relatives. In any case an unhappy event such as this can slow down and sometimes derail a transaction.

Customer Issues

Losing customers is always a concern for a company that is thinking about selling. This issue is particularly worrisome when only a handful of customers make up the majority of the company's revenues. A customer that accounts for 10 percent or more of the company's revenues is a concern. If this is the case, it is important to stay close to the customer. My advice is to be up front with these customers and inform them early in the process of your decision to sell. Without question the buyer will want to speak with them. The earlier the customer is advised of the situation the better they will feel about being important and trusted.

WAR STORY: LOSING THE LARGEST CUSTOMER

In this example an e-mail marketing company lost its major customer during the sale process. The firm provides a service to big companies that have large numbers of customers, such as airlines. It prepares and sends monthly e-mail statements and mileage plan statements. The company had a number of good customers and a few large accounts. One of these large customers, a major airline, decided that they wanted their own advertising agency to handle all of their e-mail projects. Even though it canceled its business with the seller, this customer gave the firm glowing references. The problem was that this customer accounted for 40 percent of the company's revenues and the customer canceled its business three months into the transaction process.

The transaction was eventually closed successfully. The buyer did telephone the three major customers to make sure that they would be staying with the company. The buyer also called the previous customer, the airline, just to make sure that it understood the situation correctly. Of course, the purchase price was impacted negatively because the company lost 40 percent of its business. Fortunately, the company had worked closely with this client and had done an excellent job for them. In this case the company made the best of a bad situation.

Rumors of an acquisition can scare customers. The investment banker can endeavor to keep the transaction as confidential as possible for a period of time. Eventually the word will get out. Any big customers should be informed fairly early on. Remember that after the sale transaction has been completed, customers will be better off. They will be served by a company that is larger in size and with greater resources.

Are agreements transferable between customers and the buyer? Sometimes an agreement for the company's services will have a clause that states if there is a change in control of the providing company that the agreement is no longer in force. The best thing, of course, is to not have this clause in your agreements. However, a large customer may insist upon putting this clause into the service agreement. Keeping close to the customer and providing them with excellent service is always the best solution.

Financial Obstacles

Financial obstacles are some of the worst ones. Revenues can fall off. Profits might take a downturn. Pricing levels may be difficult to maintain. Increased competition can put pressure on margins. The realities of the markets can be cruel. The best defense is knowing the market intimately, staying close to your customers, and understanding the real value of your products and services and pricing them accordingly.

Forecasts can cause problems. If the forecast is not optimistic enough it appears as if the company is not growing rapidly. If the forecast is too aggressive the seller may not be able to live up to its predictions. Both are bad situations. The solution is to develop a forecast that is based on extremely reasonable assumptions. Use reasonable projections for revenues, reasonable figures for gross margins, and reasonable expense numbers. Make sure that revenues per salesmen are consistent with past experience. Make certain that gross margins are in line with industry figures. The company must be able to back up its forecasts.

Also make sure that gross margins are not projected to increase over time. I have had many discussions on this topic. The seller can have all kinds of reasons why gross margins should increase over time; however, this does not happen in real life. As businesses grow and mature, competition always puts pressure on margins. It is a fact of business life. A believable forecast must be based on realistic assumptions.

WAR STORY: REVENUES UP, BUT NOT ENOUGH

A good example of a forecasting problem is the sale of Pi Designs Corp. We were in discussions with several interested buyers. The management of Pi Designs had put together a detailed financial forecast for the next two years. The revenue projections were aggressive, targeting 24 percent growth each year. At the time of our meetings with the buyers, the company was six months into the financial year. One meeting was going well until the seller bragged about the revenue being up 12 percent over the previous year. The buyer asked why the company was not performing. The CEO grimaced and said, "What are you talking about? Revenues are up!" The buyer responded by saying, "Yes, but the forecast calls for a 24 percent increase, so your growth is only half of forecast."

The buyer was exactly right. The company was not hitting its numbers and margins had fallen off. The buyers became disillusioned and withdrew. Not living up to their own forecast was the beginning of the end for the company. Eventually the company sold off its equipment at auction.

Hidden liabilities are one of the most threatening deal killers. Hidden liabilities, also referred to as *off-balance sheet liabilities*, are a concern in almost every transaction. A hidden liability can be anything from back pay or accrued vacation pay, to a sexual harassment suit in the wings or an environmental liability that is waiting to be exposed. The potential for hidden liabilities is one of the reasons that the due diligence process can be so demanding, particularly if the buyer is acquiring the stock of the selling company.

A good example of a hidden liability that caused a problem is accrued vacation pay. In one transaction the amount of accrued vacation pay had grown over the years. This was not a figure that was reported on the company's balance sheet. The buyer was surprised when it was eventually disclosed. In this case the buyer was purchasing the stock of the seller so in essence it was taking over the corporation. The buyer would be assuming all the seller's liabilities, including the accrued vacation pay. The buyer was unwilling to assume this liability, however, and for a good reason. It was above and beyond the price that had already been agreed upon. Eventually the deal worked out, but not without going around and around and a slight reduction in the purchase price. My advice is to disclose early on any and every off-balance sheet liability.

Contract Concerns

Outstanding contracts can have a negative or a positive effect on the transaction. A seller should review each contract and see if there are any issues that must be dealt with. Typical contracts include customer contracts, the building lease, and equipment leases.

> **Existing customer contracts.** Make sure all existing customer contracts can be assumed by the buyer. If not, see what you can do to keep the customer account.
>
> **Building lease.** The seller may have a long-term lease that could be a problem if the buyer does not want to remain in that space. Building space lease rates often increase over time so the seller can usually sublease the space for at least the same price per square foot that it is currently paying. In this situation there is no problem. However, if lease rates have fallen, the seller will take a hit when subletting the space and the seller must either make up the difference or reduce the purchase price.
>
> **Equipment leases.** The seller may have leased some of its equipment—computers, postage machines, copiers, telephone systems, and other equipment. The buyer may or may not need this equipment and any existing equipment leases must be dealt with.

Product Problems

Clear communication usually solves any product issues that arise between the buyer and the seller. However, problems can occur, including obsolete inventory and exaggerated product capabilities.

> **Inventory.** Sometimes inventory can be old, missing, or obsolete. In one transaction, the sale of a manufacturing company, there was a problem with obsolete inventory. The buyer had acquired the company including the company's entire inventory. As it turned out a portion of this inventory was older goods. The products were in good condition but the models were older and retailers no longer carried those particular models. The seller had made representations and warranties in the purchase agreement that the entire inventory was in very good condition and that none was obsolete. The buyer threatened to sue in order to be compensated for the obsolete inventory. The parties reached a compromise and the seller paid the buyer for the amount of obsolete inventory.

Miscommunication. The product may not do what the buyer thought it would do or what the buyer thought was promised. This problem does not occur often, but when it does it is a bad one. The real issue here is due diligence. The buyer should be satisfied that the products perform as promised and to the specifications of the buyer.

Technology Questions

Technology issues tend to crop up in every transaction involving the sale of an intangible company. Technology can get out of date or be incompatible with industry standards. When licensing any new technology, keep in mind how the license might impact the sale of the company.

Technology obsolescence. The technology may be old or out-of-date. It may work fine and customers may be happy with the products; however, in the buyer's eyes it may be built on an old platform and not embody the latest technological developments. This can be a serious problem and it is certainly a deal killer if the company's primary asset is its technology. If a company cannot afford or is unwilling to keep its technology current, the firm should consider selling earlier in its life. To wait until its technology is no longer up-to-date can be a fatal mistake.

Compatibility with industry standards. Occasionally, compatibility with industry standards can be an obstacle. Sometimes a smaller firm will pride itself on going its own way and developing its own technology standards. Although the firm should be applauded for its creativity, when it comes time to sell the company its unique technology may be a disadvantage if it does not comply with the technology standards of the buyer or of the market.

Licensing issues. The seller may be licensing software programs that make up portions of its applications. The company must make sure that these licenses are transferable to the buyer. Sometimes the cost of these licenses can be expensive and the buyer may not wish to take on that expense. The buyer may have its own software for that particular application. The best solution is to think ahead when licensing any software, keeping in mind that this might be an issue when it comes time to sell the company.

Intellectual Property Concerns

The ownership of the intellectual property may be in question. This is one area in which the buyer will focus significant effort during the due diligence process. If the software or technology is one of the primary assets being acquired, it is imperative that the ownership of this intellectual property be perfectly clear and well documented.

WAR STORY: WHO OWNS WHAT?

The sale of Chi Software, Inc. was going nicely and the final paperwork was being prepared by the buyer's attorneys. One issue that came up was the ownership of the intellectual property. As part of the closing process the seller is required to sign representations and warranties. These statements state that the corporation is duly organized, that the seller has the authority to execute the sale agreement, that there are no undisclosed material liabilities, that there are no lawsuits pending, and that the seller has clear ownership of all the assets.

Well, everything was fine until the seller realized that several contract programmers had performed a significant amount of work developing the programs. There was a question about who owned these programs. If the programmers were employees, there would be no problem. However, when the programmers are contractors without a written agreement, it is unclear who actually owns the software code. The buyer would not close the deal until the seller could prove that it clearly owned the software programs.

All of a sudden the seller had a huge problem. They had to go back to the programmers (who were not employees) and ask them to sign statements stating that Chi Software was the sole owner of the programs. The seller made a small payment to the programmers to make sure that the statements were signed. The transaction eventually closed; however, the seller was lucky because the problem could have been much worse than it was.

In another similar case the transaction came down to closing time and it was discovered late in the game that the trademark and brand name of the company were not registered in the corporation's name, but were actually registered in the name of the previous president. The previous president basically held the company hostage and demanded a payment of $25,000 before he would release the trademark and brand name. The company had no choice but to comply. The lesson here is to make sure that the ownership of all intellectual property assets is definitive and properly documented.

Litigation Issues

Litigation or pending litigation is the ultimate deal killer. Even the *potential* for litigation can ruin a transaction. Indirect litigation can have a negative effect as well. For example, one company that I was involved with had licensed certain technology from another firm. This other firm was being sued by a third company in the market with respect to its technology. The company decided to put the sale on hold until this legal issue was resolved. Very few buyers will move forward with a transaction if there are any litigation issues hanging over the target. These issues must be settled at almost any cost.

Securities Laws and Antitrust Troubles

The sale of an intangible company usually involves a transaction that is less than $100 million in size. As such, there are generally no problems with the antitrust laws.

The Hart-Scott-Rodino Act applies to larger transactions. This Act requires that parties to an acquisition greater than a certain size provide advance notification to the Department of Justice before the transaction can close. If the buyer has revenues of more than $120 million and the seller has revenues greater than $12 million the act may apply. If so, the parties must notify the Department of Justice and endure a 30-day waiting period. The sales of most intangible companies are usually small enough in size that they fall below the threshold for complying with the Hart-Scott-Rodino Act.

WAR STORY: NIXING THE MICROSOFT AND INTUIT DEAL

Sometimes the antitrust laws can put the kibosh on a transaction. Microsoft made an offer to acquire Intuit for $1.5 billion in Microsoft stock in 1995. Intuit produces Quicken, the checkbook software. The price that Microsoft offered was 50 percent greater than the market value of Intuit's stock. This price was also 60 times Intuit's earnings and 6 times its revenues.

The United States Department of Justice filed a lawsuit on antitrust grounds. Microsoft hoped to avoid antitrust problems by selling its Money product line to Novell. However, the Justice Department disagreed that this was sufficient to keep the market competitive. The

(Continued)

Department of Justice thought that allowing Microsoft to acquire such a dominant position in the highly concentrated personal finance software marketplace would be anticompetitive and result in higher prices for consumers. Microsoft decided not to battle the Justice Department on this issue and backed away from the deal.

Environmental Snags

Environmental issues can put a serious damper on a transaction. Most intangible companies do not have environmental issues, certainly not software companies. However, some technology companies can have environmental issues, and when they do they can be deadly. I do not mean deadly in the environmental sense, but deadly to the deal.

The problem is that environmental issues do not go away very easily and they can be extremely expensive to rectify. The cost of cleaning up an environmental problem (i.e., remediation) is difficult to estimate. By law, the liability transfers to the buyer. Rarely will a buyer move forward with an acquisition until the environmental issues have been completely resolved. Environmental issues are one of the most lethal of deal problems.

WAR STORY: OMEGA FERTILIZER

The Omega Fertilizer business had been in the family for several generations. Finally it was time for the family to sell the business. The great grandchildren had no interest in pursuing a career in the fertilizer business and several of the family members wanted cash for their shares.

A large industry buyer had made an offer that looked attractive to the family. Initial discussions went well and the parties had a rough agreement on price. Everything looked great. The due diligence effort also proceeded smoothly until the environmental issue popped up. Since this was a fertilizer business the company had used a variety of chemicals over the years in its manufacturing process. Unfortunately, in the early years, there were very few environmental regulations and the company disposed of some of the chemical waste in ways that would be frowned upon today. However, at the time they were perfectly accepted and legal.

Environmental liability stays with the property. So if the buyer purchased the manufacturing facility it would have to assume the environmental liability even though it was from decades ago. The deal was at an impasse. The buyer simply said no. The environmental liability was not their problem and they did not want to open themselves up to potential future troubles, even if they purchased the company at a reduced price.

Two years later the family solved this problem by moving the manufacturing facility to a new location. They still owned the original tract of land and they would have to contend with the environmental issues, most likely through remediation. The buyer reentered the picture and moved forward. This time the due diligence investigation revealed no problems since the manufacturing facility was on a different tract of land with no environmental issues. Although it took longer than they expected, the transaction closed successfully and the family realized its goals.

SHAREHOLDER AND MANAGEMENT ISSUES

Internal people issues can be problematic. These include management, employee, and shareholder problems. Sometimes issues among shareholder groups can be quite serious. It is critical that these issues be resolved prior to getting too far down the road with the sale of the company.

Management and Employees

Does management plan to stay or leave? Normally, management will stay for at least six months and potentially longer if the company and the manager are happy with the relationship. It is imperative that management stay with the company through the transition period, which is generally six months. A buyer will not normally acquire a company if the management will not commit to staying through the transition period. The buyer needs time to integrate the operations and to learn the intricacies of the business.

The buyer may make it a condition of the deal that certain employees stay with the company for a minimal period of time. In my experience, management or the founders will almost always remain with the buyer for six months. After that time period the odds drop off rather precipitously. Half of the managers may stay for as long as a year. Management remains longer than a year in only about 25 percent of the cases. Rarely will a manager stay longer than two years.

The managers of intangible companies are more entrepreneurial in spirit than those found in other types of companies, so they are less likely to acclimatize to the corporate organizational dynamics. In addition, the founders will often have additional new ideas they want to pursue or new companies to start.

Retention or Stay-Put Bonuses   Stay-put bonuses are incentives for the employees and management to remain with the company through the period of the sale process. For most intangible companies, the employees are the most vital assets in the company. It is very important that the employees stay on board through the closing period. Stay-put bonuses can vary widely depending on the situation and the personalities of the people involved. The nature of the stay-put bonuses depends on the temperament of the employees as well as the nature and philosophy of management.

Several examples of actual stay-put bonuses that I have run across in selling intangible companies include:

- $1 million split among the management team and employees. The CEO has the right to decide who gets how much.
- Ten percent of the deal proceeds allocated among the management team and certain employees.
- Cash bonuses of $10,000 to $25,000 to selected employees if the employees stay through the closing of the transaction, typically six or eight months.

There is no end to the variety of bonus structures that can be devised. Stay-put bonuses can be cash or stock. I have seen all of these approaches used. The form of the bonus depends on the relationship with the each employee and how essential he or she is to the firm. Management will usually know how a particular employee will respond—some may prefer stock, others cash, or others prefer a percentage of the deal. Shareholders may have a preference for formulating the stay-put bonuses, some preferring a percent of the deal, others a straight dollar amount.

In my experience, most employees of intangible companies are extremely loyal. They want to stay with the company; they want to see it succeed. In many cases, their loyalty surpasses their financial rewards.

Communicating with Employees   The relationship between management and employees drives the decision on when to communicate the topic of selling the company. It varies widely from company to company. In a well-run company, the key employees will feel that they are extremely important. They are committed and loyal and regard the company as their baby. If this is the case, management owes it to these employees to communicate with them early on about the exact situation regarding a potential sale. For the nonkey workers, it is less important and sometimes disruptive to confide in them about a possible sale of the company. Each case is different.

Sooner or later people will get wind of the situation. It is difficult to keep a secret like this for very long in any company. In my opinion, it is best if management is open and honest with employees fairly early on in the process. The section on confidentiality in Chapter 3 addresses this topic in more depth.

After the transaction closes, most of the employees will stay on board. The jobs that do not usually survive after the transition include positions such as chief financial officer, accounting manager, human resources manager, and similar staff jobs. If the selling company has less than $10 million in revenues, these jobs are not likely to be needed going forward. If a company has revenues of more than $20 million, it will still need an accounting manager and a human resources manager going forward. So the nature of jobs that will continue or be eliminated depends on the size and nature of the company. In the sale of most intangible companies almost all of the employees do stay on board.

Shareholder Issues

Shareholder issues can be quite troublesome when they arise. A transaction has enough issues to contend with without involving the shareholders and their squabbles and problems. Unfortunately, shareholder issues occur more often than one might think. The most common shareholder matter is, of course, who gets how much.

Many intangible companies have venture capital firms as shareholders. Most venture capital firms have liquidity preferences regarding the return of their capital. Liquidity preferences can be 2 or 3 times the amount of the capital invested. In other words, a venture capital firm may have invested $5 million into a company. If it has a 2 times liquidity preference, upon a sale of the company the venture capital firm would receive the first $10 million of the sale proceeds. The remaining proceeds are then split according to the ownership of common shares.

There are two primary lessons to be learned from the shareholder problems that I have experienced over the years. The first is to not use complicated financial structures in the first place. Sometimes technology people get too clever or too cute and try to solve an issue too "perfectly." A simpler and less perfect financing structure is usually a better financing structure. The second lesson is that any shareholder problems must be completely resolved before a buyer makes an offer to acquire the company.

Shareholder issues rarely arise when the company sells for a high price. The problems occur when the company sells for a price that is less than what the shareholders envisioned when the company was initially capitalized. I have seen many situations in which the common shareholders received nothing. Either the venture capital firms had preferences that gave them the right to all the proceeds or the company had liabilities that exceeded the sale price. These are not pretty transactions. Founders and shareholders need to be cognizant of the implications of their decisions when raising capital. If the company does not achieve its growth objectives, the fine print of the financing agreement can be an unwelcome surprise.

WAR STORY: GREED BY ANY OTHER NAME

In this transaction my firm was hired to sell a company that developed software for scheduling employees. The president, Bob, was instructed to sell the company by his major shareholders. Two venture capital firms (VCs) in Silicon Valley had invested $3 million in the company. The VCs were winding down their fund and needed to return the capital to their limited partners. In addition, the company's growth was slower than expected, so it was time to sell the firm and move on.

We identified a good buyer in Theta Corp., a medium-sized public company whose stock was performing fairly well. At one point I had a conversation with the chief venture capitalist and commented to him that I thought the transaction price was reasonably good and that a stock deal made the most sense. In addition, I remarked that he should be content to receive shares of Theta's stock because it was fairly priced.

However, there was a problem. The financing agreement gave the venture capital investors a liquidation preference. In other words, they got their money back first. So the VCs were slated to receive the first $3 million in proceeds. After that the pie was split according to the investors' common stock holdings. Henry, who was the founder and chief technologist, had invested $600,000—almost everything he had. This company was his baby.

The problem was that Theta's offer was $2.5 million, so the common shareholders would not receive any return of capital. Henry would get nothing.

Henry asked the venture capitalists to waive their liquidation preferences and distribute the proceeds pari passu, or proportionate to their common stock holdings. The VCs said no. Why should they give up the rights that Henry had agreed to when they originally did the financing?

The parties went around and around. They argued about the payout for a number of weeks. Each side thought they were in the right. The founder did not think he was being greedy, he just could not see outside his own ego. This was his company; he was the founder; he put up the seed capital. He was also afraid that he would be wiped out financially. He wanted his stake back even though he had spent all the VCs' money.

Eventually, the venture capitalists agreed to waive half of their liquidation preference. However, the parties squabbled for so long that Theta's offer had expired. Theta walked away, displeased with the whole turn of events.

The company pared back and limped along for the next several years. Eventually the company collapsed. If the shareholders had accepted the deal from Theta, all of them would have profited handsomely. Theta continued on its growth path and over the next three years the stock price quadrupled.

As a side note to this war story, it is important to point out that when a company sells and receives the buyer's stock the game is not over yet. The game is not over until the shares are finally cashed out. In this example the company could have sold for a low price, hung on to the Theta stock that it received, and cashed out several years later at a very handsome profit. So it does not matter if you sell for a low price to a high-growth company or sell for a high price to a low-growth company. All that matters is the return when the investment is finally cashed out.

The common shareholders usually include the founders, members of the management team, and angel investors. The founders' full cooperation is important to closing any transaction. Common shareholders also must vote to approve a sale of company transaction. If they are to receive nothing, they may be hesitant to vote in favor of the transaction.

In the situation in which the company might sell for a price that would give the common shareholders nothing, it may be a good idea for the preferred shareholders to allocate some percentage to the common shareholders.

Then the common shareholders will at least get something, even if it is a small amount.

It is very important to make this allocation early on in the sale process, long before any offers have been received. In my experience, the venture capital firms almost always want to wait to see what the selling price is before deciding to allocate anything to the common shareholders. This is not a good idea because the founders and management proceed through the transaction process with a high degree of uncertainty about whether they will receive any proceeds or not. The sale of a company cannot be successfully concluded without the committed involvement of the founders and the management team. It is in the venture capitalist firm's best interest to allocate a portion of the proceeds to the founders or management to keep them committed to the process.

WAR STORY: A SIDE LETTER TO MODIFY PREFERENCES

In this case the company was performing passably, however its growth had leveled off. It needed additional cash to achieve its growth objectives. The venture capital firm did not want to invest additional capital. Plus, the VC and the company's founder were not getting along at all. So the venture capital firm made the decision to sell the company.

The founder's involvement was essential to the company, at least until a transaction was completed. The problem was that unless the company sold for an unrealistically high number, the founder would get very little. The venture capital firm had a 2 times preference on the return of its capital, plus the venture firm had made a bridge loan to the company that also had a 2 times preference. At any reasonable sale price almost all of the proceeds would go to the venture capital firm.

The venture firm had to figure out a way to keep the founder engaged and make sure he received at least a minimal amount from the sale of the company. The best solution was a side letter from the venture capital firm to the founder outlining a modification in how the proceeds would be split upon a sale. The letter detailed an arrangement that gave the founder a minimum dollar amount for any sale. It also gave the founder 75 percent of the proceeds after the venture capital firm received the return of all of its capital. This was an intelligent arrangement because it gave the founder downside protection as well as the potential for upside gain.

Sometimes these shareholder issues are not clear-cut. In another situation, the two founders of Lambda Corp. had different opinions of how the transaction proceeds should be divided among themselves. The company's financial structure had become complicated after a recapitalization. The arrangement was problematical for a number of reasons. First, a new venture capital firm had taken over this investment for another venture capital firm that had closed down its fund. Second, when the new venture firm made an additional investment the company went through a recapitalization. One of the purposes of recapitalizing the company was to enable the founders to own a more meaningful stake in the company. Loans were made to the founders so that they could purchase additional shares of the company stock.

As the transaction got closer to closing, a number of problems surfaced. Spreadsheets went back and forth between the venture capitalist and the two founders with different opinions of who got how much under what circumstances. In addition to the share issues, the founders had also deferred a portion of their salaries for several years. This added complexity to the issue. The venture capital firm had also lent money to the company, as a note that converted into shares of stock. A question arose on the order of payment of the note. Also, if the shareholders chose not to convert the note to shares then a different series of events would play out.

The founders and the venture capitalists were on good terms with each other; there was no acrimony between them. However, this was a problem that had to be solved. It turned out that the major difficulty was not between the founders and the venture capital firm but between the two founders themselves. It was simply unclear what had been agreed to years before. Each founder had a different recollection of the intent and the specifics of the agreement. In the end the founders reached a compromise and the transaction was concluded successfully; but it would have been a smoother transaction if these issues had been ironed out in advance.

Reps and Warranty Problems

Representations and warranties can also cause shareholder problems. In one case a venture capital firm balked at signing off on the representations and warranties. The VC firm was the major shareholder of this technology company. They simply did not want to sign off on the reps and warranties. Their reason was that they could not return capital to their limited partners if there was any potential liability attached to the proceeds. The two founders were okay with signing off on the reps and warranties, but only to the extent of their capital gain. However, the venture capitalist would not go along with these provisions.

The buyer decided that if the venture capital firm would not sign the reps and warranties then it would put 50 percent of the purchase price into escrow for one year. This put a serious crimp in the deal. The VC eventually agreed to this proposal, but the problem delayed closing for several weeks.

WAR STORY: HEDGE FUND MEDDLING

Gamma Apparatus Corp. was far and away the best buyer for Mu Software, Inc. The other prospective buyers were lukewarm at best. So we really needed to close a deal with Gamma Apparatus. However, Gamma had its own problems. Competing with inexpensive labor in China proved very difficult. Sales had fallen off dramatically and the company was struggling to maintain profitability.

And then there was the real problem. The company was under siege by a large New York hedge fund. The hedge fund had begun purchasing the company's stock and it had acquired 11.5 percent of the company's outstanding shares. Since it owned more than 10 percent, the hedge fund had the right to call a special shareholder meeting and put its agenda on the table.

Gamma was somewhat alluring from a financial standpoint. Revenues had fallen from $650 million to $400 million over two years and the stock price had dropped from $42 to $12. The market capitalization was $100 million and the company had $55 million in cash. With the right glasses on, the stock looked like a bargain.

Gamma Corp. did not respond to any of my phone calls. The administrative assistant was very nice and took my messages a number of times, but there was no response from the CEO, the CFO, or the CTO. I had seen this situation before. I have learned that when a company goes dark it means only one thing—that the company is being acquired. This is a problem of course because it is hard to sell a company to someone who will not call you back.

The hedge fund had previously expressed its displeasure with Gamma's management and directors because of the ongoing losses. The hedge fund called for the board to either sell the company or replace board members with its own designees. Gamma Apparatus hired an investment bank and sought an acquirer, but no transaction transpired. Eventually, the hedge fund replaced two board members and within two months the CEO and the CFO had been fired. Needless to say, the company was in no position to make an acquisition no matter how good the fit.

PROBLEMS ON THE BUYER'S SIDE

The seller is not the only party who can have problems that delay or kill the deal. Sometimes the buyer may have problems that prevent it from moving forward with completing a transaction. Buyers can have trouble raising cash. They can experience shareholder issues as well. Buyers can also have management problems.

In one transaction everything was proceeding on schedule; the due diligence was complete and all the details had been worked out. The buyer's attorneys had almost finalized the closing documents and the closing was set for one week away. The seller in this case was a pioneer in personal computer database software and the buyer was McAfee Associates, the antivirus software company. McAfee had just hired a new CEO who had joined the company a week before the closing date. The first thing the new CEO did was nix this deal. Apparently, he had different ideas about the direction that McAfee should take. So that was the end of that. Six months of work and a major market search and we had nothing.

So it was back to the drawing board. The story did have a happy ending. A number of months later we sold the company to a Texas software firm that was looking for new software applications to spur its growth. We closed the deal and the founder was able to achieve his goal and retire after a long, successful career in the software business.

WAR STORY: LYING BUYERS

We had four potential buyers lined up for Phi Technology. They wanted to acquire my client in order to boost their revenues. All four companies offered their stock as the transaction currency. These companies were small, fast growing, and relatively risky firms. If we went forward, the selling shareholders would be accepting stock in a small, less than stellar company.

When I said "no deal" to one of the buyers, the company's chairman asked me what it would take to get the deal done. I replied that an all cash deal would work. This company was headquartered in Vancouver, Canada and the chairman was based in London. He replied, "Fine, we can do all cash." In an earlier face-to-face meeting he had mentioned in passing that the company had raised $5 million

(Continued)

through a private placement in London. This would be enough capital to close the acquisition of Phi Technology. At the time there was no reason to believe that the chairman was not telling the truth because it was still early in the acquisition discussions. As it turned out, the company never did raise this capital.

The buyer responded with a letter of intent spelling out an all cash deal. A timeline was established and the board of Phi Technology voted to accept this cash offer. Weeks went by and there was delay after delay and I became suspicious about the buyer's ability to close a transaction. I have a pretty good sense for reading people and in this situation all the alarms went off. I insisted on a cash down payment in order to keep the deal alive. Neither the chairman nor the president responded to my numerous communications, although they did keep in contact with the president of Phi Technology, telling him repeatedly that the deal was just about to close.

We moved forward to find another buyer, basically beginning the search anew. Eventually, we closed a transaction with a different buyer and the shareholders received stock in a more successful and better capitalized firm.

WHY COMPANIES DO NOT SELL

Why do companies fail to sell? What common themes emerge from these situations? Companies fail to sell for a variety of reasons. This section examines the most important and most common situations.

Intangible companies are seeking to be acquired usually because they lack the capital or resources to effectively penetrate their market. They may have experienced a minor setback: taken longer to develop the technology, shifted market focus, or had a management issue. The best way for the company to get to the next level of growth may be to team up with a larger player with greater resources rather than raising additional capital and attempting to crack the market by itself.

Four themes emerge regarding why companies do not sell:

- The problem has been solved
- The market space is polarized or fragmented
- Price expectations are unrealistic
- The president gets in the way

Problem Solved

The most common reason that a technology company does not sell is because the potential buyers have already solved that particular technology problem. In these cases, buyers either developed their own solutions in house, licensed similar technology, or acquired a company with competing technology. Another reason is that the company's technology has simply become outdated.

The selling company may have excellent, even superior technology, but unless it is remarkably better, an acquisition is unlikely to occur. Most technology buyers are sprinting as fast as they can and they cannot bother with replacing or upgrading technology if their current solution is good enough.

Timing is very important. The first company in a market space to pursue being acquired has a significant advantage because the potential buyers have not yet developed solutions and there will be more potential buyers. This is the First Seller Advantage that we address in Chapter 1. If a company decides to sell late in the game, there is a greater probability that the potential buyers have developed an alternative. If this is the case, they will not be interested in making an acquisition.

The lesson for sellers is that they should keep a watchful eye on competitive solutions in their market. If other solutions exist and the company is struggling to get its products to market in a timely manner, it may be smart to start thinking about strategic alternatives.

WAR STORY: FAST-MOVING TECHNOLOGY

This is a case of technology moving too quickly. Pi Software Corp. developed software that interacted with the multiple listing databases for real estate agents. The software offered three primary features: It displayed photos of homes for sale, the features of the home, and maps with neighborhood information.

Today, of course, everybody has this information at their fingertips on the Internet; but at the time this was a leading edge application. There was no Internet. A major problem was that each state had a different format for the data in its multiple listing database. A significant amount of work was required to interface with these different databases. As a small firm with limited resources, the database

(Continued)

problems delayed Pi's market entry. In addition, it was an uphill battle selling the software to real estate companies; they are not exactly early adopters.

Investors had invested $3 million and they were hoping to get a sale price that was close to that amount. Our search for a buyer was quite extensive and included a wide variety of companies that touched on any aspect of the real estate business, even including title insurance companies.

There were several companies that could have made good use of the company's software. The problem was that new software had been developed that performed similar tasks to each of the three application modules. The kiss of death was when companies realized that they could license equivalent software for about $75,000 for each of the three modules, for a total of $225,000. There was no way a buyer would pay $2 million or $3 million for software that it could license for $225,000. As a result, Pi Corp. did not get acquired.

Big Fish, Little Fish

If a market is polarized or fragmented, finding an acquirer may prove difficult. In polarized markets there are two sets of companies: big fish and little fish. The big fish are so big that an acquisition under $30 million is simply not substantial enough to put a dent in their revenues (say, over $500 million). The little fish are often in the same situation as the seller trying to get to the next level of growth, but they are just treading water. Smaller companies rarely have the wherewithal to make an acquisition. What about the midsized companies? By definition, there are very few midsized companies in polarized markets.

An example is the market for operations management software. This market space was totally fragmented, with more than 200 small companies and only four big players. The big companies had good technology and did not care about adding a few additional customers. The small players were too small to make an acquisition. Could this be a roll-up opportunity? Probably not. The history of roll-ups is dismal—not enough value is created. To undertake a rollup in this market would be a risky undertaking—margins were not great, and do not forget about the four major competitors.

The lesson for sellers is the same as in the previous section—pay attention to the dynamics of the market. If a company should consider strategic alternatives, it is much better to consider these options earlier rather than later. If a company is keeping its head down minding its business, it may not notice the bigger market picture. If the market should become polarized, finding a likely acquirer may be extremely difficult.

Unrealistic Price Expectations

When the asking price is too high, buyers balk at spending the significant amount of time and effort required to evaluate a potential acquisition. Time is at a premium in the technology arena and companies have plenty to do without exploring overpriced acquisitions. Unrealistic expectations result from two primary factors—bogus comparables and shareholder problems.

Bogus Comparables Bogus comparables are insidious because management can convince themselves that the numbers are legitimate. I cannot tell you how many times I have heard this story: "Acme Corp. sold 18 months ago for 3.5 times revenues and our technology is better than theirs, so we ought to sell for at least 3.5 times revenues." First of all, 18 months is an eternity in the technology world; the market changes significantly in such an interim. Second, the valuation was the result of a strategic sale. Acme's technology was an excellent strategic fit for the buyer. The price was determined by this strategic fit and by the importance of Acme's technology—not by a multiple of revenues.

Value is strategic in the technology markets. The price of an acquisition depends on how strategically important the technology is to the buyer. Acquirers are buying technological capability, not revenues—so multiples of revenues simply are not relevant. Quoting revenue multiples is kind of like a capitalist version of "Post hoc ergo propter hoc." (The Latin translates to "After this, therefore because of this.") In other words, just because a person can easily calculate price as a multiple of revenues after the fact does not mean that revenues drove the price.

If the president thinks he or she can still grow the company, his or her valuation belief is often based on what the company *could* be worth rather than what it actually *is* worth today. This is not a productive mindset and it leads to a company deciding not to sell because it believes its value is greater than the current offers.

Since technology companies rarely have intrinsic value, their value is determined only in the context of the marketplace. If no one wants it, it is worth zero. Only the market can determine value. The lesson is that if a company has decided to sell, it should not set a predetermined price that it wants to achieve, it should execute a disciplined sale process, obtain as many offers as possible, and take the highest one.

WAR STORY: THREE FOUNDERS, THREE MILLION

Zeta Medical Software Inc. was a small but successful software firm with a good product in a defensible niche of the medical software market. Zeta had three founders who worked hard for a number of years and were considering retiring and taking on new challenges.

The problem was that there were three founders and each founder wanted to net $1 million upon the sale of the company. Their opinion of the company's value was considerably higher than the offers that we received. The highest offer was $2.4 million, and it was a reasonable one.

One founder was in a bit of a mental trap. He was convinced that since Harvard Medical School and a few other prestigious universities were Zeta clients that the company should be worth more money. A big-name customer definitely adds value, but only to the extent of the revenues it provides and its value as a good customer reference account. In other words, the value of the prestigious client was already reflected in Zeta's financial statements.

The market had spoken, however, and no buyer was willing to pay more than $2.4 million. The company is worth what the market is willing to pay. The search process that we undertook was extensive, so I was confident there were no additional buyers that would step up. But, the founders wanted $3 million and the company never did sell.

Those Pesky Shareholders   Dormant issues come to a head when money is on the line. Founders and venture capitalists can be at odds about who gets how much. Companies that are seeking to sell should make sure that any differences between shareholders are settled prior to beginning the sale process.

In one transaction we had an excellent buyer in hand. As negotiations progressed, a problem surfaced between the founder and the venture capital firms. After several rounds of financing, the founder had been diluted to less than 10 percent ownership. He viewed his role as critical and wanted the VCs to give him a bigger piece of the pie. However, the VCs had invested their capital, taken the financial risk and the idea of reducing their equity share was not palatable to them. The parties went around and around and never could resolve their differences and no transaction ensued.

People can have unusual motivations that drive the price when selling a company. There is the classic case, of course, in which each of the founders wants to net $1 million, or some other even multiple of millions, regardless of what the market says the company is worth. In one situation the three founders wanted to sell their company for a minimum price of $10 million—a very optimistic price. One of the founders had a bit of a problem, however. His wife had informed him that if he did not receive $3 million for his shares then she would divorce him! True story. How is that for a pricing rationale!

WAR STORY: UNREALISTIC EXPECTATIONS

In this example the venture capital backers were seeking liquidity because their fund was at the end of its term. They needed to return the capital to their limited partners. After nine years of lackluster growth, it was time to sell Iota Corp. and move on. The president, however, wanted to continue building the company. He wanted to stay in the game and if he was going to sell, it was going to be for a very high price or not at all. Of course, the venture capitalists liked the idea of selling for a very high price as well. As the sale effort progressed several buyers indicated interest in the acquisition. The shareholders were firm and held out for the high price. The market said "no dice" and no transaction occurred. In retrospect, the venture capitalists should have relaxed their price expectation because they had other good reasons for wanting to sell the company.

President Gets in the Way

The president of a company may have objectives that differ from the shareholders or venture capital backers. The venture capitalist has the portfolio effect working in his or her favor; the president does not.

Frequently, the president does not want to sell but has been directed to by the board. Ego can be a problem. The president does not want to admit failure and, in his or her mind, selling early is failure. He or she believes that with just a little more money, success is right around the corner.

Another situation is the case in which the president's options are not yet in the money. The president will profit only if the company is sold at a very high valuation. This situation can be subtle because it may not surface until late in the negotiations. A president may be better off financially by running the show and earning an attractive salary. His or her equity stake may be too small to really care about the stock price.

The lesson: Make sure the president's interests are truly aligned with those of the shareholders.

WAR STORY: THE HALF-MILLION-DOLLAR HURDLE

The hired CEO had a small equity stake in this software company. She badly wanted her stock holding to be worth half a million dollars. This was her magic number. The founder was the major shareholder. He was getting on in years and had good reason to sell because he wanted to retire. The founder put a lot of faith in the CEO's judgment. The two of them had worked together for a number of years and there was a high level of trust.

We brought in several buyers and had several productive meetings with a very good buyer who eventually offered a reasonably good price for the company. After scouring the market I knew that this deal was the best one that we were going to find. The founder wanted to retire and the price was realistic.

The CEO, however, had made a strong case to the founder to continue growing the company to build its value in order to sell for a higher price down the road. The CEO basically scuttled the deal because she could not get the amount of money that she thought she deserved. No transaction resulted. Three years later the company sold to the same buyer at a price that was very similar to the original price.

There are many reasons that companies do not sell. The message to glean is that when a company is slow getting to market or having difficulties, it should not put off examining its strategic alternatives. A price that the market offers, especially after a comprehensive search, is probably the right price for the company. Ulterior motives by the CEO or shareholders should not influence the price decision.

RESPONDING TO AN UNSOLICITED OFFER

Receiving an unsolicited offer or an inquiry from a buyer is a fairly common occurrence for an intangible company. This typically occurs when the buyer needs a key strategic asset of the target company. Sometimes, the price offered can be quite attractive.

An offer to acquire the company may come in out of the blue. The offer may not be a specific dollar amount. It may be as simple as the CEO of the buyer calling the CEO of the target company and asking if they would be open to discussing a possible acquisition of the company. When a strategic buyer knocks on your door it is smart to take them very seriously.

An intelligent strategic buyer will keep an eye on all the companies in its space, particularly those that could be valuable acquisitions. An intangible company could fill a gap in a strategic buyer's product line or it might have technology that could be an excellent fit with the buyer.

Unsolicited offers come in several varieties, typically three. The first is an offer that is extremely good. The target has an instinctive sense that this is clearly an excellent price and the best buyer. The target company is quite sure that they should accept the offer. The second situation is one in which the offer appears to be pretty good and the target thinks they should seriously consider it; however, perhaps they should seek other offers as well. The third situation is one in which the seller is pleased but suspects that the offer is lower than what another buyer might offer. Now the seller is curious about what other companies might be willing to pay and they begin to consider the idea of the sale more seriously.

Everyone is flattered, of course, when a buyer is interested in your company. But how do you handle the situation? How should a company respond to an offer out of the blue? Should you scramble to get competitive offers? Is there time to bring in another offer? Are there any other interested buyers; and if so how should you reach out to them? These are questions that an intangible company should be prepared to answer at any point in time.

One of the mistakes that I see, and it occurs fairly often, is that a company will convince themselves that this buyer will pay the most money even though they really have no basis for that opinion. It saves them the time and hassle of having to go down the road with other buyers. Sometimes the unsolicited offer is the best offer, but sometimes the only way to know is to reach out to other potential buyers.

The first response is simply to accept the offer. Sometimes a company will accept the first offer because they do not know what else to do. They think bringing in additional offers is a difficult process, or will take too long, or will displease the buyer, or it will upset the company's business.

There are three steps that a company should take in responding to an unsolicited offer:

1. Look internally.
2. Examine the market.
3. Assess the buyer.

Look Internally

The first step is to look internally. Assemble the management team and review your growth plan. Where is your company in its development plan or life cycle? Has the technology been perfected? Is significantly more work required to build out the core technology and products? Could being part of a larger firm with distribution power be a good way to enhance your marketing and sales capabilities?

Sometimes a company will know the answer to these questions immediately. They may have an aggressive agenda for developing a comprehensive technology platform. If it is still early in the process of building out the platform, then most likely a sale of the company is not the right move.

On the other hand, if the technology and products are sufficiently developed and the company's primary emphasis is on building market share, this could be a good time to sell. Rather than spending a massive amount of time and effort building out your own sales force, it may be smart to team up with a larger company that already has an established sales force and distribution channels.

Remember the three stages of growth for the intangible company—technology development, early market traction, and broad market rollout. If the company's software or technology has been substantially developed and the company has had some good initial market traction then the company is ready for the broad market rollout. It is at this point that the company shifts from being technology driven to being sales driven. Building the sales force now becomes the primary focus of the company. At some point in time all companies will become sales and marketing driven companies. IBM is an excellent example of a company that started off in the technology business and as it matured it became a sales and marketing powerhouse.

Examine the Market

The second step is to examine the market. Sketch out a market map of your market space and the appropriate adjacent markets. Is the buyer one of three or four competitors in the market space? Is it the only company in its market space? Are there adjacent markets with additional buyers that could benefit from the acquisition of your company in order to enter your market?

Now go back and look at your marketing and sales plan. Are you ready to attack the market? Or have you already been out in the markets slugging it out with your competitors? How are you doing? Are you winning the competitive battles, the product comparisons, the bake-offs? If you are winning these contests perhaps you should continue down this road and capitalize on your success as an independent company. If a company is struggling with these market battles it may be wise to seriously consider teaming up with a larger player that has stronger sales capabilities.

Okay, now you have reviewed your company, you have looked at the market, and let us assume your sales are growing adequately—not too bad but not great either. It is probably worthwhile to enter into a dialogue with the buyer that approached you and see where the conversation goes. One of the dangers is that this process can be a major distraction to management. Not only is it time consuming, it is also emotional. Selling the company could mean wealth now, or wealth later, and certainly a big reduction in risk. At this point it is usually wise to bring in an outside adviser or an investment banker. An adviser can outline your alternatives and help you weigh them appropriately. An adviser can also give you an independent market perspective and help delineate your courses of action.

Assess the Buyer

The next step is to assess the buyer. Is the buyer perfect, reasonably good, mediocre, not particularly good, or poor? Judge the buyer by the quality of the fit, how badly the buyer seems to want the acquisition, and the company's ability to pay an attractive price. The next step is to make a short list of likely buyers and contact those buyers. It is best if a third party makes these contacts. The process comes across as more professional and it is likely to get a better response.

Given any of the three initial states, my recommendation is almost always to generate an additional offer or two. The key question is how much time the seller can afford to take in generating other offers. Now decide which of the three response alternatives makes the most sense for your situation. These response alternatives include:

- The rapid response
- The measured response
- The expanded response

The Rapid Response

One approach is the rapid response—immediately contact a handful of likely candidates. The number may range from three to six and certainly less than 10 companies. This process can be handled fairly quickly. The point is to get competitive bids as soon as possible so as not to hurt the relationship with the first bidder.

At this point the company needs to move rather quickly. The rapid response involves reaching out to a handful of companies in a short time frame. Reach out to a few buyers in order to ensure that you are getting the best price and the best terms. With a high-quality buyer in hand, you do not want to dally very long in responding to them.

In the meantime you can proceed with phone calls and meetings with the initial buyer. The important thing is to get the other buyers up to speed as quickly as possible so that the offers will come in close to the same point in time. By this I mean within a two-week period. You cannot expect the primary buyer to wait while you take your time looking for other offers. Companies do not like being jerked around and most will walk away from the negotiating table if they feel they are not being dealt with fairly and in a timely fashion.

Some potential buyers will not be able to respond quickly because they are currently consumed with their own business issues or perhaps they are considering another acquisition. You do not have the luxury of waiting two months for a potential buyer to give you its full attention. So you must let that one go and concentrate on the others.

The Measured Response

The measured approach takes a little longer but reaches out to more potential buyers. In this situation the best advice is to begin slow discussions with the first buyer and then reach out to a handful of other potential buyers. The search for additional buyers may include 10 or 20 companies and some of these may be in adjacent markets. In other words, they are not just the likely candidates. If one buyer is highly interested, it is likely that another buyer will be interested too. You never know what someone else might offer. Plus, the added value of competitive bids can be significant.

Quickly draft a memorandum that describes the company. It does not need to be lengthy but it should accurately portray the company and its strengths. This document is an excellent tool for putting the company's best foot forward. The time period for a measured response typically lasts between four and six weeks.

The Extended Response

A third response is to undertake an extensive search to identify more potential buyers. In this case we might contact 25 to 75 companies. The timeline for this approach is longer but it leaves no doubt that the best buyers have been contacted. This response takes on many of the aspects of the normal proactive search to identify buyers. The timeline for the extended response typically ranges from six to ten weeks.

SUMMARY

Every transaction will have multiple obstacles and problems that must be dealt with before the transaction can be successfully concluded. Customer, employee, financial, technology, and intellectual property issues can present a host of problems that impact the transaction. Sometimes shareholder issues and management troubles will derail a transaction as well. Occasionally, the buyer will experience problems that can negatively affect the deal.

It is imperative that any shareholder problems be ironed out prior to initiating the sale process. If these problems cannot be resolved, there is little chance of successfully closing a transaction. We presented a number of examples in this chapter that drive home the point about resolving shareholder issues.

Sometimes a company may not sell even after an extensive and disciplined sale process. A key lesson to remember is that a company should keep a watchful eye on the markets. A business does not exist in a vacuum. Technology markets move quickly; it is important for companies to know where they stand in the market with respect to their life cycle and their strategic plan. Shareholders should have realistic price expectations and the CEO's interests should be closely aligned with those of the shareholders.

If an offer comes in out of the blue, a company needs to review its growth plan, examine the market, and make a judgment about that particular buyer. Then it can decide how to best respond to the opportunity. The company may reach out to a few buyers or to many buyers depending on the situation.

As we move forward, the next chapter examines how CEOs can impact the deal process. Their involvement can sometimes be detrimental and we present 18 reasons why a CEO or founder should never attempt to sell his or her own company.

CHAPTER 10

The Problem with CEOs

CEOs can create a variety of problems with the transaction process as well as with the outcome in the sale of a company. Sometimes their influence is inadvertent and sometimes it is deliberate. In any case their involvement can have a deleterious effect on the outcome of a transaction. Many CEOs do not understand the subtleties of the deal process. They can also meddle in the transaction. Some CEOs think that they must do all the negotiating because they are the CEO.

Some CEOs do not want to sell the company until it achieves success; they view selling prior to that as failure. And the CEO may have a personal agenda that is different from that of the shareholders.

In the technology industries, CEOs are used to performing many tasks themselves. They are not particularly good at knowing when to bring in outside help. This is especially the case when hiring an adviser to assist with the sale of the company. Some CEOs believe that it is their job to sell the company. They know the company inside and out, so they think they should be the most effective at selling the business.

In this chapter we will examine the issues that face CEOs with respect to a sale of the company. Occasionally, the CEO may not fully agree with the board's decision to sell the company. In addition, we will review 18 reasons that a CEO should not sell his or her own company.

Tech hubris is a condition that comes into play in the technology industries. Founders and CEOs of technology firms are typically highly intelligent with strong analytical skills; however, many of them are weak in the area of soft skills, or people skills. We examine how these traits can have an effect on the M&A process.

First let us look at an example of one founder for whom, well, let's just say the deal could have turned out better.

FOUNDER LEAVES $50 MILLION ON THE TABLE

In this transaction the founder and CEO decided to sell the company himself and ended up leaving $50 million on the table. Let's call him Thaddeus. Thaddeus knew he was a smart guy and he enjoyed doing things himself. He and his team built a company with excellent technology and they made substantial inroads selling their software systems into the market.

Rather than continuing to build out their own sales force, they decided to seriously consider an offer to be acquired by a larger software company. The sale would mean considerable wealth to the founders. Thaddeus was quite excited about the prospect of selling to Upsilon Software Corp.

The buyer, Upsilon Software, decided that this acquisition was an excellent fit and it would bring fresh technology and a strong technical team to their company. They researched the company in considerable depth and the board approved a purchase price of up to $125 million.

Upsilon had completed several acquisitions in recent years and had assembled an experienced deal team. The team included three inside management people, the company's attorney, and an investment banker who was advising Upsilon on the transaction.

One of Upsilon's management people who was a member of the acquisition team commented about Thaddeus, "At one point I almost felt sorry for the guy," because he was naive about the whole process and he was outmatched by the experienced deal team at Upsilon Software. In other words, he was in way over his head. This was a case of he did not know what he did not know.

Thaddeus' partners even recommended that he bring in an outside adviser to assist him; but Thaddeus opted not to follow this advice and continued negotiating the transaction himself. The discussions went back and forth for a number of weeks as is typical in these situations. As the negotiations progressed, the Upsilon team realized that they did not need to raise their offer to make the deal. The parties eventually agreed on a purchase price of $75 million.

To Thaddeus, $75 million probably seemed like a lot of money. However, he had no idea of the real value of his company to Upsilon. The pathetic part is that Thaddeus thought he had done a first-rate job. This example is somewhat typical of technology company CEOs negotiating their own sale—ego and self-focus prevent the CEO from perceiving the value from the buyer's perspective. Thaddeus sold his company for $75 million when the buyer was willing to pay $125 million. The net result was that the CEO left $50 million on the table. Talk about a rookie mistake!

COMMON ISSUES

CEOs can become too emotionally involved in the transaction, particularly if they are founders. In one example the founder declared somewhat agitatedly, "This represents 10 years of my life!" He then went on to say that he should step in and handle most of the negotiations because the transaction was financially more important to him than it was to me. Actually, if you think about it, this is exactly why he should *not* be involved in the negotiations. The CEO was a smart man but his logic was overshadowed by his emotions.

A CEO may have trouble recognizing that the game is changing, that the company is being sold and will soon be part of a larger entity. It is no longer business as usual. Some CEOs want to continue business as if the company were not being sold. The firm's priorities need to shift. Long-term projects should be put on hold and the emphasis should be placed on short-term objectives and keeping customers satisfied.

Selling Equals Failure

Selling the company might imply failure—at least from the CEO's perspective. As a result, many CEOs do not want to sell the company in the first place. The venture capital backers may have decided to sell against the president's preferences. To sell before the company has become a genuine success means the CEO did not succeed at his job—that he failed.

Sometimes, in the process of selling a technology company, my biggest hurdle is dealing with the CEO. On the surface he cooperates with the sale process; but in truth he wants to continue running and building the company. "Just give me more money, I can do it," is often the CEO's attitude, whether spoken or unspoken. Success is always right around the corner.

For one thing, it is not his money. In a venture capital backed company, the CEO typically does not own a very large stake. Even founders can get substantially diluted after a few rounds of funding. The CEO has everything to gain and nothing to lose. He is playing with someone else's dollars.

Sometimes the CEO's agenda differs from that of the shareholders. What may be the best course of action for the shareholders may not be in the CEO's personal interest. The CEO may be biased towards one buyer because of future employment opportunities. Selling to that buyer might give the CEO a better career boost compared with the other buyers.

Little Patience for the Subtleties of the Process

Many CEOs, particularly the smarter ones, have very little patience with the subtleties of the process. I had a client once—let's call him Ernest—who was a very smart man but he did not understand the dance associated with the negotiating process. He wanted to move immediately to the details rather than address the larger issues. Ernest's approach was a little like having one date with a woman, deciding that he liked her and asking her to marry him right away. Human interaction just does not work that way. Patience can be a good thing.

Completing tasks as soon as possible is generally a good tactic in business, especially in the fast-moving technology arena. But it is not a smart tactic when selling a company. There is a rhythm to the sale process—it is a dance. A negotiation is like a high-stakes poker game: If you have a terrific hand, you do not just bet high immediately. Timing is critical.

Trying to gauge the other party's level of interest is one of the most difficult parts in the negotiation dance. How quickly or how slowly the other side responds can be a good indicator of their level of interest. How and when they respond is good information. If the CEO makes a second contact before receiving a response from the first contact, this timing information is lost.

The subtleties of the deal process are where the challenges are. Tech CEOs are smart; there is no question about that. However, smart does not translate into appreciating the importance of subtlety. Smart is about the ability to focus, deductive logic, thinking clearly, analytical skills, and so on. These are all excellent skills; however, they do not engender subtlety. Understanding the subtleties of the transaction process is critical to successfully completing a deal at the best price and with the least problems.

Let me give you another example. This is about our friend Ernest again. In a deal that went south, Ernest insisted on negotiating the terms of his own compensation plan before the deal terms were agreed upon. The venture capital backers and I suggested that Ernest have a telephone conversation regarding the basic compensation issues. The potential buyer asked Ernest to put it in writing. So Ernest e-mailed a compensation plan to the buyer outlining in great detail the terms he would like including salary, bonuses, stock payouts, and even an earnout portion. This was a big mistake. I told Ernest that he had gone into too much detail and caused a problem with the deal. His reply was that the buyer asked him to put in writing, so he did so. My point is this: Just because the buyer asks you to put it in writing, that does not mean you should put it in writing. The buyer is the opponent in the negotiation. Ernest let the buyer lead him down a path. Ernest had absolutely no judgment about the appropriate method and depth of his reply. The buyer and the seller were so far apart on the compensation issues that it torpedoed the deal. There was no reason to continue negotiations and the transaction fell apart.

No Scorecard

When a CEO sells the company himself there is no objective way to measure if the deal was an optimal transaction or not. There is no scorecard to appraise the deal—no way to know if the CEO achieved an excellent price, a mediocre price, or a poor price. In the example of Thaddeus, the CEO who left $50 million on the table, he probably thought he was a hero. Only the opposing side knew that his shareholders could have been $50 million richer.

Most of the time if a transaction closes, the board and the shareholders generally assume that it was a very good deal, or at the very least a good deal. However there is really no way to know.

As an investment banker, I have witnessed transactions from a variety of perspectives. A great number of these deals are not done optimally. There might have been a better way to structure the terms of the transaction; the timing and incentives of the earnout could have been better; a royalty could have been structured differently; and most of all, the price could have been higher. But since there is no transaction scorecard there is no way that the CEO or board will know if the transaction was priced right or structured optimally.

WAR STORY: FOUNDER'S PERSONAL AGENDA

In this transaction the founder and CEO of Chi Corporation decided that he wanted to take over the negotiations himself. I had contacted slightly over 100 firms and identified three companies that were definitely interested in the acquisition. The first buyer, Big Omega Corp., was one of the larger players in the industry and had experienced exceptional growth in recent years; it was on a good roll. The seller tried to complete a transaction with Big Omega 18 months earlier, but to no avail. Now they were back in the picture and the founder wanted to close a deal with them. As their investment banker, I had lined up two other very interested and well-qualified buyers that wanted to make offers for the company. The management of one buyer had already made a cross-country trip to meet with the company. They were definitely serious.

The net of the story is that the founder went ahead and signed a letter of intent with Big Omega. I encouraged him to slow the process down for a week or two in order to get offers, at least preliminary

(Continued)

offers, from the other two buyers. He did not want to follow this course of action and he moved forward to close a transaction with Big Omega.

The conclusion I draw from these events is that the CEO/founder was more interested in his personal agenda of going to work for Big Omega than he was in getting the best deal for the shareholders, even though he himself was a shareholder. (The company had 35 outside shareholders.) Plus, he could boast to his friends that he sold his firm to this well-known company. This was not a large dollar transaction and it included the assumption of debt, so the shareholders only received a mediocre return. In my opinion, the founder's career going forward with Big Omega overshadowed the value of his stock holdings and his duty to his shareholders.

As a follow-up note, I am convinced that, given the level of interest by the other two buyers, we could have leveraged that interest into achieving a higher price from Big Omega, probably an extra $1 million.

We have just reviewed some of the issues and problems that can arise regarding the CEO and the sale of an intangible company. The following section outlines 18 reasons why a founder or a CEO should not attempt to sell his or her own company.

18 REASONS WHY A CEO SHOULD NOT SELL HIS OR HER OWN COMPANY

Actually, anyone can sell a company. It is not really that difficult. All you have to do is make some phone calls, give the buyer the information it asks for, and then say yes to the offered price. How hard can that be? Anyone can give a company away. It is not difficult to sell dollars for fifty cents.

CEOs and founders can sell their own companies—unquestionably. It happens all the time. But can they do it effectively? Can they be objective about the process and effectively overcome the obstacles that invariably occur? Can they do it without letting the company languish in the meantime? Can they do it in a way that generates competitive offers? Can they get the best price for the shareholders?

At first glance, it is tempting for a CEO to try to sell his or her own company. After all, they know the company and the market very well. A CEO's mindset can often be characterized as: (a) I know the industry; (b) I know how to negotiate; (c) I'm a smart guy... I can handle this. In addition, we will save a fee.

Technology and software people are interesting. They are independent and they take pride in doing things themselves. They are used to arranging a variety of transactions—licensing deals, employment agreements, leases, intellectual property agreements, and so on. Sometimes CEOs want to sell their own companies simply for their own egos—so they can say they did it themselves.

Business, however, is a different matter entirely. Business is not about doing things yourself. Business is about organizing people, building a team, and taking advantage of the skills of others. Many technology CEOs need to delegate more effectively, trust others, and not do everything themselves.

A CEO can make a number of mistakes when attempting to sell his or her own company. The M&A process involves many important subtleties that CEOs often fail to notice. A CEO should spend time where he can create the most value—running the company, setting goals, monitoring progress, executing the business plan, and leading the team. If Thaddeus had brought in an adviser to assist him with the sale there is a good chance he could have avoided some of his naive missteps and the transaction price might have been significantly higher.

Over the years I have observed many CEOs attempting to sell their own companies. Most CEOs do not engage in a transaction process that leads to an optimal deal structure. Selling a company at the best price and terms to the best buyer with minimal problems is a difficult endeavor. A founder or a CEO should never attempt to sell his or her own company. It is all too easy for a CEO to make rookie mistakes and these blunders can cost the shareholders real money.

What follows are 18 common mistakes that founders and CEOs often make when trying to undertake this task themselves.

1. This Will Be Easy

Many CEOs think selling a company is easy. The process seems quite straightforward—find a buyer and agree on the price. Sometimes CEOs think they have a head start because the company currently has licensing deals with several firms that might be potential acquirers. A founder typically enjoys a good challenge—that is why he or she started the business in the first place. Selling a company appears to be a new and interesting challenge as well. This is particularly true for technology CEOs.

What they fail to consider is the tremendous amount of time and effort required to do the job right. Without significant experience in M&A, they miss the subtleties that can lead to a higher price, more favorable terms, and a smoother process. Even if a CEO has previous M&A experience, he or she cannot be fully objective and still has to run the company—usually a full-time job in itself.

The situation is analogous to taking on your own home-remodeling project. On the surface, it looks fairly straightforward. However, halfway through the project you uncover some unforeseen problems that are beyond your expertise, or you get busy at the office and cannot devote the time to keep the project moving forward. In hindsight you would have been better off bringing in a professional, saving both time and money and with a better end result.

2. Lack of Objectivity

A founder or a CEO simply cannot be objective about his or her own company. The CEO is entwined at the center of the company, at least he or she should be. The CEO is too close to the situation and cannot possibly manage the sale process or negotiate objectively.

A CEO's industry knowledge can actually hamper his or her efforts to view the industry in a creative, fresh way. Not to mention the fact that selling a company is a full-time effort. CEOs who try to sell their own companies rarely contact enough companies and they have preconceived ideas about the preferences of the buyers.

CEOs limit themselves with accepted wisdom about the companies and the market. Their knowledge constrains them. The boxes are already drawn.

3. Poor Positioning

CEOs generally are not practiced at positioning the company to potential buyers. How should the company be presented? What strengths should be emphasized? Which assets have the most value in the marketplace?

CEOs can be self-focused, company-focused, and not outwardly looking. Technology assets may carry a different weight in the market than they do internally. Assets should be viewed from an external perspective, not from management's internal perspective.

Since value is extrinsic, not intrinsic, each buyer will view value differently from each other and from the CEO. One buyer may want to acquire the products; another may embed the seller's core technology inside the buyer's technology. A third buyer may view the customer base as the most attractive asset. Most CEOs will think that their technology is far and away the most important asset.

4. Are You Serious?

Third-party representation signals to the market that the seller is serious. Buyers have at least some assurance that they are not wasting their time with a tire-kicker. If a potential buyer receives an inquiry from an investment banker, it means the company is being represented professionally. It means they are serious about selling the company. In addition, the deal has been screened; it has passed the muster of the investment banking firm. Buyers do not want to waste time with a company that is not serious about selling.

5. Too Narrow a Search

CEOs tend to pick the low-hanging fruit. Their search process is rarely exhaustive. CEOs typically contact six companies. Yes, six companies. Not 10, not 20, not three, but six companies. This has been my observation over a number of years.

They think they know the market, know who the buyers are. This is hubris and overconfidence. "I know my market." I hear this all the time. Of course the CEO will know some of the good buyers. However, half of the time the buyer is from outside the market; the buyer uses the acquisition as market entry. CEOs neglect these potential buyers. CEOs rarely seek out the tangential and fringe companies that often can be excellent buyers.

My guess is that they think they know the market so well that they know which companies would be good buyers and which companies would not be interested. A CEO can avoid the search problems entirely by convincing himself that a particular buyer will pay the highest price. It also may be that they do not want to be turned down so they do not pursue certain buyers.

Once CEOs begin discussions, they stop looking for additional prospects. They are content to engage one or two potential buyers. CEOs can get locked into their own preconceptions. They do not see the market with fresh eyes. There is a lot to be said for beginner's mind—you go down roads you might never have gone down.

Deals can fall apart. It is imperative to get multiple offers and create competitive bidding. However, generating competitive bidding involves too much work for most CEOs. They delude themselves into thinking that the buyer in hand will pay the highest price. Many CEOs tacitly assume that the incremental price will not be worth the incremental effort. This is simply not true.

6. Setting the Wrong Price

A CEO's prejudices can cloud the value issue. Unrealistic value expectations can be deadly. What the market is willing to pay may be very different from what the CEO thinks his or her company is worth or ought to be worth.

A CEO may want to sell only if the price is greater than a certain threshold, often where his or her stock options are in the money. This may put strains on pricing the deal and may not be in the best interests of the shareholders.

7. Adversarial Beginnings

Sometimes things can get a little heated, with friction developing between the buyer and seller. To avoid an adversarial relationship between the parties it is best to have a third party handle the negotiations. An experienced intermediary will be more adept at steering conversations productively and knowing what paths not to go down.

A case in point is negotiating the president's salary and option package. Who can best negotiate these items—the CEO himself or an independent third party? Let the third party be the bad guy.

8. No Full-Time Commitment

Identifying and contacting candidates is a full-time task that can continue for a number of months. This process can be very tedious—something that an executive-level person may not want to undertake. A CEO who is running a business cannot possibly give his or her full attention to a comprehensive search process. Selling a company is a full-time endeavor. A CEO cannot execute a disciplined sale process and at the same time effectively run the company.

9. Ignoring Opportunity Cost

A CEO who attempts to sell his own company is ignoring the opportunity cost of his time. Where can the CEO create the most value? Trying to sell the company or continuing to build the company and leading his team? More value is created when the CEO continues to increase market traction, grow revenues, keep customers happy, and lead his team. The value of these activities is far greater than the amount of any fee saved. The CEO should spend his time building and enhancing the business.

10. Selling the Future

Most CEOs are accustomed to raising capital and they perceive the process of selling a company as very similar to raising capital. They think this experience is transferable to selling a company. When trying to sell the business, they paint the same picture. They sell their vision—large markets, rapidly growing revenues, and substantial profits. They focus on where they are going, not where they are. In other words, they are selling the future.

A business plan is forward looking. It is about growth; it is about the future. A descriptive memorandum for selling the company, on the other hand, focuses on the present. It is a coherent snapshot of the current situation. This is where the company is today. This is the technology that is complete today. There is a big difference between selling a future vision and selling the company as it exists today. Buyers can get frustrated with this future-focused approach because they are not sure what is fact and what is future.

11. Presenting the Wrong Information

CEOs do not take the time to develop the proper documentation to promote the sale. Most fail to draft a selling memorandum or even a one-page summary of the acquisition opportunity. Most CEOs just send out the business plan, not a selling memorandum, without realizing that there is a difference.

Since they are not well-versed in the process, CEOs are not usually aware of what information should be communicated at different stages of the M&A process. They will often give the wrong depth of detail—too much information too soon or too little information too late.

12. Glossing over the Negatives

CEOs love to portray their companies in a good light (e.g., "Everything is going great." "We have great marketing, great technology, and great people."). CEOs are so close to the situation that it is difficult for them to view the transaction from the buyer's eyes.

When a serious buyer completes its due diligence, it will know almost everything about the company, warts and all. It does no good to start off by saying the company has no warts—this just wastes everyone's time.

CEOs rarely admit that they have done a poor job of marketing or sales. However, a company with excellent technology that has not had the time or capital to undertake a comprehensive sales and marketing effort can be positioned as a good opportunity for the buyer. What may have been a weakness can be presented as an opportunity.

13. Unable to Ramrod the Transaction

CEOs cannot push the transaction without appearing somewhat desperate. They cannot call the buyer every other day. An intermediary, however, can ramrod the transaction. The banker can call the buyer four times a week to keep the deal moving forward, which is the advantage of being a third party; he or she is just doing the job. Buyers expect an investment banker to be aggressive, to be persistent. A persistent CEO, on the other hand, is perceived as a desperate seller.

14. Failure to Manage the Process

The sale of a company involves many detailed activities. Time lines must be met, questions answered, approvals obtained, documents provided, and so on. You do not just locate a buyer and then have a few meetings. Countless tasks need to be accomplished along the way.

A CEO is almost always too busy running the business to pay attention to all the minor details involved in the sale of a company. Too often time schedules slip and activities are not well coordinated. A proactive, hands-on approach can keep small issues from turning into major problems. Without a constant watchful eye on the transaction, a CEO too often lets small issues slip and they become bigger problems later.

15. Not Listening

Buyers will tell a third party all kinds of things they would never tell the CEO directly. A third party can pick up clues along the way about how strategic the technology is to the buyer, about how the buyer regards the management team, about how the buyer perceives value, and how much they might be willing to pay.

A CEO usually focuses on what points *he* wants to make and what *he* wants to say. This is not very productive. One must listen with big ears. What is the buyer saying between the lines? What are they really after? What is the feeling you get from them? A good negotiator is really a professional listener.

The negotiator's job is to figure out the other side's motivations and continue progressing to the next step. There are many ways to solve the problems that inevitably pop up. The biggest danger is not being aware of a problem before it becomes full-blown. You cannot head it off if you do not know it is there.

16. Uncreative Structuring

There are so many ways to structure a deal, so many ways to be paid—it is not only stock or cash. Since they are not professional deal makers, CEOs are generally not very imaginative at solving problems or devising creative structures where both parties could be better off. The key to good structuring is to fully understand the objectives of each party and have an open, creative mindset.

The CEO may actually believe what his or her venture capital investors tell him or her about their price expectations. An experienced deal person, who has dealt with many venture capitalists, will have a better idea of what the VCs will find acceptable. I have seen CEOs ask wildly unrealistic prices, sending buyers running. This approach is not at all productive.

17. Incorrectly Valuing the Buyer's Stock

If the seller receives stock from the buyer, what is the value of that stock? A private company's last venture capital valuation may be totally arbitrary and a public company's stock price may not represent its true value. CEOs are not valuation experts. They have difficulty developing a rationale for negotiating with the buyer regarding the price of the buyer's stock.

18. The Fallacy of Saving a Fee

CEOs must ask two questions regarding saving a fee: First, is the amount of fee saved greater than the opportunity cost of the CEO's time? In other words, is the fee greater than the incremental value that the CEO could add by focusing on building the business? Second, is the amount of the fee saved greater than the incremental price paid as a result of having several bidders?

Rarely is the amount of a fee saved greater than the opportunity cost of the president's time, nor is it greater than the value derived from competitive bidding. Everyone loves to save a fee. But is trying to save a fee really worth it? Actually, the fee amount is usually negligible in the context of the deal.

CEOs can create the most value for their shareholders by building revenues, keeping customers satisfied, and leading their teams. Selling their own companies may be interesting and they may save a fee, but the process is too time consuming to do an adequate job and run the company at the same time. In addition, selling a company is a specialized skill, one in which experience pays substantial rewards.

Remember Thaddeus, the CEO who left $50 million on the table? Well, look at the bright side—he saved a fee!

WAR STORY: A VALUATION ABSURDITY

Lambda Corp. had two choices—it could raise additional capital or sell the company. The market was too small to interest venture capital firms and the existing angel investors were unwilling to invest additional capital. My firm was hired to sell the company. As we moved forward we realized there was a third alternative: The company could obtain capital from a corporate partner. Normally this is not a viable alternative, but the nature of this market, in the financial reporting area, was such that several companies might make very good corporate partners. In a partnering deal a company would invest capital in Lambda Corp. but not acquire the whole company.

Approximately $4 million had been invested in Lambda Corp. and the founder and his team had done a good job of building the business. Although revenues and profits were not on target, the company had solid market traction. As a result the founder determined that the valuation for financing purposes should be $16 million. The founder was very firm on this valuation. This number was also influenced by the fear of dilution for the current shareholders, including the founder. As a result none of the corporate partnering candidates decided to move forward; the valuation was simply too high.

So we moved forward with the sale of the company and identified several interested buyers. Of three potential buyers, one seemed to show a much higher degree of interest than the others. At this point the founder stepped in and took over the negotiating process. He went back and forth with the buyer and eventually settled on a price of $3 million for the sale of the company.

In retrospect I was amazed by the turn of events. The founder was very firm on the $16 million valuation for an investment. However, to sell the whole company he was okay with $3 million! In my view, $3 million was probably a fair price for the company. What was wrong with this situation was the $16 million valuation for a financing transaction. The shareholders would have been much better off selling half the company for, say, $5 million than selling the whole company for $3 million! In this case the founder was so close to the situation that he was blind to the valuation absurdity.

A TALE OF TECH HUBRIS

Over the years I have been involved in transactions in a wide variety of industries—technology, software, and service, in addition to manufacturing, distribution, and retail. This diversity of experience has given me a unique perspective from which to draw generalizations about how people differ in these various industry sectors. These personality traits have an impact on the merger and acquisition process.

Technology people are extremely smart, analytical, and highly focused. However, their people skills and ability to empathize are not as well developed. Technology people are often colorblind to the nuances of communication and interaction with others.

Meet Joe Techman

Many technology people—founders, CEOs, venture capitalists, and others—are extremely intelligent, with high IQs and powerful analytical abilities. Trained as engineers or computer scientists, their analytical skills are exceptional. Let us refer to these people by the term "Joe Techman." By the way, man here is a collective noun—it applies to women as well as men.

Summarizing the positive aspects of Techman's character, a handful of points can be made. Joe has:

- exceptional intelligence
- strong analytical skills
- the ability to focus very sharply
- a high degree of honesty

Technology people are very smart, capable people. Techman is more proficient at quantitative tasks than he is at qualitative tasks. The strength of his intelligence, however, can also be a weakness. Joe Techman wants to solve every problem by analyzing, by drilling down. He tends to overthink and overanalyze everything. Analyzing is an extremely powerful tool; however, it is not the only tool. For some situations a highly focused analysis is not the appropriate approach.

Techman tends to be narrowly focused. A narrow focus can be a good thing in business and particularly in technology development. But as one rises in the organization, an individual needs to have a broader purview. Sometimes the best way to solve a problem is to step back, get the lay of the land, observe the bigger picture, and then approach the issue from a new angle.

One of the things I enjoy about working with Techmen is that they are extremely honest—they are honest to a fault. Most would not dream of providing any information that was not absolutely accurate. And they would never want to give someone an incorrect perception about either them or their business. The downside of honesty in an M&A context is transparency. Their positions and stances are totally transparent. Joe Techman cannot bluff.

Another strength of Joe Techman that I admire is his courage to become an entrepreneur in the first place, for putting himself on the line and being exposed to possible failure.

Like most human beings, exceptional strengths beget some weaknesses. Joe Techman has a few weaknesses. They include:

- a need to do everything himself
- the need to control
- limited people skills

Joe Techman wants to do most things himself. Not only does he enjoy doing everything himself, on some level he needs to prove to himself that he can do everything himself. It is almost a personal affront to suggest that he could not do everything himself. He views it as a weakness to bring in outside help. Techman can also have a strong need for control. He realizes that he is smarter than most people in his organization. He wants to control too many aspects of the business. Many Techmen can be micromanagers.

Successful companies do not attempt to do everything themselves. They focus on their core competencies and outsource everything else. A business does not develop into a thriving company by doing everything in-house. A company should not reinvent things that it can obtain from someone else. The goal of a business is to serve its customers and create value for its shareholders. If a company draws on outside help there is no asterisk on the scorecard. It is simply about results.

Cisco is a great example. Cisco's objective is to solve its customers' problems with "end-to-end solutions," as the president expresses it. It does not matter if the solution embodies their own technology or if they must license outside technology. They will even acquire a company if that is what it takes to solve the customer's problem.

"We can do that ourselves" is a phrase I have often heard in the technology arena. The point is not about whether you *can* or *cannot* do things yourself. That is ego talking. The wise business person knows which tasks the company should perform itself and which tasks to outsource.

Soft skills are not one of Joe Techman's strengths. Soft skills include the ability to understand people, empathize with, and recognize the needs of others. Techman is generally not a good people person and often not a good listener. His people-judgment skills are not as developed as his analytical skills. Techman lacks the judgment to know when to trust someone and when not to trust someone. If Techman has been burned in the past he may have difficulty trusting people in the future.

People communicate on a number of levels in every conversation. Nuances of situations often escape Joe Techman. He can be quite literal, placing too much weight on the exact words that were spoken or written. This limits Techman's ability to work and communicate effectively with people. It also restricts his ability to be effective in arranging transactions. Techman usually concentrates on what he wants, not what others want. This is another reason that tech people are not good deal doers. They have difficulty viewing issues from the perspective of the other person.

WAR STORY: THE NEUROSURGEON'S WIFE

An extremely bright neurosurgeon brings his wife to important meetings to help him read people. The surgeon is a highly intelligent individual. He is exceptionally focused, analytical, and literal. His technical skills are superb. However, he has a hard time communicating and understanding others. He is so literal that he will miss significant parts of a verbal communication.

After a few instances, he realized his wife possessed very strong people skills. She could pick up things that he had no idea about. So he asked her to accompany him to important meetings—for example, when negotiating a certain issue with the hospital. She would perceive that the president of the hospital might be saying let us take action X in order to improve medical care when he really meant we must take action Y in order to reduce costs. The president was not being duplicitous; he was just negotiating his position. Without his wife's input the surgeon would not have noticed this and would have come out on the losing end of the negotiation.

The surgeon and his wife also arrange social situations with his colleagues when changes are in the offing at the hospital. The social setting combined with having his wife present enables him to assess the

(Continued)

situation better so he can formulate his approach more effectively. She would occasionally review communications with his staff, commenting for example "that makes me feel defensive, let's reword it." The result was that his staff was more supportive of him and he was more effective in dealing with the hospital in a variety of matters.

The neurosurgeon is essentially colorblind to the nuances of communication. He does not understand that body language and tone of voice convey important information. However, he was smart enough to realize that his wife's people skills could be a huge benefit to him as a doctor.

Joe Techman versus Bill Businessman

Joe Techman differs from a "Bill Businessman" in a number of ways. Each has a different way to define his business. They have different opinions on the importance and meaning of *smart*. One is focused; the other more opportunistic. And of course the major difference is their individual ability to work effectively with other people.

It is important to Joe Techman that he be smart—to do smart things, to make smart choices, to think in a smart way, and to be perceived as smart. Bill Businessman, on the other hand, is not concerned with being "smart." Bill Businessman thinks of smart in a different way. The Businessman views smart as a way to run the business that makes it successful. Smart is not about him at all. In fact, the Businessman could care less about the word *smart*. He is more concerned about being effective and being profitable.

There are two kinds of smart—processing power and "are you paying attention?" Tech people are smart in the sense of processing power, but they are not smart in the sense of paying attention. It is similar to IQ smart versus commonsense smart.

Joe Techman is usually very focused on his own technology. Proprietary technology is certainly a key component of any technology or intangible business; however most tech people focus too acutely on this aspect. "Our technology is better," he says, as if that is all that matters in a business. (I have seen many companies go out of business that had previously won distinguished awards for their technology.) Customers will not adopt a new technology solely because it is better. The switching costs of making a change are usually quite high. The "total cost of software" is not only the software's purchase price, but also the costs of installation and training. The learning curve has a cost as does the temporary disruption of the business.

To the contrary, business is about solving the customer's problem. The customer does not care how you do it. Bill Businessman is customer focused, not technology focused.

This important difference raises the question of how to define a company. Bill Businessman defines his business by its customers, not by its products or services. The company is defined by the answer to the question, "What problem do we solve for the customer?"

Joe Techman, on the other hand, defines his company by its technology. "Our technology this, our technology that." Take a look at technology company web sites. A majority of technology firms define their businesses by their technologies.

Another contrast between Techman and Businessman is whether they are focused or opportunistic. Most technology people are good at employing a singular focus. Focus is a good thing; but it is not the only thing. Opportunity can play an important role in business as well. One does not analyze in order to find opportunities; one explores to find opportunities. Markets are always changing and companies must explore new avenues to find fresh opportunities. The Businessman is open to new opportunities.

Bill Businessman is quite good at working with and understanding people. It is one of his most essential business skills. This is not one of Joe Techman's strengths. One of my clients was a software company that could not increase its revenues beyond $2.5 million. Sales had been flat for a number of years. The problem was that it had gone through four vice presidents of sales in two years. Now I am not saying it is easy to find a good VP of sales, but to go through four people in two years says something about management's ability to hire. They were simply not good at making decisions about people. They recognized that this was the case and it was one of the reasons they decided to sell the company.

Joe Techman needs to become a Businessman—to quit analyzing everything, to relinquish control, to delegate authority, and to let people take responsibility. Being a Businessman means making decisions under uncertainty. It means making judgments with imperfect information. Often there is a paralysis to act on Techman's part—"Give me more data." This is not how decision making works. If all the data were available, the spreadsheet would make the decision by itself. Judgment would not be necessary.

Another aspect of tech hubris is that Joe Techman often does not know what he does not know. Bill Businessman, on the other hand, is generally pretty aware of what he knows and what he does not know. He also knows when to ask for help.

The Businessman's mindset is practical and opportunistic. Often good enough is good enough. Bill Businessman is people oriented and he realizes that action is more important than intellectualizing.

How Tech Hubris Affects the M&A Process

This idea of "we did it by ourselves" is a common theme in the technology sectors. Whether it is selling the company or undertaking an acquisition search, companies often retort, "we can do that ourselves." Of course they can do it themselves. A company can do absolutely everything itself if it so chooses. However, it may not be the smartest course of action.

If an entrepreneur builds a company and decides to sell it himself that is fine. But when outside shareholders come into the picture, the game changes. He has an obligation to these shareholders. When it is time to sell the company, that obligation includes obtaining the best price and terms. It is no longer the entrepreneur's prerogative to learn a new talent and sell it himself. He should seek experienced advice and assistance because he is playing with other peoples' money.

Joe Techman needs to understand his real goal. Is the goal to do everything himself? For an entrepreneur, the goal should be to serve the customers and create maximum value for the shareholders. For the venture capitalist, the objective should be to create value for the limited partners. Techman needs to understand what game he is playing. Is it the "we did it ourselves" game or is it the "return to shareholders game?"

Over the years I have negotiated with many different types of people. Without question, technology people are the easiest to negotiate against. All I have to do is observe which thought process they utilize and then it is straightforward from there. Joe Techman is a prisoner of his own thought process.

In one situation I was negotiating the breakup of a company. The two founders reached an impasse and were trying to decide how to split the company and part ways. Up until that point the parties had gone around and around and made no progress. The opposing founder believed that discounted cash flow was the only correct way to view the company's value. He was totally locked in to this approach. Once I discovered that, it was relatively easy to arrange the pieces in such a way that he thought he was getting an acceptable deal.

Joe Techman is great to negotiate against. Tech people are so linear and so narrowly focused. They often miss the bigger picture and have a hard time seeing the situation through the other party's eyes. They are easily led and easy to get off track. They are also extremely literal. As a consequence, they are easy to manipulate.

In another situation the CEO for the buyer sent an e-mail to my client, the founder of the seller. The e-mail posed four questions. My client proceeded to discuss with me how he would answer these questions. My response was that we should not answer three of the questions at all and only answer the fourth question in a general and vague manner. It never occurred to the founder not to answer all four questions; he was locked in.

The antithesis of this mindset is the quarterback who sees a situation on the football field and calls an audible play. Joe Techman is the polar opposite of this quarterback. Once the play is decided Techman will keep his nose down and execute no matter what the outside world is doing. This narrow focus is great for developing technology but it can be a real detriment in negotiations.

WAR STORY: $100 MILLION ... OOPS

Psi Software Technology was an up-and-coming firm that developed systems management software for broadband infrastructure systems. The company had been in business for four years and had received three rounds of venture capital totaling $12 million. The company employed about 150 people. Psi Software was developing innovative technology and it had a number of partnerships with other companies selling components into the same market. The technology was in the prototype stage and the company's revenues were minimal.

One of its larger partners made inquiries about acquiring the company. This buyer sold complementary products and was convinced that if it owned Psi's core technology it could capture the number one market position. The buyer was a fast-growing technology company with a market capitalization of $2 billion. After several rounds of discussions the buyer offered $100 million to acquire Psi Software. $100 million for a company with minimal revenues! This is truly a no-brainer.

The founder owned 50 percent of the company and he had a blocking vote. Given the liquidity preferences of the venture capital firms, the founder would have received $40 million in this transaction. However, he thought that the offer was 20 times less than Psi's eventual potential. In other words, he thought the company could grow to be worth $2 billion. The venture capitalists also viewed the offer as too low, so Psi turned down the $100 million offer.

The company went forward and eventually raised $26 million of additional capital at a $100 million valuation, for a total of $38 million in invested capital. Seven years later Psi Software Technology is still in

(Continued)

business. It employs 15 people and has revenues of less than $2 million. The founder is still running the company.

The fatal flaws on the founder's part include believing in the potential of his technology to an extreme degree, being blind to alternatives, placing too much weight on his own opinion, and having no appreciation for the downside risk. He also wanted to remain in control. This tech hubris cost the founder and his investors $100 million.

Market Hubris

Joe Techman often expects perfect market knowledge. Tech people think that they can simply analyze the situation and figure out who the best buyer is and then negotiate with that one company. Many Techmen try to out-think the market. "We know our market space. We know who the best buyers are." This is market hubris.

The idea that one can think the outcome through ahead of time and select the best buyer is erroneous. It presupposes perfect market knowledge and no one has perfect market knowledge. One cannot intellectualize about who the best buyer is. One has to go out to the market, contact a wide range of companies, and discover exactly which buyers are interested and which are not. Joe Techman is not comfortable with a situation in which he cannot analyze it all the way through.

Technology markets are fast moving, dynamic, and ever changing. Six months is an eternity in the technology arena. New players pop up all the time. In the technology markets it is impossible to see very far down the road because the roads keep changing. As I have discussed before, half of the time the best buyer is from an adjacent market, not from the seller's core market. In other words, half of the time the best buyer is a company that the seller is not familiar with.

The sale of an intangible company is an inexact and sometimes messy process. Techman prefers that the M&A process be antiseptic. In order to find the best buyers one must make contact with many potential buyers. Every search holds surprises. In every assignment I am surprised by who *is not* interested and by who *is* interested.

Technology M&A is an exploration. It is about working the process. This process requires a significant amount of effort and there are no shortcuts. You must go to the market and find out. Do not overthink it. You cannot out-think the market.

Board Hubris

The boards of technology companies can also exhibit hubris. In my experience, board members who have been through the sale process attach an inordinately high degree of confidence to their experience. If they were involved in one or two transactions that had certain transaction dynamics, then they are quite certain that all transactions have those same dynamics. The problem is that transactions differ significantly from one to the next. Each transaction has its own set of issues and challenges—they are all different. Preconceived ideas are dangerous.

Board hubris makes the intermediary's job more difficult. The CEO does not know who to believe—the board member or the investment banker. It becomes an uphill battle to help the company make the right decisions and take the right actions on the path to selling the company.

VC Hubris

Most venture capitalists (VCs) understand the process for large M&A very well. They may have been investment bankers at New York investment banks or they may have made acquisitions for high-tech companies. Many do not realize that small M&A, transactions under $30 million, is a different process than large M&A. The auction method is not effective and there are more alternatives when it comes to deal structure. Plus, any number of obstacles can derail a small transaction. VCs should not assume that just because they lop off a few zeroes that the process is the same.

Venture capitalists can fall into the trap of selling companies themselves as well. A VC may have worked as an investment banker prior to becoming a venture capitalist. But this raises a question: Is this the highest and best use of the venture capitalist's time? Certainly as a board member they should weigh in on the sale process. But should the VC spend their time actually selling portfolio companies or should they be seeking out new investments and advising their companies?

A venture capitalist will create more value acting as a venture capitalist than acting as an investment banker. Even if the venture capitalist was an investment banker in his or her previous job, he or she should still outsource the assignment of selling the company. Behavioral economics comes into play here. This well-known bias in human beings is called *loss aversion.* Loss aversion is the tendency for people to much prefer avoiding a loss than making a gain. People will spend much more energy trying to avoid a $500 loss than trying to make a $500 gain. Research studies have shown that people will expend 2 to 2.5 times the effort to avoid a loss than the effort to achieve a gain.

The parallel is that a VC will spend more effort trying to sell the company and save a deal fee than he or she will using that same time creating value as a venture capitalist. Some VCs think it is part of their job description to sell their portfolio companies. This is not a task that a venture capitalist should perform. Yes, the VC knows the market and can make a few phone calls to his or her contacts. This is the casual approach. The casual approach is not effective when selling an intangible company. A venture capitalist simply does not have enough time to execute a comprehensive sales process. The details get ignored and the process gets shortchanged.

A venture capitalist will create more value performing VC tasks—working with successful portfolio companies and identifying new investments. It is not like venture capitalists have plenty of spare time on their hands. It is the disciplined venture capitalist who engages outside help so that he or she can stay focused on his or her primary objectives.

SUMMARY

Most CEOs vastly underestimate the time and effort required to do a thorough job selling a company. There are many moving parts surrounding the sale. The right thing for the shareholders is to have an experienced intermediary sell the company, not the CEO. Rookie mistakes are all too common for the CEO that decides to sell his or her company him or herself.

As the technology industries evolve and mature, tech companies will be managed by businessmen not by technology people. Almost every large technology company is run by a businessman, not a technology person. Smaller firms need to learn a lesson from the big companies. An intangible company with as little as $10 million in revenue can afford to hire an experienced businessman with strong people skills as CEO. The founder, the tech guy, does not need to run the company. Running a business is about interacting with people, about dealing with customers and employees. People skills are paramount.

Technology can only take a company so far. Sooner or later every company must become sales-driven. First adopter customers may beat a path to the door for a limited time, but eventually regular customers will require a typical marketing and sales effort.

Business is business. It does not matter if it is a technology business, a service business, or an old-line manufacturing business. Business is about dealing with people and the best businessmen are those who are skilled at dealing with people. This is not going to change. Regardless of Moore's Law or any other technological advance, people skills will always be the most important talent in business.

The next chapter delves into structuring alternatives. A company can sell its stock or sell its assets and it can get paid in cash or stock or a combination of both. We consider some innovative structures including royalties, licensing, and assumed liabilities. Consulting contracts and non-compete agreements are common in the sales of intangible companies so we review those agreements. We also touch on how a buyer accounts for the acquisition.

CHAPTER 11

Structuring the Transaction

et us examine the basic structure and alternatives and then discuss some of the twists on these issues. First of all, what is the company selling? Is it selling its stock or is it selling its corporate assets? What is the buyer paying with—cash or stock? What legal structure will the transaction take?

The terms can get confusing. For example, is a stock deal a transaction in which the buyer purchases the stock of the selling company, or is it one in which the buyer pays with stock? It can mean both; however, most of the time a *stock transaction* refers to the purchase of stock.

In some sales of intangible companies the full potential of the selling company has not been realized at the time of the transaction. In such cases it is common to use an earnout to bridge the gap between what the buyer is willing to pay and what the seller thinks the company is truly worth. There are pluses and minuses to using an earnout and we examine these in Chapter 13.

The two primary structures are a sale of assets and a sale of stock. A third transaction structure, the merger, is rarely used in the sale of an intangible company. The seller usually wants a stock sale and the buyer usually wants to purchase assets. Normally, from a tax and corporate liability standpoint, what is favorable for the buyer is not favorable for the seller and vice versa.

SELLING ASSETS

For smaller transactions, less than $10 million or $20 million in purchase price, buying the assets of the company can be the simplest transaction structure. Assets might include software, technology, and other intellectual property; patents, brand names, and trademarks; as well as contracts with customers and the typical business assets such as accounts receivable, inventory, equipment, computers, and so on.

An asset sale is practical for transactions involving intangible companies because a company with intangible value generally has few physical assets. A sale of assets is not a complicated deal structure. Asset sales are best for companies that sell for relatively low prices because the tax impact will be minor. If a company sells for a high price an asset sale will not be attractive because the corporation (if it is a C corporation) must pay tax on any gain and corporations are taxed at ordinary income rates, not capital gains rates. Taxes would also apply when the proceeds of the asset sale are liquidated and paid to the seller's shareholders. This is the so-called *double taxation* that applies to C corporation shareholders in this context. The S corporation and limited liability company forms are taxed differently and generally more favorably to the selling shareholders.

A purchase of assets is attractive from the buyer's perspective because it eliminates or reduces the possibility of hidden liabilities—claims and other actions against the corporation that occurred before the purchase.

The Bulk Sales law may apply to a sale of assets depending on the state. The term *bulk sale* refers to the sale of a majority of a company's assets not in the ordinary course of its business. The Bulk Sales law prevents owners from defrauding creditors. In order to comply with the Bulk Sales law a company must notify each creditor regarding the sale of assets. The Bulk Sales law only applies to asset transactions, not stock transactions. Most states have repealed their bulk sales laws in recent years because they were viewed as too onerous.

SELLING STOCK

The purchase of stock is a fairly straightforward transaction structure. If there are a large number of shareholders, the deal can get more complicated. One of the major issues surrounding the purchase of stock is the presence of unknown liabilities or off-balance sheet liabilities. Because of this additional potential risk, due diligence can require a longer time for the buyer to become comfortable with the potential risks of the transaction.

If a company sells its stock in exchange for stock in the buyer the transaction will be tax free in most situations. If stock is sold for cash the shareholders will have to pay tax on the capital gain. One of the advantages of selling stock is that gains are taxed at the capital gains rate of 15 percent. If the transaction includes payment in the form of both cash and stock, only the stock portion is tax free.

Sometimes when a company sells its stock there may be an issue of who gets the cash left in the company's account. If a seller has an appreciable amount of cash it is important to make it clear who gets this cash. Sometimes the buyer assumes that it will get the cash while the seller also assumes that it will keep the cash. The best way to solve this problem is to work off a balance sheet as of a specific date. The parties may also simply agree on the amount of cash that will be left in the company's account. It is important that this issue be negotiated early so as not to cause problems down the road.

FORMS OF PAYMENT

The currency used to pay for an acquisition of an intangible company is cash, stock, notes, or a combination of these. The buyer can also assume liabilities from the seller or make future payments based on performance, known as an earnout.

Cash is very straightforward. It is usually paid in full at closing. Typically, the funds are wired from the buyer's bank to the seller's bank. Sometimes the buyer may place 10 to 15 percent of the purchase price in an escrow account in case any problems surface after the transaction has closed for which the buyer seeks reimbursement.

Sellers almost always state upfront that they want all cash. However, most of the time, they do not really need all cash. Stock from a sound and well-capitalized public company can be just as good as, or sometimes better than, cash because of tax reasons. If the selling shareholders are primarily individual investors they do not really need the cash back. Typically, any cash received will be invested in another investment. The point is that sellers always think they must have cash and most of the time they do not actually need the cash.

Getting Paid in Stock

Getting paid in stock may be much more attractive for sellers than they might initially think. No, it is not liquid. But it may be more liquid and less risky than the stock they currently hold in the seller. There may be a reasonable chance that the stock of the buyer could become liquid in the next few years. Plus, the stock could increase in value. In addition, taxes can be deferred until the stock is eventually sold.

It is important to understand the shareholders' objectives. For individual investors, or angel investors, they may be better off with a different stock that might grow in value. Wealthy investors rarely need their money back. They knew they were buying an illiquid stock when they made the investment and if they receive stock in a larger and more successful company, they are better off.

Accepting stock puts an additional burden on the seller because now it is becoming a shareholder of the buyer. In this case the seller needs to do some homework to determine the issues surrounding the buyer's stock. If the stock is publicly traded, is the price a sensible one? Is the price-earnings ratio in line with the industry? If the buyer is a private company, what valuation is being used to determine the price of the buyer's shares?

The transaction proceeds can be a combination of stock and cash. The cash portion should be less than 20 percent of the total deal consideration in order to qualify as a *reorganization* for tax purposes, which is tax free for the sellers. The cash portion is not tax free.

WAR STORY: OVERVALUED BUYER'S SHARES

I had initially negotiated the price of this transaction in terms of shares of the buyer's stock. We had reached tentative agreement on a price of $48 million in stock. At this point the two primary shareholders of the seller began to look more closely at the buyer's stock. This was a fairly risky stock.

The buyer was on a roll. It had been growing rapidly and achieving strong growth in both revenues and earnings. As a result the stock market had responded favorably and bid up the price of the company's shares. The market capitalization was around $250 million. Of course the buyer wanted to use this high-priced stock as its acquisition currency.

The price-earnings ratio was fairly high and the company had experienced very rapid growth. Even though the transaction price was quite attractive, the sellers decided that this stock was much riskier than they were comfortable owning. They had just spent the last 12 years building their company, overcoming all kinds of difficulties and dealing with risks. They were now ready to retire and reduce their level of risk.

So it was back to the drawing board on negotiating price. My first step was to take a hard look at the buyer's stock. Was it overvalued? Was the price-earnings ratio in line with the industry? Was management capable of growing the company to the next level? Was there much danger of the price falling significantly and thereby reducing the value of my client's stock? After considerable analysis and industry research I came to the conclusion that the stock *was* overvalued and that there was a very real possibility that the share price could drop.

Knowing my client's preference for less risk, I concluded that taking stock was not in my client's best interest. The next step was to determine what amount of cash the buyer could afford to pay that was high enough to satisfy the sellers. This is not the kind of analysis that is appropriate for a spreadsheet. It is more holistic in nature, taking into consideration all the subtleties and nuances of the transaction and the personalities involved. I concluded that $30 million in cash was the appropriate number. I reopened negotiations and the buyer accepted the deal. The transaction closed successfully and both parties were very happy with the deal.

A few months after the closing of the transaction, the share price of the buyer began to decline. It edged down gradually and over the ensuing eight months the buyer had lost about a third of its market value. It is easy to look back with hindsight and say how smart we were. On the other hand, one could say we left $18 million on the table. In the end the preference for cash instead of stock was not about money, it was about risk. The sellers were smart to recognize their own risk preferences and close the transaction for significantly less money but they were able to sleep soundly.

When the buyer is a public company and makes an offer with its shares of stock as consideration, it can make the offer in terms of number of shares or in dollars. If the offer is made in dollars and if the price of the stock changes between the letter of intent and the closing date, the buyer will adjust the number of shares upward or downward so that the dollar goal is met. If the offer is made in number of shares, it may be wise for the seller to negotiate a collar. A collar is a maximum or minimum number of shares that the seller will receive.

For example, a collar can be established with a minimum price per share of $30 and a maximum of $35. If the stock price falls below $30 before the closing date, the seller will receive more shares. Similarly, if the price exceeds $35 the seller will receive fewer shares. If the price stays within the $30 to $35 range then no adjustment is made. The collar protects both sides from extreme or even moderate swings in the share price.

The price of the seller's stock is usually determined as the average of the last 20 days of trading. This is a common practice; however, there is no reason that it needs to be this way. The stock price can be established in any way that the parties agree. I have seen transactions in which the stock was valued using the average closing market price over the two-day period before and after the sale was announced.

WAR STORY: STOCK OR CASH? ARNIE AND BERNIE

Two founders sold their software company to Microsoft for $5 million. Each founder received $2.5 million. One founder, Arnie, opted to receive cash, the other founder, Bernie, chose to take Microsoft stock. Arnie was going to enjoy his new-found wealth. Within six months Arnie had purchased a new house, a new car, and taken a month-long overseas trip. He also paid a considerable sum in taxes. Bernie, on the other hand, held onto the Microsoft stock.

A few years later a look at Arnie's and Bernie's net worth showed remarkably different pictures. Arnie's net worth was $2 million. Microsoft stock had tripled in value and Bernie's net worth was now $10 million. So Bernie's net worth was 5 times that of Arnie. Sure, Bernie was a little lucky but he also was thinking about the future.

All stock deals do not work out this favorably. In fact, I have heard plenty of horror stories from founders who took stock in less than stellar buyers that ended up being totally worthless. There are a number of points to this story. Do not be greedy. Look to the future. And make sure you understand the risks as well as the upside potential associated with the company whose stock you are accepting.

Assuming Liabilities

Assuming selected liabilities of the selling company is an effective way for a buyer to raise the price of the transaction without having to put up additional cash. The buyer usually does not assume *all* of the seller's liabilities, but *selected liabilities*. For example, if the buyer will be taking over the seller's business it makes sense for the buyer to assume the accounts payable—because it wants to make sure these bills are paid. The buyer will usually assume the accounts receivable and service contract liabilities as well because it wants to maintain the relationship with customers. The buyer may assume the building lease or a bank loan. The buyer will not likely assume previous payroll obligations, deferred compensation, investment banking fees, accounting fees, or attorney's fees.

In some cases the assumption of liabilities can be a significant portion of the transaction value. For closely held and family owned companies it is not unusual for the principals to sign personally for any bank loans or lines of credit. In one transaction the founder and his wife had personally guaranteed a $3 million line of credit. About $2.5 million had been drawn down at the time the company was sold. The transaction terms stated that the buyer would pay $2 million in cash and assume the outstanding debt. Thus, this was a $4.5 million transaction and the assumption of debt accounted for more than 50 percent of the purchase price.

Promissory Notes

Occasionally, a deal will be structured in which the buyer pays the seller a portion in cash and a portion in a promissory note. The note will usually have a moderate interest rate and be payable over a period of two to five years. Buyers like using promissory notes because they can purchase a company without requiring as much cash upfront. Although a promissory note is a very straightforward form of payment, notes are rarely used in acquisitions of intangible companies.

WAR STORY: TOO MANY SHAREHOLDERS

The number of shareholders can be an issue. In this case, Zeta Software Corp. had 47 individual investors as shareholders. The buyer, Alpha Corp., only had five shareholders, including the three founders and two venture capital firms. It did not want to add 47 new shareholders to its shareholder list. It would be too cumbersome if Alpha Corp. were to be acquired in the near future, as it expected.

The buyer chose to pay for the acquisition with stock. It was on a fast growth track and wanted to conserve its cash to finance this growth. Alpha Corp. insisted that the structure be such that it did not acquire 47 new shareholders. So, Alpha simply purchased the assets of the seller and the seller's corporation remained intact.

Zeta Software essentially became a holding company with one asset—shares of stock in the buyer, Alpha Corp. The seller also changed the corporate name as part of the deal requirements.

This was not a liquidity event for the shareholders of Zeta Software. However, they now own shares of Alpha Corp., a much better

(Continued)

capitalized and faster growing firm. Alpha Corp. is likely to be acquired or go public within the next two or three years and the shareholders of Zeta Software will then achieve liquidity. In addition, Alpha Corp. might sell at a higher price than the valuation at the time of the Zeta Software acquisition.

The events played out in exactly that way. Two years later Alpha sold at a much higher valuation and Zeta's shareholders were rewarded handsomely.

Tax Issues

In an asset sale, the corporation must pay taxes on any gain. The gain is the amount that the sales price exceeds the assets' basis. The corporation then distributes the remaining proceeds to its shareholders and the shareholders must pay tax on any capital gain. Thus, the tax cost can be significantly higher for an asset sale.

Double taxation can be a problem when a C corporation sells its assets. It must pay tax on any gain at the corporate level and then the shareholders pay tax on their capital gain. A limited liability company (LLC) or S corporation will not have a problem with double taxation since neither entity pays any tax itself.

In a stock sale, the corporation does not pay any taxes. The proceeds are distributed to shareholders and shareholders pay capital gains tax on the amount of the gain that exceeds their basis. If shareholders sell their shares of stock in exchange for shares of the buyer, the transaction is tax free.

One section of the IRS Code (Section 338) allows the buyer to treat a stock acquisition as an asset acquisition for tax purposes. The buyer acquires the stock of the seller. Then it records the seller's assets on its books as if it had completed an asset transaction. This transaction structure is beneficial when the seller has a net operating loss or tax credit carry forward that the buyer would like to take advantage of. The buyer can also step up the tax basis for the acquired assets. (A stepped-up basis gives the company a higher value for depreciation, which is a tax advantage.) One disadvantage is that technically for liability purposes this is a stock purchase so any liabilities of the seller, known or unknown, still remain.

The tax issues surrounding the sale of a company can become quite complex. Get the advice of an attorney and an accountant who have experience working with merger and acquisition transactions.

Securities Issues

Securities issues apply to any issuance of securities by a buyer. The issuance of the securities is treated as an *offering* to the seller or the seller's shareholders, depending on the structure of the transaction. Any such offering is subject to the same federal and state securities regulation as an offering of the buyer's securities to raise capital. Thus, a private buyer must consider whether the number of seller shareholders, or the number of lower net worth shareholders who do not qualify as *accredited investors* under applicable securities laws, makes such an offering impractical. If the offering cannot be made as a private offering exempt from registration, few private companies will wish to make it. A public buyer has the advantage of being able to more easily register securities offered to complete an acquisition. Selling shareholders receiving stock of a publicly traded issuer also have an easier path to liquidity.

WAR STORY: SHAREHOLDER DILEMMA—STOCK OR CASH?

This software company had been in business for 10 years and it was time to sell. The company had progressed reasonably well, but not well enough to be a strong player now that the industry had matured and competitors were larger. Individual investors had invested several million dollars in the company and they knew they should either sell the company or bring in a new management team and contribute additional capital.

The sale proceeded on schedule and the shareholders realized that they would not be getting a high price for the company. The company's software was good; however, the buyers had their own software. The primary asset was the company's customer base. With no buyer willing to pay a premium for the software technology, the price would simply be mediocre.

After a comprehensive search, we met with the board to discuss four potential buyers that had shown an interest. All four of the buyers proposed transactions using their shares of stock as the acquisition currency. One of the buyers, actually the least promising buyer, was a young company with an optimistic growth plan. However, the board did not believe the company could execute the plan so we informed the buyer that we were not interested in doing a transaction with them.

(Continued)

Another buyer was based on the East Coast of the United States and was larger and more profitable than the others. The choice seemed like an easy one until we received an all cash offer from the first buyer, the least promising firm. Now the shareholders had a decision to make. Do they take stock in a private company that is based on the opposite coast and hope for a larger liquidity event, or do they take the cash and be done with it? The stock deal was about 35 percent higher in value than the cash deal. Plus this company was on an aggressive growth track. After some deliberations the board decided to accept the stock deal from the East Coast buyer. The shareholders did not need their cash returned immediately and the idea of holding shares of a growth company was consistent with their original investment objectives.

Two years later the buyer was acquired for $150 million—an excellent price. The shareholders were rewarded for their patience and earned an attractive return on their investment.

CREATIVE STRUCTURING

Creative structuring can solve transaction problems when there are issues that are somewhat unusual. Over the years I have employed a wide variety of creative structures that solved exceptional problems. In one transaction we structured the deal as a marketing agreement, not a sale of the company, because the primary asset was the company's customer base, which was gradually transferred to the buyer.

Royalties can be an appropriate structure if the selling company's primary assets are its product lines, or perhaps a technology. Royalties are more directly related to the success of specific products in the marketplace. Royalties are used when acquiring products; they are not typically used in the acquisition of entire companies.

In one transaction a Canadian software company was seeking to sell off some of its software technology in order to concentrate on its primary area of expertise. An in-depth search did not turn up any buyers that were serious about acquiring the software. Several companies had shown interest in licensing the software however, so we shifted our focus to putting together a licensing transaction. Zeta Software, a large software company, appeared to be the best candidate to license the software.

As a large company, one of the problems that Zeta had encountered over the years was lawsuits regarding the ownership of intellectual property. As a result, Zeta was hesitant to license this software technology. In order to overcome this obstacle I proposed a rather creative structure. Rather than Zeta licensing the software from the Canadian company, I suggested a reverse deal—Zeta could purchase the software and then license it back to the Canadian firm. Now Zeta would own the technology outright and the ownership issue would be clearly established. This transaction went full circle: from selling to licensing to selling and some creative thinking brought about a successful transaction.

WAR STORY: BUYING CUSTOMERS ONE AT A TIME

Nu Software was a small software company and it had developed a nice niche software application for a specific vertical market. Like many small software firms, they could not effectively achieve the next level of growth on their own. They needed to be part of a firm with greater sales and marketing resources. Their technology was good, but it was a little dated. The primary asset was the company's customer base.

In our search for potential buyers, we discovered that buyers were not interested in acquiring Nu's software technology. However, the customer base was an asset that buyers responded to. So we ended up structuring a transaction in which the buyer paid a specific dollar royalty amount for each customer when that customer converted to the buyer's software. Nu Software remained in business until all the customers converted to the buyer's software. The founders of Nu Software received royalties for several years and were pleased to capitalize on their efforts. This was a much simpler transaction structure than a purchase of assets or stock.

CONSULTING CONTRACTS AND NONCOMPETE AGREEMENTS

Consulting contracts and noncompete agreements can be very useful instruments in structuring transactions. Although not specifically part of the purchase agreement, these contracts can be an effective way to distribute the proceeds disproportionately. With the proliferation of preferences on venture capital investments, I have witnessed many deals in which the founders have received very little for their common shares. Consulting agreements can give key management people, who do not have significant shareholdings in the company, a bonus that is separate from the shareholders' proceeds.

A consulting contract typically has a term of one or two years and the consultant's compensation is specified. There are a few additional terms and conditions, but the primary points are how much and for how long. A consulting agreement has the added benefit that it often does not fall under the buyer's internal salary structure or normal budget category. A company's internal salary structures can limit the amount of salary that can be paid to an employee. Especially for smaller acquisitions where a buyer has set firm limits on the purchase price, a consulting agreement can be used by the buyer to work around those limits (and salary parameters) in a way that is beneficial to both parties, plus consulting payments are deductible to the buyer.

In one instance I negotiated a very lucrative two-year consulting contract for a senior management person from the seller. The amount of the annual compensation was well in excess of his previous salary. He had been an instrumental part of the team but did not have any ownership stake in the selling company. The buyer wanted to reward him as well as keep him on board after the acquisition.

A noncompete agreement is a fairly standard instrument used in the context of an acquisition. By signing a noncompete agreement an employee agrees not to work for a competitor for a period of time—usually two years and sometimes as long as three years. Key employees will often know sensitive and confidential information that could be damaging if it got into the hands of a competitor. In California a noncompete agreement is not enforceable unless the person is a selling shareholder. The argument is that it deprives a person of the right to make a living.

The buyer can attach a dollar amount to a noncompete agreement. It is not unusual for a buyer to pay from $50,000 to as much as $400,000 as consideration for a noncompete agreement. It is important to note that the amount paid for a noncompete agreement is not extra cash paid out because the buyer is generous. Rather, it is an allocated portion of the total purchase price that was previously negotiated.

WAR STORY: A NONCOMPETE AGREEMENT PROBLEM

In this transaction the two founders were asked to sign noncompete agreements by the buyer. Both founders were offered employment by the buyer and their hiring was an important component of the trans-action. However, the buyer was unwilling to offer them employment contracts for a specific length of time. It was simply employment at will. In addition, the buyer expected both founders to sign noncompete agreements with terms of two years.

Neither founder was very excited about this situation. Either of them could be dismissed at any time with only normal severance pay and they could not work for a competitor for two years because of the noncompete agreement. The founders initially proposed that the buyer pay a dollar amount for the noncompete agreement. The amount suggested was slightly more than each person's annual salary. However, the buyer was unwilling to go along with this suggestion. The founders countered with a proposal in which, if they were terminated, the buyer would pay the founders 80 percent of their salary for the remaining portion of the noncompete period. The parties dickered for a while and then eventually reached an agreement along those lines.

A FEW OTHER ISSUES

Acquisition Financing

Rarely is bank financing involved in the sale of an intangible company. Either the buyer is large enough to have sufficient cash on hand; or the buyer will use its stock as the acquisition currency. Occasionally a company will go back to its venture capital backers to obtain additional funds for an acquisition.

In some cases a small buyer must raise additional equity capital to do a deal. In one example, a Canadian firm was interested in acquiring a company in the United States; however, it did not have sufficient cash on hand and the seller was unwilling to accept stock as the transaction currency. The buyer had to go back to its shareholders including one institutional investor to raise additional funds to complete the acquisition. The transaction took a little longer because of these events, however this buyer was clearly the best one and the seller was willing to wait for the financing to be put in place.

In another situation the transaction was very near closing. It was a stock transaction so no cash was required. However, the venture capital backers voiced their opposition to the deal and the transaction fell through.

A venture capital firm can have a strong influence over a deal even if it does not have voting control.

Reverse Mergers and Shell Companies

One structure to be aware of, and usually to steer clear of, is a reverse merger with a shell company. This transaction is used for taking a company public (and sometimes for financing) although technically it is a merger transaction. The essence of this transaction is that a publicly traded company exists that has no business and no assets other than perhaps some cash—it is a shell company. The shell company then acquires the target company. The shell company may change its name to that of the target. After the transaction is completed the target company will have a new group of shareholders and a stock that can be publicly traded.

On the surface a reverse merger appears to be an inventive and financially clever transaction. Technically there is no reason that a deal should not work out for the target company. In actual practice however these maneuvers should be avoided. The first problem is that the shell company could have a bad history, undisclosed liabilities, irritable shareholders, and legal problems. Second, there are rarely enough shares traded in the market to provide real liquidity. (If the company's only asset is cash, there is no reason shares would be actively trading.) And third, these transactions are sponsored by financial promoters, not strong management looking to build companies. Often their only interest is to dump their stock on the market as soon as they can. Some reverse mergers have actually worked out successfully, but the majority of the time they come with a lot of baggage and should be avoided.

Loss Carry Forwards

If a target company has experienced losses for a number of years it may have a loss carry forward. A loss carry forward or net operating loss (NOL) carry forward allows a company to offset taxable income in future years. Loss carry forwards are no longer as attractive to buyers as they were in the past. The actual rules are fairly complicated.

The net operating losses may offset taxes due on current profits; however, the loss may be carried back up to two years and carried forward for 20 years, so the amount available in any one year is only about 5 percent of the amount of the loss carry forward. This kind of takes the fun out of the loss carry forwards. (The amount of losses that the acquiring company can use each year is limited by Section 382 of the Internal Revenue Code. This section was designed to prevent a corporation acquiring another one simply to use the acquired corporation's NOLs.) The present value of a loss carry forward that extends for 20 years is a much smaller number. The effect of this change is to make loss carry forwards considerably less attractive to buyers.

BUYER ACCOUNTING FOR THE ACQUISITION

An intangible company that is seeking to be acquired should have basic understanding of how the acquisition will be accounted for by the buyer. The purchase price includes the total of payments made plus assumed liabilities. The buyer allocates the purchase price among the acquired assets and records the fair market value of each asset on its books. The allocation of the purchase price must be the same for the buyer as for the seller according to Internal Revenue Service rules. Both parties report the allocation on the IRS form entitled the Asset Acquisition Statement.

In 2007 the Financial Accounting Standards Board (FASB) made some changes on how accounting is done for acquisitions. Acquisition costs are now expensed. Costs such as fees paid to investment bankers, attorneys, and accountants that were formerly capitalized and amortized are to be expensed immediately. Another item called *in-process research and development* is no longer to be written off when acquired, but capitalized and recorded on the balance sheet.

Goodwill is the amount of the purchase price that is greater than the fair market value of the assets, both tangible and intangible assets. Goodwill is recorded on the books of the buyer. It is no longer amortized as it once was. Instead, goodwill remains on the books forever as long as it does not lose its value. It must be tested annually for impairment, and, if its value has declined, the company must write down its goodwill as an impairment charge.

Intangible assets are becoming increasingly important economic resources for many companies. Not surprisingly, a large portion of an intangible company's assets are intangible assets. An intangible asset is not physical in nature. Intangible assets include items such as distribution rights, patents, trademarks, trade names, trade secrets, customer lists, capitalized software, and other technology. Goodwill is not technically an intangible asset from an accounting point of view.

Intangible assets have real economic value and they are recorded on the buyer's books at their estimated fair value. This value is determined by several methods: replacement cost approach, the income approach (using discounted cash flow analysis), and, to a lesser extent, the market approach.

Each intangible asset has an estimated useful life. The useful life of many intangible assets is usually about three to five years and perhaps 10 years for those with a longer life such as trademarks and patents. Each intangible asset is amortized over the period of its useful life.

Goodwill is not treated as an intangible asset; it is a separate accounting item. Remember that goodwill is the excess of the purchase price after subtracting the fair market value of the assets, including tangible and intangible assets.

WAR STORY: AN EXAMPLE OF PURCHASE PRICE ALLOCATION

Smith Micro Software, Inc. acquired Allume, Inc. Smith Micro develops and markets wireless communication and utility software products. Smith Micro is publicly traded and had revenues of $20 million and $30 million in cash, which included $21 million from a private placement financing earlier that year.

Allume develops compression software for JPEG, MPEG, and MP3 platforms. The company's StuffIt Wireless technology compresses an already compressed JPEG file by up to 30 percent more without losing picture quality.

The purchase price was $12.8 million, consisting of $10.6 million in cash and 397,547 restricted shares of common stock worth $1.86 million. Smith Micro also spent $320,000 on acquisition costs. The common stock was valued at the average closing market price over a two-day period before and after the sale was announced. $2 million (15 percent of the purchase price) was placed in an escrow account to secure certain representations and warranties in the purchase agreement.

Smith Micro's allocation of the purchase price is summarized as follows:

Allocation of Purchase Price	($ in thousands)
Cash and accounts receivable	868
Inventory and equipment	303
Other	244
Intangible assets	4,863
Goodwill	7,573
Less: payables and liabilities	(1,051)
Total purchase price	12,800

Notice that the intangible assets and goodwill account for almost the entire purchase price. This is typical in the sale of an intangible company. The allocation of purchase price to certain types of assets can have tax rate implications. Tax advisers may see opportunities to characterize the purchase price in a more favorable manner for either party (often at the expense of the other party) by allocating relatively more purchase price to categories that result in the lowest tax rates (for sellers) or highest deductions and tax bases (for buyers).

SUMMARY

In this chapter we reviewed the basic structuring alternatives for the sale of an intangible company. The acquisition currency usually includes stock or cash and sometimes a combination of both. An acquirer can purchase the stock of the selling company or it can purchase the assets of the selling company. If purchasing assets, the buyer often assumes selected liabilities of the seller.

Shareholders of the selling company have to make a decision about whether they prefer to receive cash or shares of the buyer's stock. There are pluses and minuses to each of these alternatives. Generally, an exchange of stock is a tax-free transaction. Sometimes the shareholders opt to receive stock in a privately held buyer in the hope that the stock will increase in value and eventually become liquid.

Occasionally, a transaction will have unusual dynamics that will require creative structuring on the part of the investment banker. Keeping each side's interest in mind is essential in trying to develop creative solutions that each side will be happy with. On small transactions, consulting contracts and noncompete agreements can be an important part of the transaction structure.

Now that we have reviewed the basic structuring alternatives, let us turn to the subject of documenting the transaction and the agreements that are employed.

CHAPTER 12

Documenting the Deal

The first document that comes into play is the letter of intent, often referred to as an LOI. We will discuss when a letter of intent is not appropriate and we will identify some key drafting points. Due diligence can be one of the most arduous tasks in the transaction process and this chapter outlines the primary components of this process.

The chapter also reviews the purchase agreement, which is the definitive document that specifies the details of the transaction. We also review the period prior to closing that can be a critical time for the seller.

CRAFTING THE LETTER OF INTENT

The letter of intent (LOI) is a useful tool that can facilitate a deal going together smoothly. This section answers several questions:

- What is a letter of intent?
- What are its primary uses?
- Should your company use one?
- What are the important issues that should be covered?

In addition, several pointers on how to draft an effective LOI are included.

The LOI summarizes the intentions of the parties and describes the general price, terms, and conditions of the transaction. One of the key attributes of the LOI is that it is a letter of agreement, usually not more than three or four pages in length. It is a very effective summary of the deal points. The letter of intent is generally drafted by the buyer and presented to the seller. If both parties agree to the terms, each party signs the letter and the transaction moves forward. The buyer then begins a detailed due diligence process and directs its attorneys to draft the definitive purchase agreement.

The LOI is the first step in the closing process. This letter demonstrates commitment on the part of the buyer. It shows that the buyer is serious and proceeding in good faith. It is a rare situation when a buyer will send a letter of intent without a serious intent to purchase the company. Firms are simply too busy to bother with an LOI unless they are serious.

The letter of intent is an excellent tool for moving a transaction forward in a clear manner. In addition to demonstrating the level of seriousness on the part of the buyer, the LOI is an effective way to solve issues early on so that they do not need to be negotiated later. It can prevent later misunderstandings. The letter clarifies the major issues before the buyer begins drafting the definitive documents, which is a time-consuming and often expensive task. Fewer deals fall apart if a letter of intent has been issued.

The LOI encourages the parties to negotiate in good faith and introduces an atmosphere of cooperation. The letter should be drafted quickly, simply, and with minimal back and forth between lawyers. The more issues that can be resolved prior to the letter of intent the better. However, a letter of intent should not be delayed in order to negotiate minor issues. If minor issues happen to be agreed upon in the process of negotiating larger issues, it is acceptable to incorporate these in the letter of intent so that they do not have to be dealt with later; but do not spend time discussing minor issues.

If there are any key issues or deal breaker issues, they should be negotiated before the letter of intent is drafted. If the seller wants to continue discussions with any other buyers, these discussions should be held prior to signing a letter of intent.

Most of the clauses in the letter of intent are not binding; however, the paragraphs that are binding can have serious teeth. The letter should state specifically which paragraphs are binding and which are not. Even though most paragraphs are not binding, buyers do not issue LOIs casually.

For large acquisitions, another reason to use a letter of intent is that the LOI serves to start the clock for complying with the Hart-Scott-Rodino Act (covered later in this chapter). Parties must wait a specified time period before consummating large transactions and the LOI begins this time period.

The Basic Elements of a Letter of Intent

The letter of intent usually covers five primary topics:

1. Price and basic terms.
2. No-shop clause.
3. Employee matters.

4. Confidentiality.
5. Closing date.

Each of these is covered in detail in the following.

Price The price is almost always specified in dollar terms. If the buyer is a public company and using shares of its stock as the deal currency, the LOI should state whether the price is a specific number of shares or whether it is a dollar amount. It may be a good idea to set a minimum or maximum amount in case the share price fluctuates appreciably in the market. Sometimes the price may be expressed as a formula, such as a multiple of earnings for the last 12 months.

The deal structure should be specified. The structure is usually phrased as a "purchase of assets" or "purchase of the outstanding shares" of the company. If there are any unique or significant deal issues, it is a good idea to include them in the LOI. Minor terms are not typically specified in a letter of intent.

The buyer can adjust the price later if it discovers problems in the due diligence process that warrant changing the price or terms. However, changing the price stated in the letter of intent without a good reason is not a good thing. A buyer who does this should be regarded with suspicion.

No-Shop Clause One of the most important binding terms is the "no-shop clause," sometimes called a *stand still clause*. The no-shop clause states that the seller will not communicate with any other companies regarding the sale of the business for a certain period of time. The no-shop clause is usually stated something like: "The seller will not solicit proposals or engage in discussions with other potential buyers."

The no-shop time period can vary widely. An acceptable time frame ranges from one month to two months. Six weeks is a very good time frame. If the buyer cannot perform its due diligence tasks within that period of time, the seller should be free to talk with other parties. Any time period longer than two months is overreaching on the buyer's part. There is no good reason for a company to cease contact with other buyers for more than 60 days.

During this period the buyer will undertake its due diligence research to investigate the target company in depth. The buyer will expend significant resources during the due diligence process. The no-shop clause protects the buyer by giving it a window of time to perform the necessary due diligence.

Employee Matters Another important and binding clause is the "no-hire clause." This clause protects the seller because it prevents the buyer from hiring, or attempting to hire, any of the seller's employees. Without this clause there could be a real problem. The buyer will have just spent time meeting with and interviewing various employees of the seller and will have a clear idea of which employees they would like to hire. Without the no-hire clause the buyer is free to contact and hire away any of the employees. A well-drafted letter of intent should always have a no-hire clause.

Some letters of intent will include a paragraph in which the buyer promises to make written offers to hire the employees of the seller after the transaction closes. The offer letters will specify terms substantially similar to the terms of their current employment and describe any stock options. The purchaser may make the acceptance of these employment offers a condition to closing the transaction.

Confidentiality   For most transactions, a confidentiality agreement will have been signed long before the parties reach the letter of intent stage. If, for some reason, they have not signed a confidentiality agreement, the LOI should specify that they do so or include confidentiality language in the letter. If a confidentiality agreement was already in place, the parties may wish to tighten up the terms of this agreement. The paragraph on confidentiality is binding.

Closing Date   The letter of intent should specify a closing date. This date is not set in stone. It is usually an estimate of a likely time frame. The date can be changed later by the parties to accommodate their schedules.

The letter of intent may also contain numerous conditions to closing. These conditions include items such as disclosures, approvals, access to records, successful due diligence, legal issues, and the signing of a definitive agreement. The letter usually specifies that the seller will conduct its business in its normal fashion and not change its compensation to employees. These paragraphs are nonbinding and are generally boilerplate.

The letter of intent should also include the date that the letter expires, which is usually about two to five days from the date of the letter.

When a Letter of Intent Is Not Appropriate

If the basic price and basic terms have not been agreed upon, it is too early to draft a letter of intent. It is important that the parties reach an agreement on the basic price and terms before employing an LOI. The LOI simply summarizes this agreement in written form.

If the seller is not ready to commit to a specific buyer, the seller should not enter into a letter of intent with the buyer. If other parties are still interested in acquiring the company, it is best to explore these avenues before signing an LOI.

If the buyer is a public company it may not wish to issue an LOI. The reason is that publicly traded companies are required by SEC regulations to disclose any "material event." Issuing a letter of intent for an acquisition is a material event. Companies typically disclose an upcoming acquisition through a press release to notify the public. If a publicly traded company wishes to keep a potential acquisition secret, it will not utilize an LOI.

A letter of intent sometimes can create problems. The drafter may inadvertently make all or a portion of the letter binding. It might commit one or both of the parties to something before they know all the facts. It may also tip one's hand in negotiations; the company may want to hold some items back to use as negotiating points later.

Another reason for not using a letter of intent is that it may slow down the process. It is one more thing to negotiate. Sometimes attorneys can get a little overzealous and the LOI can take a significant amount of time to hammer out.

Tips for Good Drafting

Occasionally the letter of intent discussions can run amok. I have seen situations in which the buyer and the seller both try to include so many items in the LOI that it gets ridiculous. This can actually create more problems than it solves. Good judgment is required to know what items to include and what items to exclude. An experienced adviser can help the parties decide which items to include in the LOI and which ones to leave for later.

An LOI should be simple and straightforward. A few tips:

- Focus just on the major points; omit the details. Make sure that agreement is reached on the important issues.
- The letter should only be two to four pages long; otherwise, too much detail is going into it.
- Mention specifically which terms are meant to be binding and which are not.
- Draft the letter in the future tense.
- Specify that the transaction depends upon the execution of a definitive agreement.
- If a number of minor items have been agreed upon, you might as well include them in the LOI. As long as they do not open up discussions for new arguments, the more that can be agreed upon the better.
- The no-shop clause should be six weeks in length, not longer.

WAR STORY: A TOTALLY BINDING LETTER

This was an odd transaction in which the buyers were afraid they might lose the deal and they wanted to move fast to lock in the seller. So they drafted a letter of intent in which all the terms were binding. The letter stated that both parties agreed to close a transaction; however, the details of the transaction were not yet determined.

In my opinion, this could have been a legal and negotiating nightmare because the parties were agreeing to a transaction without knowing what all the terms were. The seller signed the letter because this was the best buyer and there were no other good buyers in the picture. The seller was not desperate; however, they did not have many alternatives.

In the end the deal worked out fine, although it was an unusual and risky way to proceed.

NAVIGATING THE DUE DILIGENCE PROCESS

The due diligence process seems to cause a lot of concern for many sellers and buyers as well. Misconceptions about the topic are common. What is due diligence exactly? When does due diligence begin? How long will it last? Due diligence is a critical part of any acquisition transaction.

A good way to think about due diligence is to consider it from the viewpoint of the buyer. What is the buyer trying to achieve or discover? What does the buyer want to learn about the seller? What are they worried about? One of the difficulties is that often the buyer does not know what it does not know. This is one of the reasons that due diligence takes so long. The buyer wants to have a high degree of certainty that it has investigated all the important issues.

What is the buyer trying to accomplish through the due diligence process? First, the buyer is trying to understand what it is actually buying. Second, the buyer wants to confirm that the company's business and assets are as portrayed. Third, the buyer wants to identify potential risks and satisfy itself that that the seller does not have any undisclosed problems. In addition, it wants to know if there are any issues that would cause the buyer to make an adjustment to the purchase price.

Through the due diligence process the buyer researches and reviews a wide range of information about the selling company. A good portion of the due diligence process centers around confirming that the information provided by the seller is true and accurate. The buyer will review the financial statements, sales forecasts, customer lists, product information, and so on. If the seller has patents, the buyer will want to review these as well.

Prior to issuing an LOI, the buyer will have completed fairly extensive research into the selling company. I like to think of this as the businessman's review phase. This first look into the target company begins when the buyer decides to make a serious assessment of the acquisition. It involves basic research about the company and is focused more on market opportunity, technologies, and product capabilities. Secondarily, it includes investigation into the development team, the management team, and sales capabilities.

The formal due diligence effort begins after the LOI has been signed by the buyer and the seller. In this phase, the buyer looks into almost every aspect of the target company's business. When does due diligence end? It ends when the buyer is satisfied that it has turned over all the stones and researched everything that might be of concern. The due diligence process usually lasts about six weeks. The process may take shorter than this or longer than this depending on the depth of research and the time constraints on the buyer.

The buyer will begin the process by sending the seller a lengthy checklist of items that it wants to review. A due diligence checklist can be quite extensive, running as many as 20 or more pages in length. Many of these items are requests for a wide variety of documents. Each situation is different. Some companies will have areas that require more digging into than others. It depends on the specific assets and the characteristics of the company that is being acquired.

The due diligence process is a laborious one. Many buyers keep asking for more and more documents. The best response is to provide them with whatever they ask for. It is a good practice to have one person in charge of providing the due diligence information. This person can interface with the buyer and take charge of providing the right information. The more information that can be organized early on in the process the easier the due diligence effort will be.

If the buyer is purchasing the assets of the target company, and not its stock, the due diligence burden is considerably less. The buyer only needs to check out the assets to make sure that they are as represented. How current are the accounts receivable? Is any of the inventory obsolete? Is the intellectual property ownership clear?

One the other hand, if the buyer is purchasing the seller's stock, the due diligence burden is considerably greater. The buyer must make sure that there are no hidden or off-balance sheet liabilities. It must satisfy itself that there are no lawsuits in the wings, that no sexual harassment suits are threatened, that no employee grievances could create problems.

A complete due diligence checklist can be provided by a number of sources including your investment banker or attorney. Many due diligence checklists present such a minute level of detail that they can be overwhelming. Remember that every deal is different and not all parts of the due diligence checklist will apply to every transaction.

During the due diligence phase the selling company should try to operate its business above expectations. The seller needs to keep revenues growing and customers completely satisfied.

The FTP Site: A Useful Tool

A relatively new tool that can make the due diligence process easier is an FTP site. An FTP site is a way to exchange files between the seller and the buyer using the Internet. FTP stands for file transfer protocol. It is a much more efficient way to transfer large files than to simply e-mail them. (FTP is how most web pages are posted on the Internet by the administrator or owner of an Internet web site.) To be more accurate, a Secure FTP site should be utilized and it is referred to as SFTP. In essence, an SFTP site is a web site created for the purpose of exchanging documents. Files are uploaded to the web site by the seller and downloaded from the web site by the buyer.

It works something like this. The buyer will request documents from the seller such as contracts, legal agreements, financial information, and so on. The seller will track down these documents (and scan them into a computer file if they are not already). The seller will then upload these documents to the SFTP site and send the buyer an e-mail notifying them that these specific documents have been transferred. The buyer will download the documents and then notify the seller by e-mail that the documents have been received. This process may go on for a number of weeks until all the required documents have been received by the buyer.

The next section reviews the basic areas that due diligence focuses on. These are the main areas that a buyer will want to review when making an acquisition.

Financial Statements

The buyer will want to review the financial statements for several years. Three years of statements should be provided. However, some buyers may want to go back as far as five years depending on the transaction. These statements include income statements, balance sheets, and cash flow statements. The current budget and projections for two or three years are usually requested as well. Unlike acquisitions of tangible companies with a history of profits, the buyer will rarely perform ratio analysis since it does not pertain to intangible companies.

Supporting schedules may be requested for certain areas such as aged accounts receivable. Two important schedules are revenues by product and revenues by customer for the last 12 months. It is a good idea to have a written explanation of unusual items such as write-downs, write-offs, prepaid or deferred income, or expenses and other unusual items. Any off-balance sheet liabilities or commitments are important to mention.

Contracts and Agreements

The buyer's team will review all contracts, agreements, and licenses. An important issue is whether these contracts can be assigned to the buyer.

Is the buyer required to provide service and support for previously sold products? If so, the liability for warranty services should be described. All loan documents should also be provided.

Intellectual Property

A full review of all intellectual property is a key part of due diligence. Intellectual property includes patents, copyrights, software, trademarks, as well as trade secrets. For a technology company the patent portfolio can be a significant part of the seller's value.

The ownership of all intellectual property should be well documented. The buyer will want a schedule of trademark and copyright registrations. Patents should be in order. A schedule of patents and patent applications are important documents. Some buyers may want to see copies of specific patents. Any licensing agreements related to patents should also be disclosed.

Software

Many intangible companies are software companies. Sometimes ownership issues surrounding software can be particularly troublesome, as software projects have become increasingly complex. Many software projects include components from a variety of sources: a single project may include portions developed internally, by outside contractors, and licensed.

Software firms often use outside contractors to assist with the development of software projects. It is imperative that the ownership of all code developed by third-party contractors be clearly defined. Other questions regarding software ownership pop up. If a company has purchased software, were the rights conveyed properly? Are there any ongoing royalties that are payable? Has all licensed software been licensed correctly?

In addition to the ownership issues, the buyer will want to do an in-depth technical review of the company's software. Sometimes this can be a problem if the transaction does not come to fruition. The seller will have shared potentially secret and proprietary information with the buyer. If the buyer is a competitor of any kind this could be a real problem.

The solution is to use a trusted third party to evaluate the software. A qualified third party can provide an independent evaluation of the software source code including design and architecture reviews, code quality assessments, and development capability reviews. This arrangement also protects the buyer because it reduces the chance they might be later sued by the seller.

Customers

The buyer will want to review a list of all customers. They may want to have a telephone conference, and possibly meet with any key customers, especially those who account for more than 10 percent of revenues. The buyer will also want to obtain a schedule of revenues by customer. The buyer will want to find out if the company has any unprofitable customers.

Products

The buyer will want to see complete product descriptions including the technical specifications. Information on any products in development will also be important to the buyer including product development time lines, regulatory clearance, and manufacturing requirements. Sales by product and pricing for each product are important schedules. Usually the buyer will like to see a description of each competitor and how the seller competes with each of these competitors.

Employees

Information on employees includes the organization chart, a list of all key employees including position and description information, salary, and time with the company. Biographies on the senior management team should be prepared.

Copies of any employee agreements, incentive and bonus plans, deferred compensation programs, and employee benefit plans should be made available for the purchaser.

Operations and Facilities

The buyer will have a number of questions about the seller's operations. What services do you outsource and who provides you with these services? What computer services do you utilize? What internal software systems do you employ? What is your data architecture and IT infrastructure? Who maintains the web site? Where is it hosted? Provide a description of all your facilities including real estate. Provide a copy of your building lease.

Corporate Information

The buyer will want to review all the corporate documents including the articles of incorporation, corporate bylaws, and so on. The buyer will probably want access to the corporate minute books, reports to shareholders, and filings with any government agency.

The buyer will also want copies of the capitalization table and any agreements among shareholders, stock option plans, and any other documents relating to the ownership, voting, sale, or issuance of securities of the company.

Other Items

Due diligence also includes several areas that do not fall under the aforementioned categories, including:

- **Litigation.** A description of any pending or threatened claim, lawsuit, or investigation should be provided.
- **Environmental Matters.** The seller should provide the buyer with any internal company reports concerning environmental matters including notices from the Environmental Protection Agency (EPA). Reports concerning compliance with any waste disposal issues and any other records reflecting any environmental problems should be disclosed.
- **Tax Matters.** Tax returns for the last three years should be provided to the buyer. Any tax problems or outstanding issues should certainly be reported. The seller will want to assure the buyer that all employment taxes have been correctly withheld and paid. Are there any outstanding tax liabilities? Are there any tax benefits that the buyer can realize?

WAR STORY: EASIER THE SECOND TIME AROUND

The buyer of Gamma Corporation had developed a problem with its financing for this all-cash deal. After a number of months the buyer could not come up with the cash to make the deal happen, so Gamma Corp. had to go back to the drawing board and effectively start the sale process over again. We identified a very good buyer who was new to the market space and we negotiated a deal. After the LOI was signed, it was very easy and straightforward to provide all the information that the buyer required for its due diligence. Almost all of this information had been gathered and organized for the previous buyer.

The result was a smooth and orderly due diligence process. The transaction closed ahead of schedule. Getting all the due diligence documents prepared ahead of time can make a transaction go together much more smoothly.

Representations and warranties are another topic related to due diligence. Representations and warranties are statements made by the seller in the purchase agreement that certain information is true. For example, the seller will represent that the corporation is duly formed, that the intellectual property is properly owned by the corporation, that the financial statements are correct, and so on. The buyer uses due diligence to confirm an assortment of issues. These are usually issues that can be researched in a straightforward fashion. Representations and warranties by the seller assure the buyer that certain information is correct, and thus can alleviate some of the work on the buyer's part to independently ascertain these facts.

The more due diligence information that can be gathered and prepared ahead of time, the more smoothly the whole process will proceed. If a company has a high degree of confidence that it will be acquired it should begin preparing due diligence information early on. The chief financial officer or a trusted administrative person can coordinate the gathering of documents long before the buyer requests them. In most transactions there will be a number of documents that were not anticipated or that were not readily available and the seller must scramble at the last minute to pull the information together. Early preparation can pay huge dividends.

THE PURCHASE AGREEMENT

The purchase agreement specifies the details of the transaction. There are six or seven sections to the agreement. The document delineates the price and the terms of the transaction as well as the closing date. One section defines the terms used in the agreement. Another section that is somewhat lengthy describes the representations and warranties by the seller and by the buyer.

The all-important section on price typically only requires a paragraph or two to describe. The agreement states the price and how the price is to be paid. If the price is in shares of the buyer's stock, the number of shares and any other pertinent information is described.

Other provisions in the agreement include items such as the seller promising to operate its business in its ordinary fashion and the seller will not enter into any new contracts or make unusual payments to employees. If the agreement is for a purchase of stock there will be several additional clauses. The agreement describes how a variety of employee matters should be dealt with such as benefit plans, employment offers, and so on.

Representations and Warranties

Both the seller and the buyer will make representations and warranties regarding a variety of corporate issues. Basically the "reps and warranties" (as they are usually referred to) confirm that the seller has disclosed everything of importance to the buyer. One of the issues is who is making the representations? Is it the selling company and its shareholders, or just the selling company?

The representations and warranties can pose significant problems in some transactions. To the buyer many of the risks are unknown so they want assurances that things are exactly as they appear. The buyer's attorney will draft the agreement so that the seller must represent and warrant that certain items are true. The buyer also makes reps and warranties, but they are much less extensive than the seller's.

A representation is a declaration of a specific fact. A warranty is an assurance. Representations and warranties cover a wide range of areas. Typical reps and warranties by the selling company include items such as:

- The corporation is duly organized and in good standing and has the power to enter into this agreement. The company is not in violation of any provisions of the certificate of incorporation or corporate bylaws.
- The capital stock of the company has been duly authorized and issued. The number of shares is specified for common stock and preferred stock.

- The board of directors and/or shareholders have authorized this agreement.
- The attached financial statements are accurate and are prepared according to generally accepted accounting principles (GAAP).
- The company has no material liabilities other than those shown on the balance sheet.
- The accounts payable are collectible within 90 days, less the amount shown for doubtful accounts.
- There have been no changes since the balance sheet date that would have a material adverse effect on the company.
- The company has legal title to all of its assets including all intellectual property.
- The company has properly licensed all the intellectual property it utilizes and its patents and trademarks have been duly registered.
- The company's agreements and contracts are valid and in full force.
- The seller has provided the purchaser with a copy of each assumed contract.
- The company has complied with all environmental laws and there are no environmental claims outstanding.
- There are no lawsuits pending or threatened and the company has no knowledge of any reasonable basis for litigation.
- The company has conducted its business in compliance with all laws.
- The company's tax returns have been filed and are correct in all material respects.
- No key company employee has any plans to terminate employment with the seller.
- The company is in compliance with all provisions of its employee benefit plans.

The buyer typically wants the representations and warranties to be as broad as possible. The reps and warranties are usually very general in nature. The buyer will insert all kinds of things that it wants assurances on. If the seller has a problem with the representations and warranties they can attempt to make them narrower in scope. The reps and warranties are typically in effect for a period of two years after the document has been signed.

The "Schedule of Exceptions," also called the "Disclosure Schedule," is one of the most important documents. The schedule of exceptions details how the reps and warranties should be modified to represent the truth. It qualifies and limits the reps and warranties. This is the document that the lawyers spend significant time on—it is where all the finer points are spelled out.

Sometimes reps and warranties can create problems for the transaction. Frequently, although not always, the seller's major shareholders, or some of them, will be asked to make representations and warranties in addition to the company. This may be an issue if venture capital firms are the primary shareholders. VCs typically do not readily sign reps and warranties as shareholders. There is no problem representing that the company has title to its assets, the capacity to do a transaction, and that there are no encumbrances. However, some of the representations could be problematic. VCs are required by their partnership agreement to distribute any cash proceeds to their investors. The venture capitalists cannot call money back from their investors in case reimbursement must be made to the buyer.

In one transaction the venture capital firm was very hesitant to sign the reps and warranties. The seller was a small instrument company and it was being acquired by a very large buyer. A minor issue arose regarding the certification of the seller's products and their compliance with certain standards. This was not a big deal for the seller; however, the buyer viewed it as a potential problem. In the worst-case scenario the products must be redesigned to be in compliance. The buyer and the VC had extensive conversations to work out a compromise. Initially, the buyer requested a one-year escrow for half the purchase price. Eventually, the parties agreed on a six-month escrow for half of the amount that the venture capital firm would receive.

The buyer will also make representations and warranties; however, these are much more limited in scope. The buyer will state that its corporation is duly organized and has the power and authority to enter into the agreement. The purchaser will also state that it will not be in violation of any laws and that it has the financial capacity to consummate the acquisition.

Covenants and Other Items

The agreement will include a number of covenants. A *covenant* is a promise to do something or to not do something during the time period from the signing of the agreement until closing or following the closing. For example, the seller will promise to conduct its business as it ordinarily does. The seller will promise not to enter into contracts or incur liabilities above a certain dollar amount and not to change the compensation to its management or employees.

The purchase agreement also has a section on indemnifications. These paragraphs specify that the seller will indemnify the buyer against all claims or losses as a result of any breach of a representation or warranty of the seller. For example, if any litigation is pending, the seller might indemnify the buyer against the cost of the litigation.

The purchase agreement typically includes a number of appendices and exhibits. These appendices include items such as: financial statements, schedules of patents and intellectual property, assumed liabilities, accounts payable, employee lists, allocation of purchase price, list of contracts, and trademark assignments.

Escrow is utilized in some transactions. If escrow is used a portion of the purchase price (cash or shares), typically 10 percent is held back and put into an escrow account with a third party for as long as one year. If there are any later discrepancies, the buyer has an easy mechanism to recover these amounts.

Restricted Stock and Registration Rights

Just because the seller receives stock in a public company as part of the purchase price does not mean that the seller can immediately sell these shares. These shares may be restricted or the buyer may require a lockup for a period of time. Restricted stock can only be sold after six months, subject to certain volume limitations, and can be sold without restriction after one year. This requirement was relaxed in 2008, reducing the prior holding periods from one year and two years, respectively.

It is to the seller's advantage to negotiate "registration rights," which allow the shares to be sold without any restrictions. There are two types of registration rights: demand rights and piggyback rights. Demand rights allow the seller to force the company to register the shares so that the seller can sell the shares. Piggyback rights allow the seller to sell its shares whenever the company files a registration statement with the SEC. The fee for filing a registration statement can be expensive, costing between $50,000 and $100,000.

Sometimes the buyer will insist upon a "lockup agreement" for some period of time, often as long as a year or more. The lockup is simply an agreement between the buyer and the seller regarding the terms under which the seller can dispose of its shares. The buyer requests a lockup because it does not want the seller to dump the shares of its stock on the market, which could hurt the stock price.

The "basket" is a useful tool for avoiding arguments over small amounts of claims or discrepancies. The basket amount is stated in the indemnification section of the agreement. The basket is a dollar amount that is typically 1 or 2 percent of the purchase price. The idea is that small amounts of claims would go into the basket and the seller is not required to pay these claims until the basket is filled. So on a $10 million transaction, a 1 percent basket would mean that up to $100,000 of claims would not have to be paid by the seller. If the amount of claims totaled more than $100,000, the seller would pay the buyer the amount greater than the basket. A negotiable point is whether the seller pays the total amount of claims or just the amount exceeding the basket.

The document will mention the time and place of closing. The signing of the legal documents and the closing of the transaction usually occurs on the same day; however, in some cases the closing may be delayed for as long as four weeks. Approvals of governmental agencies and approval of the shareholders can impact the date of closing.

R & W Insurance

Companies can purchase insurance for representations and warranties, called R & W insurance. This is a relatively new and creative insurance product. It covers loss resulting from breaches or inaccuracies of the seller's representations and warranties and can reduce or eliminate the amount of funds placed in escrow. R & W insurance is appropriate for deals greater than $25 million in transaction size and is often used in transactions involving private equity groups.

In a hypothetical $75 million transaction the seller will provide indemnity of only $15 million for one year. The seller also does not want a portion of the purchase price placed in escrow. The buyer can supplement this indemnity with additional coverage of say, $10 million and for a longer period, up to six years. The cost of this coverage ranges from 2.5 to 5 percent of the amount of insurance. There is also a deductible amount that runs 2 to 3 percent of the transaction value. On this transaction the R & W insurance would cost about $400,000. This is based on a premium of 4 percent for a $10 million policy. The deductible amount would be $1.8 million. The insurance company assumes some of the risk of the transaction, making it easier for the buyer and seller to agree on the terms.

THE PRECLOSING PERIOD

Will the deal close on schedule? What if it drags out? Will it close at all? What happens during the closing process? After the letter of intent has been signed there are three primary activities to complete: the due diligence review, drafting of the legal agreements by the buyer's attorneys, and the resolution of any outstanding issues that arise.

The closing process generally takes six to eight weeks and sometimes longer if there are due diligence questions that need to be addressed. If there are problems that require some effort to resolve, this time frame can extend to as long as 10 weeks.

Closing the transaction always presents some surprises. Even when you think the deal is as simple as possible something always pops up. The fewer surprises there are, large or small, the better your chance of successfully closing the transaction. The seller should provide all the schedules that are requested in a timely fashion; answer every question the buyer asks; and help the buyer understand any aspect of the business that it has concerns about.

A good indicator of the likelihood that a deal will close is the amount of time and effort that the buyer spends prior to closing. It is a good sign of their level of seriousness. It is a bit like sweat equity. You might call it "deal sweat equity." What do they have invested in the transaction? How much time and effort have they put in? The more time, manpower, and resources the buyer has devoted to the transaction, the greater their deal sweat equity and the higher likelihood of successfully closing a transaction.

Business As Usual... Only Better

What is the most important thing the selling company can do during the preclosing time period? By far the most essential thing a company can do is to keep market momentum at its highest level. Stay focused on running the business and generating revenues.

The period before closing is when the selling company is the most vulnerable. It is a critical time and should be managed very carefully. The seller must perform during the preclosing period. The CEO needs to be fully engaged in running the business.

Negative news can have a serious consequence on the price. Any number of events can cause the buyer to rethink the price of the deal—the loss of a customer, reduced profit margins, scaled-back sales pipeline, delayed product development, as well as employee problems. It is critical for management to be absolutely on top of these issues.

Business people are human and therefore emotional. How will they react to problems that arise or to positive news that occurs during the closing period? The seller should try to make the buyer feel as confident and optimistic as possible during the preclosing period.

There are several beneficial things the seller can do. First of all, make sure there are no surprises—that there are no customer cancellations, no key employees leaving, no downturns in sales, and no reduction in profits. Show that the company is vibrant and growing. Bring in new sales. Prove to the buyer that customers are willing to part with their cash to obtain the company's products and services. Keeping the sales pipeline full and growing is one of the best things a seller can do during the preclosing period.

Use innovative pricing to get customers to lengthen the terms of their contracts. This locks in revenues for a longer period of time and reduces the risk of customers leaving. The buyer will want to interview some of your customers at some point. You will want to have a glowing report about how the company takes care of its customers.

Do not overpromise. There is a tendency in the early discussion stages to paint a rosy picture of the company's sales potential. The problem arrives weeks later when the buyer is in the middle of due diligence and these promised sales have not been realized.

Closing a transaction does not follow a recipe. What worked on one deal, may not work on another deal. Deals are done between people; they are not inert transactions. When you deal with people you have emotion, ego, personal agendas, and a whole host of issues that truly are moving targets in the context of a transaction.

A shareholder vote is sometimes required for the sale of a company. State law and the company's bylaws will dictate the requirement in most cases. The first step is that the board of directors will vote to approve the transaction. If a shareholder vote is required, the company will either hold a shareholder meeting or send letters to all the shareholders. In a typical transaction, the company will send letters outlining the transaction terms to each shareholder. The shareholders have 30 days to respond. Shareholders reply with their proxy vote.

Hart-Scott-Rodino and Antitrust Issues

The Hart-Scott-Rodino Act requires that parties to a merger or acquisition greater than a certain size provide advance notification to the Department of Justice and the Federal Trade Commission before the transaction can close. These agencies assess whether the proposed transaction violates any antitrust laws.

There is a 30-day waiting period after filing the notice. During this time regulatory agencies may request additional information. The transaction cannot be closed until the end of the waiting period.

There are two size requirements for notification to be required. First, the acquisition must result in the buyer having securities or assets greater than $63 million in value. Second, one party must have revenues or assets greater than $126 million and the other must have revenues or assets greater than $12.6 million in value. If the transaction value is greater than $239 million a notification must be filed regardless of the parties' sizes.

The reason that these numbers are odd amounts is because originally they were even numbers like $10 million and $200 million but the law allowed for inflation adjustments so the threshold amounts have crept up over time. These figures are effective as of 2008.

The Actual Closing Procedure

At closing the parties meet in the attorney's conference room and sign all the documents. Checklists are consulted to ensure that all the documents are at hand and organized. There always seems to be a few schedules or documents that were not prepared earlier and the attorneys scramble to make sure that everything is in place. Dates are inserted in any documents where they had been left blank. Typically, closing can be accomplished in a couple of hours.

SUMMARY

The letter of intent is an effective means for communicating the basic deal terms and it sets the stage for moving the transaction forward. We examined the key terms in the letter and discussed the concept of binding terms. We also reviewed the pluses and minuses of an LOI and identified some key drafting points.

The due diligence review is a very important part of any transaction. The purpose of due diligence is to understand all the relevant details about the selling company and ensure that the important records and documents are complete. One of the more subtle functions of due diligence is to determine if there are any reasons why the transaction should not go forward.

The purchase agreement is the definitive document that spells out the details of the transaction. This agreement is usually drafted by the buyer's attorneys and then reviewed by the seller's attorneys. In addition to the deal terms, we discussed representations and warranties, an important part of the purchase agreement. The period prior to closing is a crucial time for the seller. It is during this time that transactions tend to fall apart. It is imperative that the seller maintain strong sales momentum, keep customers happy, and avoid any setbacks.

In the next chapter we evaluate the concept of earnouts. We address when they are appropriate, when they are not appropriate, and I offer a few structuring tips.

CHAPTER 13

Earnouts

Earnouts can be a flexible technique for bridging the price gap in the sale of a company. More and more intangible companies are selling early in their lives and earnouts are becoming increasingly prevalent. This chapter discusses when to use an earnout, traps to avoid, and six rules for successful earnouts.

Earnouts can be versatile tools for structuring the sale of a company when there is a disparity between what a seller thinks his or her company is worth and what the buyer is willing to pay. On the other hand, earnouts can put a strain on the new working relationship if not structured properly.

What is an earnout? An *earnout* is a mechanism in which part of the purchase price is contingent upon future performance. A typical earnout might include payments to the seller every year for three years based on a percentage of revenues or operating income that exceeds a certain threshold.

Earnouts are effective when the parties have different views about the degree of certainty of achieving future objectives. Earnouts allow the seller to receive full compensation for creating value, especially if much of the value has yet to be realized and the buyer is unwilling to pay the total amount up front.

In the technology arena, many companies are acquired after they have created valuable technology, but before they have had time to prove that value in the marketplace through revenues and profits. To borrow a concept from physics, intangible value is similar to kinetic energy—it is stored up but not yet used. New technologies are often developed by small, innovative firms and sold to larger companies that have the marketing, sales, and distribution resources to capitalize on the opportunity.

The acquisition of an intangible company is often difficult to value because the profits and revenues may be minimal or nonexistent. An earnout may be a way to obtain a higher purchase price by proving the market value of the technology to the buyer. One drawback with earnouts in the technology sector is that acquired companies are often tightly integrated into the buying company, making it difficult to ascertain which revenues or profits were derived solely from the target company. This situation makes earnout measurements more unwieldy.

Earnout discussions can be fruitful even if an earnout is not included in the final transaction structure. Exploring an earnout will flesh out many issues in more depth than might otherwise be the case. Earnouts can provoke a number of questions: What is the marketing budget for this division? Who will control spending decisions? What are the gross margin objectives? Are we sacrificing long-term objectives for shorter term profits? This deeper discussion can be effective in bringing the parties closer together on price.

WHEN EARNOUTS ARE APPROPRIATE

When should an earnout be used? Earnouts can be an appropriate structure when the buyer and seller cannot agree on the price to pay for the upside potential of the acquired company. If a large portion of the value depends on future events, such as the completion of a product line, an earnout may be suitable. Earnouts are most successful when the operating entity continues to be independent after the acquisition.

If the selling company remains fairly independent an earnout based on gross profits, operating profits, or pretax profits can be employed. This structure is also appropriate when a seller's earnings are more than just minimal. A typical earnout structure starts with a baseline number for profits. The earnout computation is based on the amount of profit exceeding this threshold. In structuring an earnout like this, it is critical that the exact method for calculations be agreed upon beforehand. Buyers usually prefer an earnout that is based on profits.

An earnout based on revenues is simpler to calculate and can be more appropriate if the acquired company does not remain as a standalone entity. If the target becomes a division of the buyer tracking revenues is fairly straightforward. Sellers typically prefer an earnout that is based on revenues because many expense items may not be under their control if the company is partially integrated with the buyer.

WAR STORY: A CLEAN AND SIMPLE EARNOUT

In this example, Tau Corp. sold out to a much larger company. Tau Corp. had revenues of about $7 million per year; however, the company had experienced flat profits and even a loss in the most recent year. Tau Corp. had intangible value because of the innovative designs of its products.

The purchase price of $3 million included the purchase of all Tau Corp.'s assets and the assumption of all Tau's liabilities. Tau had good growth potential but it needed to be part of a larger firm with well-established sales and distribution capabilities. The buyer had these strengths and being part of this larger organization would benefit Tau considerably.

It was unclear how Tau Corp. could increase margins or profits on its own. The buyer had excellent manufacturing efficiencies that would help. However, there was no reason the seller should be paid for improvements made by the buyer. Since Tau Corp. would be part of the large company there would be very fuzzy lines on administrative and other expenses, making it difficult to clearly track profitability. So the parties agreed on earnout that was based strictly on revenues. This was a good arrangement because it was easy to monitor and there were no vague areas.

The parties agreed to an earnout for three years. The amount of the earnout was equal to 2 percent of the gross revenue of the business. Payments were to be made annually and the earnout had a cap of $1.75 million.

Philosophically, I am opposed to caps on earnouts because there is no logical reason to do so, plus if the sales are greater than expected then the seller deserves to benefit from that situation. (See the next War Story in which the absence of a cap paid large dividends to the seller.) In this case the cap of $1.75 million was extremely high given that Tau's revenues were only $7 million. Do some quick math: Even if Tau doubled its sales to $15 million, the earnout portion of 2 percent would be $300,000 per year. To reach the cap, Tau would have to generate revenues for three years totaling $87.5 million—an unlikely occurrence. So in this case the cap was acceptable.

WHEN EARNOUTS ARE NOT APPROPRIATE

Earnouts should not be used when the operations are tightly integrated. It is too difficult to determine if objectives were achieved because of the entrepreneur's efforts or because of the buyer's sales team, distribution channels, or other assets. Earnouts should also not be used when the new owner wants to impose his or her own operating methods on the company.

In most software and technology acquisitions the selling company will be closely integrated with the buyer; thus, an earnout is not a good structure. The buyer is acquiring product lines or technologies and will sell them through its existing sales channels. If the selling company will not remain a stand-alone business it is difficult to develop an earnout structure that makes any sense.

Earnouts are not appropriate for companies that are fully developed. It is not a good idea to use an earnout to acquire a company that has been in business for more than about 10 years. A 10-year-old business is a known quantity. Just because the seller wants more money does not mean that an earnout is suitable. This is simply not a good reason. In addition, sometimes it is the buyer who deserves the credit for growing the company, not the seller.

In one transaction I was representing the buyer and the investment banker for the seller suggested an earnout in order to give the seller more money. This was a business that had been in operation for 23 years—it was a totally known quantity. There was no mystery about what the company was or what it might achieve. Earnouts are appropriate for companies that have not reached their *stride*, so to speak. This company had reached its stride many years ago so there was no reason to include an earnout. This investment banker was asking for too much and there was no reason to unnecessarily complicate the transaction with an earnout.

WAR STORY: A VERY LUCRATIVE EARNOUT

Sometimes an earnout works out in a very surprising way. Rho Corporation was growing nicely; however, one of its products did not perform as well as a product from its competitor, Sigma Technology. Even though it had a pretty good product, Sigma was a small firm and it was struggling. The plan was for Rho Corp. to acquire the product and take over all of Sigma's customers. Sigma would then close its doors. Sigma Technology was asking for a purchase price of only $250,000.

Rho Corporation was experiencing healthy growth and it needed all of its available cash flow to fund this growth. Even though Rho wanted to acquire Sigma, it would have been a stretch to use cash for the acquisition. So, the two companies worked out an earnout arrangement.

Rho acquired the product and took over the customers. In return it agreed to pay Sigma 10 percent of revenues from product sales for the next 13 years. The percentage stepped down after five years and then stepped down again after eight years. As Rho Corp. continued its growth, sales of the new product did very well. After two years Rho was paying Sigma $160,000 annually in earnout payments. Over the term of the agreement Sigma will eventually receive $2 million in earnout payments. The $250,000 purchase price is looking very attractive in hindsight.

Actually, the CEO of Rho Corp. has no regrets. The earnout enabled him to acquire a good product at a time when his cash was tight. He projected revenues for the product at a much lower level than what turned out to be the case. He was quite pleased of course when revenues exceeded his projections. And do not forget, even though he was paying 10 percent to Sigma Corp., Rho got to keep the other 90 percent of the revenue stream.

STRUCTURING TIPS

Earnouts can be based on revenues, operating income, development goals, or any number of factors. A good negotiator will uncover as much as possible about each side's risk preferences, needs, and motivations in order to structure an earnout that meets each party's objectives.

The performance goals should be obtainable, not pie in the sky. Gross profit is a better measure than net profit since it is less subject to nonoperating influences. Graduated payments are better than an all-or-nothing scheme. The time frame for the earnout should be one to four years—any longer than that and the mechanism becomes too burdensome.

Traps to Avoid

Definition problems can plague an earnout. How is operating income or profit calculated? How are sales defined—are they gross or net? Should depreciation or nonrecurring events affect the measurement? What about technology that is only a small part of a product?

Most problems in earnouts stem from control and budget issues. The biggest trap to avoid is agreeing to an earnout without having sufficient control over the division and its marketing and sales budgets. The entrepreneur must make sure that he or she will have full access to the resources needed to run the division, in both dollars and people. The marketing budget or development budget should be definitive.

Six Rules for Earnouts

1. Use easily measurable milestones. Revenues are easier to measure than profits. The payout should be directly associated with the performance of the acquired company. Make sure the calculations for the earnout formula are straightforward. Vague definitions and complex calculations can muddy the water, create bad blood, and take a manager's focus away from running the business. Keep it simple.
2. Management should have the operating freedom and the resources necessary to achieve their performance objectives. Management must have control over the division's operations.
3. Commit to a budget, especially a marketing and sales budget. Be sure the needed resources are under the control of the manager. If an earnout is based on revenues and management has no control over the marketing budget this can be a problem.
4. Put a time limit on the earnout. At some point operations will become integrated and it will make sense to eliminate the nuisance of earnout calculations. The longer an earnout goes, the more difficult it is to identify separate financial metrics for the company.
5. Do not put a dollar cap on the earnout. This makes eminent philosophical sense, but in practice it can be difficult to overcome the emotional element in buyers who think, "How could we pay that much for this company?" It is somewhat analogous to the salesman who earns more than the president—it makes sense but is a little hard to swallow.
6. Last, try to structure the transaction without an earnout. Life will be much simpler down the road. There is enough to worry about in most fast-growing companies without compounding the situation with a complicated earnout structure and differing management objectives.

The buyer can always add normal incentives, such as stock options and bonuses, as part of an employment agreement. One transaction we structured included an up-front payment in stock combined with an employment agreement that included a sizable bonus. The bonus depended one-third on certain product development goals, one-third on the performance of the division, and one-third on the financial performance of the parent. This structure was cleaner than an earnout and provided a strong incentive for management to work toward the buyer's objectives.

SUMMARY

An earnout can be a good way to bridge the price gap when the buyer and seller cannot come to a meeting of the minds regarding price, but they should be used only in appropriate situations. We discussed some structuring tips and some traps to avoid.

The next chapter reviews the decision to use an investment banker to assist with a transaction. We discuss how an intermediary adds value to the process and how a company can work effectively with the banker. We also examine the deal skills that are critical for an investment banker.

CHAPTER 14

Using Investment Bankers and Third Parties

Investment bankers, attorneys, accountants, and other professionals can be a great help in successfully closing a deal. Their broad range of experience and specialized knowledge can be invaluable. Certainly there is a cost for this expertise, but the cost is almost always worth the value added.

Let me introduce this chapter with some comments from Peter Drucker, one of my favorite management philosophers. I had the pleasure of interacting with Mr. Drucker briefly when I wished to include some of his writings in my newsletter, *The Technology Acquisition Update.* We had a brief e-mail exchange regarding how much he should charge me for including a few paragraphs of his writings in my newsletter. It ended up costing me $150, but it makes me smile every time I think of it.

Utilizing the skills and experience of an investment banker is a type of outsourcing. Peter Drucker had a number of comments regarding outsourcing. He said that companies

> *don't yet really know how to do outsourcing well. Most look at outsourcing from the point of view of cutting costs, which I think is a delusion. What outsourcing does is greatly improve the quality of the people who still work for you. I believe you should outsource everything for which there is no career track that could lead into senior management.... When you outsource you may actually increase costs, but you also get better effectiveness. (*Fortune Magazine, January 12, 2004)

Buyers are typically more skilled at the acquisition process than are sellers. A buyer may have made one or several acquisitions in the past. They know the drill. A seller, on the other hand, sells only once. So there is a disparity in the level of transaction experience between the parties. The best way for a seller to avoid rookie mistakes is to hire an experienced adviser.

In this chapter we review the decision to hire an investment banker or intermediary. (I use these terms interchangeably.) We examine the tasks that an investment banker performs and the advantages that an experienced adviser can bring to the company. Investment banking firms can be categorized into three groups by size, and we comment on how to choose the right sized banker for a transaction.

The chapter also addresses the issues of fees, including retainers, the engagement letter, and some interesting terms that these agreements contain. I comment on how to work effectively with an investment banker and make the most of this relationship. Sometimes a less experienced banker can cause problems for his or her client. And last we take a look at seven critical deal skills that an investment banker should possess.

MAKING THE DECISION TO WORK WITH AN INTERMEDIARY

Why use an intermediary or an investment banker? To answer this question, you must first revisit the company's goal. How can hiring an investment banker help the company accomplish its goal? Companies usually have three primary objectives when seeking to sell the business:

- Get a transaction closed.
- Close it with the best buyer at the best price and best terms.
- Close the transaction in a timely manner, with the fewest problems, and a minimum of disruption to the company.

The sale of a company is an important job and it is essential that the process be performed competently. Mistakes can be costly; it is simply not worth it to try to go it alone. An investment banker has transaction experience that is different from that of a CEO or a venture capitalist. As an independent third party, the banker can be truly objective. He or she will see and hear more information and perceive it differently.

Selling a company requires a tremendous amount of time and effort. There is no way a CEO can run the company and competently manage the sale process at the same time. The transaction will always be shortchanged. Selling a company is a full-time endeavor and there are no shortcuts.

What does an investment banker actually do? There are four primary activities that the investment banker handles during the sale of an intangible company. The investment banker:

1. Manages the overall sale process.
2. Identifies and contacts potential buyers.
3. Overcomes obstacles and generates multiple offers.
4. Negotiates, structures, and closes the transaction.

Another way to view hiring an investment banker is to consider it as a type of "transaction insurance." More buyers will be contacted and negotiations will be conducted professionally. The participation of an experienced investment banker increases the odds that the transaction will be concluded at the best price and with the fewest problems.

The benefits of using an investment banker include:

Objectivity. Objectivity is a key concern when selling a company and obtaining advice. Even if a CEO has been through the sale process a few times, it is vital to get expert help. The ability to listen from an impartial point of view is constructive. Many CEOs are so focused on what they are going to say next that they do not hear the true concerns of the other party. A third party can be much more objective.

For example, as an investment banker, I will often sit in a meeting and listen and observe, speaking only when I can guide the discussion in a helpful direction. But I listen to everything. I ask myself—what does the buyer really mean by that? Is he serious? Is he bluffing? Why would she bring that point up? What is her true concern? In addition, I always take good notes; note-taking pays dividends later on.

The Third-Party Dynamic. The third-party dynamic is an interesting one. A buyer will tell things to an intermediary that he or she would never tell the seller directly. These may or may not be major revelations, but they can provide useful information. For example: "No way are we going to keep the CTO on board (the president's brother); he is indecisive and petty. Good developers will not want to work for him." This is not a statement that a buyer could ever say to the president of the company. Without expressing this reservation to a third party the issue might remain unresolved until late in the preclosing period. The more issues like this that are not communicated the greater the chances that the transaction will stumble.

The third-party dynamic applies to acquisition searches too. The first contact with a potential acquisition candidate is more effective and less threatening if it comes from an intermediary rather than from the buyer itself. Companies are more open and less guarded

when communicating with a third party. This dynamic reflects the
nature of human interaction.

Pushing the Deal. An intermediary can push the transaction. They can
keep the transaction moving forward without the seller appearing
desperate or too anxious to sell.

Negotiating. An objective third party can be more effective in negotiations. An intermediary can establish a constructive atmosphere, help
defuse unreasonable claims and minimize extreme posturing. They
can gauge reactions and devise compromises. A knowledgeable deal
maker has a wealth of experience overcoming problems, head-
ing off issues before they become serious, and keeping the parties
on track.

In addition to negotiating the deal price and terms, an intermediary can also be effective when negotiating employment contracts
and salary amounts for the management team. If the parties will be
working together after the transaction closes, it is better to let the
investment banker be the bad guy when negotiating these issues.

CHOOSING THE RIGHT SIZE INVESTMENT BANKER
FOR YOUR TRANSACTION

Companies often face a dilemma when choosing an investment banker to
sell an intangible company. What size investment banker is right for your
transaction? Should you choose a small boutique firm? Should you choose
a midsized investment bank?

First of all, if the transaction is a large one—greater than $150
million—a large New York investment bank is probably the right choice.
The deal is big enough to command their full attention. When a company's
value approaches this level the firm usually has significant profits and the
value is shifting to be more tangible in nature.

Most intangible companies, however, sell for less than $150 million.
Two categories of investment bankers are relevant when selling a smaller
company—the midsized firm and the boutique firm. A midsized investment
banking firm is the right choice for the sale of a company with a transaction
size ranging from $20 million or $30 million to $150 million. On a smaller
transaction—less than $30 million—a boutique firm is the best choice.

A transaction that is greater than $30 million or so will require the
skills and resources of the midsized investment bank. The midsized firm will
employ from 15 to as many as 50 people. The deal team typically involves
one or two principals and several associates, and they can marshal significant

resources to assist with a transaction. Antitrust issues and securities issues can require specialized expertise, and a midsized firm typically employs bankers with a variety of capabilities. Their business model enables them to dedicate the necessary resources and attention to the client. A midsized firm may have offices in several cities and perhaps one overseas.

For a transaction less than $30 million (sub-30), a boutique investment bank is the best alternative. Some boutiques have just one principal, usually an experienced deal maker working independently. Other boutique investment banks may have as many as five or six principals and a few junior associates.

The principals of the boutique firm normally perform most of the work themselves, so the client receives senior attention. On a small transaction the boutique firm usually provides greater attention and more personal service. A small deal is likely to be more important to the boutique firm. And remember that you hire the person, not the firm.

On a sub-30 transaction, the deal size is not significant enough to command the full attention of a midsized investment bank. The firm's business model simply will not allow it. Their minimum fee is normally $1 million. They cannot earn a large enough fee to make a sub-30 transaction worth their while. Be wary of a midsized investment bank that wants to take on a small transaction. They might be doing it to keep their people busy during slack times or to use it as a training ground for junior associates. The bank may assert that it will give attention to a $15 million deal, but it truly is small potatoes and they will not give it their full attention. Plus, a midsized investment bank is likely to run the same auction process on small deals that it does for larger deals—not the appropriate process for a small transaction.

Ego can come into play. An owner would rather tell his friends that he has hired Goldman Sachs to sell his company than some less familiar boutique firm. Companies typically want to hire the biggest name investment bank that will work with them. The client is not always well served in these instances. Choose an investment bank that is the right size for your transaction.

A WORD ABOUT FEES

An investment banker's responsibility is to help his or her client achieve its objectives—usually the successful completion of a transaction. The banker's compensation is tied to this result. In most fee arrangements the banker gets paid for results—for closing a transaction.

The most important factor in a fee arrangement is alignment. The client's objectives should be tightly aligned with the investment banker's fee structure—so that the banker gets paid only if the client achieves its objectives. The fee is usually large enough that the banker has an extremely strong incentive to work diligently to complete a transaction and at the best price.

Another aspect of alignment is risk sharing. One of the reasons that investment banks receive large fees is that they take significant risks. Other than the retainer, 90 percent of the investment banker's compensation is paid only if a transaction is successfully completed. For a period of six or seven months the banker is working without pay. In the transactions that I have worked on, I typically spent between 200 and 350 hours working on the deal. This is a significant number of hours to work without compensation.

Bear in mind that when selling an intangible company the value is an unknown. Some may think that paying a 4 percent fee simply means that the seller receives 4 percent less than it would have otherwise received. In the sale of an intangible company there is no value per se, so the price you receive is the price you negotiate. If an investment banker can help negotiate a price that it is 5 percent or 20 percent greater than what the company might have otherwise received, the fee is a good value.

Some CEOs and owners resist paying fees—and resist strongly. Of course, no one wants to pay for something without receiving good value. In most cases the investment banking services are worth the money; the value added is greater than the amount of the fee.

Retainers

Most investment bankers charge a retainer up front. Retainers typically range from $15,000 to $75,000 (or even more for very large transactions). Most retainers are paid up front; occasionally, a retainer may be paid in monthly payments. A retainer demonstrates to the investment banker that the client is serious about selling the company and that the company is committed. Otherwise, there is a danger that the client is simply trying to see if he or she can achieve a very high price.

Accepting a retainer obligates the investment banker to the client. Now the banker owes the client a significant work effort. Without a retainer there is a tendency for the banker to merely go after the low hanging fruit, to contact only the obvious buyers, and to put in less than a full effort. The client is not well served in this case.

A top-tier investment bank, whether it is a midsized firm or a boutique firm, will always charge a retainer. They want to know that the client is serious and committed.

The Fee Agreement

Principals of intangible companies are often unsure how to view the relationship with the investment banker. In my opinion, the best way to view this relationship is to consider the banker as being part of the company's team, working toward the company's goal. He or she should be viewed as a partner of the company. The fee relationship should be structured in a way that reflects this partnership.

Many tech CEOs put undue emphasis on the finding aspect. They think the greatest value added is in identifying the buyer. This is not the case. Certainly, identifying the right buyer can be a critical aspect of the transaction. However, most of the time generating a list of good buyers is not difficult. The difficult part is managing the process, getting buyers to the table at the same time, negotiating the best price and terms, and making sure that the deal actually closes. This is why the investment banker gets paid for results—the client's goal is to conclude a transaction, not simply find potential buyers.

A well-drafted fee agreement leaves no questions unanswered and no room for arguments or misunderstandings. The agreement should cover all eventualities, so that there is no uncertainty or disagreement later on. For example, what happens if the deal is done with stock? What if there is a promissory note? What if there are royalties? What happens if there is an earnout?

Some CEOs are more concerned with how to reduce the fee than how to align the banker with the client's goals. The CEO may want to modify certain terms in the agreement. It is important to understand how a change might affect the alignment between the investment banker and the client. Changes can have the effect of reducing the investment banker's incentive to put in a diligent effort. This situation is not good for either party. A CEO should consider any proposed change through the eyes of the investment banker. What actions are they encouraging or discouraging with the changes?

The next few sections outline some of the pitfalls you want to avoid regarding the fee agreement. Almost all investment banking agreements are exclusive agreements, and for good reason—the seller will get a better effort. A selling company should also be mindful of its primary objective and not get caught up in the game of these contacts are mine and those contacts are yours. A carve out does not align the banker's motivations with those of the client.

Exclusivity   An exclusive arrangement means the investment banker gets paid no matter what transaction is concluded. Some people think the *exclusive* is a negative because it locks you in or commits you to an undeserved fee.

The reverse is actually true. With an exclusive arrangement the investment banker knows that if a transaction closes then he will be paid, so it is worth it for him to devote the significant effort required to manage the process and close the best transaction. Closing a deal is a long and difficult road. If an investment banker is embarking on this journey with a committed effort, he wants to be sure that he will be paid.

Without an exclusive there is an incentive for the banker to take the easy road and just pick the low hanging fruit. The client will receive a much stronger effort with an exclusive arrangement.

My Contacts versus Your Contacts   Sellers can get caught up in the game of "my contacts versus your contacts." Some clients are willing to pay the banker only if a deal closes with a buyer that they were not aware of. The CEO does not want to pay a fee to close a transaction with a buyer they already know.

Selling a company is not about "these are my contacts and those are your contacts"; it is about closing a deal at the best price. This mindset is not productive. The investment banker is not on the opposing team; he is on the client's team. The goal is to close a transaction, preferably at the highest price and the best terms. The investment banker is not simply a finder. The banker's job is to negotiate and close a transaction. Identifying buyers is certainly a part of the process, but the banker gets compensated for completing the transaction, not for identifying buyers. Identifying buyers is the easy part. Negotiating the best price is the hard part.

There are two deal states—closed and not closed. The transaction is not finished until it is finally closed. Quite a few CEOs that I have dealt with thought that if they already had conversations with a buyer then the deal was halfway to closing, and therefore why pay the banker a full fee? The singular objective is to close the transaction. The value added is not finding the buyer but closing the transaction.

Carve Outs   The most common issue that arises regarding modifications to a fee agreement is when the seller has already had discussions with a potential buyer. The typical reaction is to carve out this buyer. A *carve out* is an exception in which the banker gets no fee or a reduced fee if the company is sold to a particular buyer.

The problem with carve outs is that they encourage the investment banker to reduce the effort or drag his or her feet. Why should I put in a fully committed effort if I will get no fee or a reduced fee? Sellers should not propose terms that that will diminish the investment banker's motivation to put in a fully committed effort. Carve outs diminish effort.

There is also the issue of fairness. An investment banker could add significant value and not be compensated. For example, let us say the company had prior discussions with Buyer Alpha before hiring an investment banker, and therefore carved it out of the fee agreement. In this case Buyer Alpha offered $7.5 million to acquire the company. The banker worked diligently and brought three buyers to the table with offers of $7 million, $8 million, and $9 million. But now, because of the competitive bids, Buyer Alpha raises its offer to $9.5 million. The client is pleased with this price and sells to Buyer Alpha. Why should the banker receive no fee or a reduced fee? Even if the banker never contacted Buyer Alpha, his efforts created an extra $2.0 million for the seller.

Another point that seems to escape many CEOs: Even if they are already talking to Company Alpha about acquiring their company, would it not be a good idea to bring in an experienced adviser to help with the negotiations? Once again, they see the value as finding, not negotiating or closing the deal. Just because company Alpha has already made an offer does not mean that the negotiations are over. This is where investment bankers can really add value and earn their fee. Many CEOs are more concerned with saving a fee or doing the transaction themselves than they are in getting the best result. This mindset is penny-wise and pound-foolish and it is very common in the technology industries.

Tails   Most investment banking fee agreements have tails. The *tail* states that the banker will be paid if a transaction closes within a certain period after the agreement is terminated. For example, the banker may work on a transaction for six months and bring in two offers. The seller wants a higher price, declines both offers, and terminates the agreement with the investment banker. Nine months later the seller changes his mind and closes a transaction with one of those buyers. In this case the banker would be paid for the transaction.

The tail issue arises when the seller wants a price that is greater than the offers. I know of many examples in which a company sold to the same buyer that had made an offer within the previous two years. The company did not like the price so they turned down the offer. No other buyers offered a higher price. A couple of years later the sellers decided that it was a pretty good price after all and they closed a deal.

On several transactions I put in a diligent effort and produced good offers but received no fee because the sellers declined the offers. Later on, the sellers realized that their price expectations were unrealistic and they closed a transaction with one of the companies that I brought to the table. Unfortunately for me, the tail had expired and I did not receive a fee for these transactions.

WAR STORY: NO FEE FOR ME

In this case, after an exhaustive search I brought in an excellent buyer headquartered in Australia. My client was based in Seattle and had a well-designed product for a specific sector of the software industry. The buyer and I had exchanged numerous e-mails and telephone calls and eventually the buyer traveled to the United States to meet with the company in person. After several lengthy meetings, the parties were at an impasse. The fit between the companies was quite good. However, the seller wanted a high price for the business and the buyer was unwilling to pay that price. So no deal was completed.

Two years later a transaction was consummated with this same buyer. By then the tail on my fee agreement had expired and I received no fee. In retrospect, I think I earned the fee. I identified the buyer, introduced the parties, arranged multiple calls and meetings, and participated in the negotiations. Clearly, the deal happened as a result of my efforts. Had the seller not had unrealistic price expectations we would have closed the transaction earlier and I would have been compensated for my efforts. But, those were the terms that the client and I agreed to in the fee agreement. It was a tough break for me but that is the way it goes sometimes.

The operative word regarding tails is *fairness*—fairness for the client and fairness for the investment banker. What is a fair time frame for both parties for the tail? The tail should be long enough so that the investment banker is compensated for his or her efforts. However, it should not be so long that the client is paying for little value added by the investment banker. For many years across a broad spectrum of industries the standard tail was always 24 months.

In my opinion, a tail of 24 months is a good time frame—it is fair to both parties. Longer than that is probably not fair for the client; and shorter than that is probably not fair for the investment banker. This judgment is based on knowing how long it takes to complete transactions, knowing that deals close as a result of my efforts, and knowing that sellers often have unrealistic price expectations. Of course, the tail only applies if the transaction closes with one of the companies that the investment banker had previously contacted. If the company sells to an entirely different buyer then no fee is due. To protect both parties it is a good idea for the banker to provide the company with a list of all the buyers that were contacted.

Additional Fee Issues

A few additional fee issues are worth noting that arise in the context of fee discussions. It might be helpful to sellers to understand some of the reasons behind these issues.

Timing of Payment. My fee arrangement is to be paid in full at closing. Some buyers want to pay me only when they get paid, in other words potentially not at closing. Well, one could use that arrangement in the fee agreement; however, that is not how I choose to run my business. It would be like selling your house and paying the realtor her commission each month for 30 years. One could do it that way, but if you are the realtor it may not be the best business model. If there are contingent payments then, of course, I would be paid later for that portion.

Form of Payment. I have also been asked to get paid in the same form as the seller. In other words, if they get stock then I get stock as payment. One problem with accepting stock is that it can cause structuring problems. If the buyer is a closely held company it may not want the investment banker to own its stock. There are also securities issues surrounding stock ownership that make the situation problematic. And, quite frankly, I do not want stock. I want cash. If I were to accept stock, the fee percentage would be higher.

Sometimes sellers are concerned about having enough cash at closing, particularly on small transactions. As a practical matter this should never be a problem. The buyer will always have cash. If they do not have cash, they have no business acquiring an intangible company that will require cash to grow. If the seller is short on cash and the transaction is a stock deal, the buyer's cash can be used to pay the banker's fee and any other liabilities that need to be paid at closing. The price is reduced by the amount of these liabilities. I have negotiated a number of transactions in which we altered the deal terms to include additional cash at closing to pay my fee as well as other liabilities of the seller.

WAR STORY: PAID IN STOCK—BUMMER... JACKPOT

In this situation the founder was insisting very strongly that if he were to be paid in stock then I should be paid in stock as well. He was

(Continued)

worried about having enough cash at closing. This was early in my career as an investment banker and I did not fully understand the implications of accepting stock. I did not really want to accept stock at all, but the client was very insistent about it, so I said yes in order to appease him. Thus, the bummer from my point of view.

We moved forward with the transaction and identified a number of good buyers. One buyer was clearly more interested than the others so we ended up negotiating solely with that company. The price we negotiated was an excellent one. In fact, it was more than double what the founder expected to get for the company. So everyone was happy.

When the deal closed, two-thirds of the transaction currency was cash and one-third was in stock of the buying company. So I received some shares of the buyer's stock. (Fortunately the buyer went along with this arrangement. Most buyers would not be amenable to such a structure.) To our good fortune, only eight months later the buyer was acquired by Network Associates. The value of my stock (and the seller's) had tripled in just eight months. I assumed that this was my reward for being so agreeable. Actually, it was the first and last time I ever took stock as compensation; but in this instance all parties were quite happy.

Intentions. In my fee agreement there is a list of the different types of transaction structures for which I will be compensated: sale of stock, sale of assets, financing, debt assumption, royalty agreements, licensing agreements, and so on. This confuses some sellers and they respond saying that they do not want to do a licensing agreement or a royalty agreement. The fee agreement is not a statement of the seller's intentions; it simply articulates how the banker gets paid. The structure can take many forms and the banker should be paid for a successful transaction no matter what structure is employed; this language protects the investment banker in case the transaction is structured in an unusual way.

Problems with Inverted Fees. An inverted fee is one in which the percentages increase instead of decrease as the price goes up. The problem with inverted fees or "incentive fees" is that they make great philosophical sense but are difficult to formulate in practice. I have encountered a number of CEOs and venture capitalists who proposed inverted fees. A normal fee structure might be 6 percent of the first few million dollars and then step down to 5 percent, then 4 percent, then 3 percent, and so on, breaking every few million dollars. An inverted fee structure might be 3 percent on the first $10 million and 7 percent on the amount over $10 million.

The concept is a good one; however, in reality there are three problems with this arrangement. The first and biggest problem is setting the threshold amount. It is difficult to set a threshold value that is reasonable for an intangible company. The seller usually wants a high threshold—not what I would call a reasonable price. The threshold might be set at $8 million because the venture capitalist firms invested $8 million. A reasonable threshold number is the company's financial or baseline value; typically 5 or 6 times earnings before interest and taxes. (This has been the standard multiple among private equity buyers for many years.) However, the seller will view this as extremely low.

The second problem is that if the company sells for a low price then the investment banker is getting a much reduced fee—and not a fair fee in my opinion. Small deals are difficult and require as much, if not more, work than larger deals. If the seller wants to give me a bonus for achieving a price greater than $10 million that is fine; however, that is no reason to reduce the fee for a $3 million deal.

The logic of inverted fees is very appealing—"the banker will have a greater incentive to achieve the high price." This is a naïve assumption. It can actually turn a transaction into an all-or-nothing situation.

A third point to make on this topic is that the investment banker *does* make more on a $10 million deal than on an $8 million deal. Just because the percentage decreases does not mean the fee decreases. Dollars are what count, not percentages, and the banker makes more money on the higher priced deal, so his or her incentives line up with the client's.

Another problem with inverted fees is that there is a greater probability of closing a deal at a price lower than the threshold amount. In my experience, the probability is 70 to 80 percent that the price will be lower than the suggested threshold amount. So why would an investment banker accept a reduced fee for closing a transaction that has an 80 percent probability of occurring? An investment banker is supposed to be a good negotiator. If he cannot negotiate a reasonable fee for himself, he probably will not do a very good job for the client.

I cannot speak for other investment bankers, but I give a fully committed effort on every transaction that I undertake. I do not work harder on a $10 million deal than I do on a $5 million deal, even though I will make a bigger fee on the $10 million deal. A deal is a deal and as a professional I do whatever it takes to get the transaction successfully completed for the client.

PROBLEM BANKERS

If a banker has limited experience or has not worked on similar types of transactions, his or her participation can do more harm than good. Let me give you an example in which the client lost $3.5 million. In this case I was advising the buyer. My client really wanted to do this deal. They had a large amount of cash in the bank and they needed to make some aggressive moves in order to continue building the business.

The investment banker representing the opposing party, the seller, was totally ineffective. The banker had limited experience and he was pushing for the wrong things. My guess is that he wanted to mimic the two-step auction process because he thought that is how big deals were done. First, he asked me to commit to a preliminary price before my client had investigated the company. It made no sense to commit to a price range this early in the process. And it is not my practice to promise a price range and then change it later. If I am going to propose a price range, I want it to be meaningful.

This acquisition would have been perfect except for one thing. The company was asking a ridiculously high price. The banker kept bringing up the point that two other companies had made offers a year earlier, one for $9 million and one for $10.5 million. He was suggesting that these offers set a value range or a market price for the company. I tried to explain that just because someone made offers in the past does not mean the company is worth that much now. And furthermore, why did the seller not accept those offers? I labeled them "phantom offers" in order to make my point. I was surprised that he was clinging to this argument. In addition, the company's profit history did not even remotely support the price.

I advised my client to offer a maximum price of $7 million. We initially offered $5.5 million and the seller turned it down. My client wanted the deal so badly that they raised their offer several times, finally to as high as $7 million. I strongly advised my client not to go higher than $7 million. The buyer turned down the $7 million offer. My guess was that the magic number in the buyer's mind was $9 million.

After the deal fell apart, I thought the seller would muddle along and eventually fade away. The seller had some problems that were going to get worse before they got better. A year and half later, the seller came back to the bargaining table. My client acquired the company for $3.5 million.

The lessons to be learned from this example are several: Do not be greedy; be realistic with respect to price; and do not cling to magic numbers. There is no doubt that this deal could have been successfully concluded a year and a half earlier at a price of $7 million. The seller would have made an extra $3.5 million and the buyer would have paid an extra $3.5 million, and both parties would have walked away happy. This mistake cost the seller $3.5 million. This investment banker was inexperienced and he did not really understand the dynamics of the situation; as a result, he gave his client poor advice. An experienced intermediary would have advised the company to be more realistic regarding price and might have saved the client more than $3 million.

WORKING EFFECTIVELY WITH AN INVESTMENT BANKER

The founders and CEOs of many intangible companies do not have a great deal of experience working with investment bankers, so they are unsure how to work as a team or how to include them in the transaction process. Having an experienced investment banker work with you on a transaction can add significant value and help generate the best price.

The client should take advantage of the banker's experience and his objective point of view. Bounce ideas off him. Discuss any and all open issues with him. One of the benefits of working with an investment banker is that the banker knows how to run a disciplined sale process and where problems might crop up. He has been down these roads before.

I have worked on many transactions in which the CEO or founder took over the negotiations. In looking back at these situations, I would say the reason why this occurs so often is because: (a) CEOs and founders have a difficult time delegating—they want to control everything, and (b) they do not truly appreciate the advantages of utilizing an objective third party.

A Few Tips

How does the CEO view the role of the investment banker? Does the CEO think the banker's job is only to identify potential buyers? The banker should manage the transaction process and drive the deal to closing. As an independent and experienced third party, a banker can be more effective in negotiations. The investment banker should also negotiate the CEO's compensation package going forward. If the banker has been out of the loop during the due diligence phase, bring him back into the discussions. And sometimes when working with an unsophisticated buyer, the investment banker can work effectively in the background.

Here are a few tips on how to work effectively with an investment banker.

Let the Banker Do His Job   First of all, let the investment banker do their job. Let them do what you hired them to do. Let the banker put their skills and experience to work for you and earn the fee. The banker should manage the sale process and handle the communications with buyers. He should also be the primary point person for negotiations.

Not Simply a Finder   In many transactions that I have been involved with, the founder or CEO thought that my role was solely to identify potential buyers and then he would step in to negotiate and close the transaction. This is a big mistake. An investment banker has significantly more experience closing merger and acquisition transactions than does the CEO. Even if the CEO does have M&A or negotiating experience, an objective third party has many advantages.

An investment banker is not simply a finder. Even though identifying good buyers is a critical part of the transaction, managing the process and negotiating the best price are the prime skills that an investment banker brings to the party. That is what the banker is paid for—closing deals. Do not assume that when conversations begin with buyers that the investment banker's job is finished. The game is just beginning. This is where the investment banker can really earn his or her fee.

The Banker Should Handle the Negotiations   The founder or CEO should defer to the investment banker in handling negotiations. A banker will likely have a much broader spectrum of experience in negotiations than will the founder or CEO. Plus, as a third party, the investment banker will have a more objective view of the negotiating situation.

An experienced investment banker has well-developed people skills and will know how to read people. This is particularly valuable in the technology sectors, where reading people is not typically one of the CEO's strengths. Good people skills enable a negotiator to be alert to the nuances of the other side's positions. Is the other side telling you the straight scoop? Are they serious? Are they being honest? Are their questions and concerns legitimate?

In one case, the founder wanted to handle all the negotiations with the buyer. This buyer was a large and successful company and the founder clearly wanted to close a deal with that company. He had never sold a company before but he did not include me, his investment banker, in any discussions with this particular buyer. This was a mistake. He did not entertain offers from two other interested buyers and, in my opinion, the price was suboptimal.

In another case, the founder told me that at the end of the day, he had to be the one negotiating and closing the deal. I disagreed and said that actually he did not. I remarked that he did not need to be involved in the negotiations at all. He had a very deep-seated assumption that this was his role as the CEO. He proceeded to negotiate the transaction himself and it eventually fell apart at the 11th hour.

In one of my most successful negotiations, I was representing the seller. The two founders met the buyer's team at the initial meeting when the buyer's management flew in to visit the company. After that meeting, the founders had absolutely no contact with the buyer until the transaction's celebration dinner, after the deal was closed. It was much easier for me to negotiate effectively with the founders out of the picture and they were very pleased with the price that I negotiated.

Let the Banker Be the Bad Guy   If the founder or CEO plans to stay with the company going forward, it is important that the buyer and founder get to know each other and build a positive relationship. They need to develop mutual trust and respect and discover how they can best work together. The CEO does not want to be the tough guy in the negotiations. Let the investment banker be the tough guy, the bad guy. If the CEO will be employed by the buyer, he will negotiate too softly. This is the ideal situation for the intermediary to negotiate the challenging points. This enables the CEO or founder to maintain a constructive and cordial relationship with the buyer. Let the investment banker be the bad guy—after the transaction is completed he or she is out of the picture.

Negotiate the CEO's Compensation   In a similar vein, the investment banker should negotiate the founder's or CEO's salary and compensation package. In one transaction, the founder strongly insisted that he negotiate his own pay package with the buyer. I commented to him that the situation was similar to a sports agent who negotiates a contract for a star baseball player. The baseball player should not negotiate the contract himself, even if he is an excellent negotiator and a smart guy. The same is true for CEOs and their compensation packages.

This founder did step in to negotiate his own pay package and he ended up being quite disappointed with the result—but he *had* to do it himself. This particular founder was quite stressed about his salary package and he had some serious control issues. This is all the more reason to use an experienced third party. Having an objective intermediary negotiate the salary package takes the personal issues out of the situation.

Keep the Banker in the Loop   There will be times when the buyer will be having extended conversations with the seller, particularly during the due diligence phase. The price and terms have been decided and the buyer is plugging along, gathering due diligence information. The seller's staff is assembling documents and schedules for the buyer. The investment banker may be out of the loop.

Occasionally, issues will arise during this time that can impact the price or terms of the transaction. It is important to keep the banker apprised of the situation and the details. The investment banker's judgment can be invaluable during the final stages of a transaction. The smart CEO welcomes outside advice and will keep the banker involved.

The investment banker should also keep the client in the loop. Good communication between the parties will make for a better relationship. The banker should report regularly about the status of the transaction and where things stand with each particular buyer. I have found biweekly reporting to be the best time frame for regular reports. I also use exception reporting: When a significant development occurs, I call or e-mail the client to inform the management or board about the development.

Unsophisticated Buyer... Work in the Background   Occasionally, an unsophisticated buyer will think that they can get a better price if they go around the seller's investment banker and cut him out of the process. They will talk directly to the principals rather than dealing with the seller's banker. If a buyer wants to go around me, they do so by not returning my phone calls or emails; they always contact the CEO. If that is how the buyer wants to play it, then you have to play their game. You cannot make them call the banker.

I have worked on a number of transactions in which I was a very active participant, but in the background. After every single phone call or meeting the CEO and I would debrief. Given my many years of experience, I could put the buyer's comments into perspective for the CEO. I provided guidance on where the buyer was coming from and what his or her motivations might be. I also helped the CEO frame his or her ideas to communicate with the buyer. This process worked extremely well. The buyer thought that the CEO was acting alone and possibly naïvely; but in the background was the active involvement of an experienced investment banker.

Some of the best deals I have completed have been with an unsophisticated buyer who went around me and dealt exclusively with the CEO. It does create more work for the CEO, but that is his or her choice.

On the other hand, an experienced buyer will welcome an investment banker's participation (i.e., representing the seller). The third party removes the emotional element from the transaction and enables the deal to go together more efficiently. This is particularly true when dealing with founders who own a large portion of the company's stock. In a number of transactions the buyer—who was not my client—thanked me for my involvement because it made the deal go together much more smoothly.

Summary

Too many CEOs interject themselves into the deal. They enjoy being part of the process and they like being in control. However, they do not know when to step back. The CEO's most important responsibility is running the company, building revenues, and leading his or her team. Let the investment banker do his or her job.

The banker typically has significantly more experience closing deals than does the founder or CEO. Take advantage of this experience. Most investment bankers have worked on a multitude of transactions and have a wealth of experience negotiating deals. In my case, having been an investment banker for 25 years, I have worked on well over 100 transactions. I have interacted with many personality types with different styles, nuances, and approaches. This experience gives me a valuable perspective.

In summary, trust your adviser and let him do the job that you hired him to do. An experienced intermediary can be much more effective in negotiating and closing a transaction than the founder or CEO.

CRITICAL DEAL SKILLS FOR INVESTMENT BANKERS

As a boutique investment banker specializing in selling companies with intangible value, I have long pondered what key deal skills lead to successful transactions. Over the years that I have been structuring deals, I have come up with a brief list of the consummate deal skills that can be applied across any sector or industry.

Good deal skills are manifested by the outcome of a transaction: First of all, the deal gets closed and the client gets the best price, typically by getting multiple offers. All the best buyers are contacted, especially the less obvious ones. The transaction gets back on track after it breaks down. (Forty percent of all deals blow up at least once.) The deal gets completed smoothly, with fewer problems, fewer delays, fewer arguments, fewer hassles, and in a reasonable time frame.

The best deal makers have two attributes that are more important than all others—an exceptional understanding of human nature and the ability to read people. These talents include understanding peoples' personalities, communication dynamics, motivations, and insecurities. A savvy deal maker knows how to read people, how to respond to them, how to question them, how to work with their egos, how to motivate them, and how to tell when they are stretching the truth. Closing a transaction of any kind is all about interacting with people.

Some people believe that industry knowledge and contacts in a certain market sector are the most important qualities for closing a transaction. These topics are addressed in Chapter 2 on myths. Industry knowledge is beneficial; however, most investment bankers are highly skilled at drilling down on a particular market sector and gleaning the pertinent information. And making contacts is a very straightforward process—one that investment bankers are also skilled at.

Deal skills are far and away the most important component of successfully closing the sale of an intangible company. Deal skills can only be acquired through experience. When it comes to getting a deal closed at the best price and with the least problems, the following seven deal skills are the key to success:

1. Read people effectively.
2. Listen between the lines.
3. Identify the less obvious buyers.
4. Perfect your horse trading.
5. Apply creative problem solving.
6. Pace the transaction.
7. Structure the deal appropriately.

1. Read People Effectively

The quintessential deal skill is understanding and reading human beings. What kind of person are you dealing with? What is their level of risk tolerance? What kind of communicator is he or she? People are always changing their minds, not sure what they want; one day they want to buy (or sell) the company, the next day they do not. There are many shades of gray enshrouding those quirky creatures.

Consistent patterns emerge among people, and recognizing these patterns can be helpful in working with someone new. What is their communication style—is it direct or indirect? Do they have the courage to face tough issues or do they shy away from them? An experienced deal person is flexible in dealing with different personality types.

A good deal person will see through the stated objection to the real objection. People do not always tell you the real reasons for their actions and motivations. They even get their own objectives mixed up. They can be insecure. Sometimes they have to save face. Knowing how to read people is a consummate deal skill.

By the way, the best deal people are not generally technology people. The skills that make a good engineer, programmer, or inventor are not the same skills that make a good deal person. Tech people are smart and highly analytical, but they are usually not good at putting themselves in other people's places, understanding their motivations, and relating to their points of view.

2. Listen Between the Lines

When principals meet, they rarely listen well. They are thinking about what they are going to say next, rather than really hearing the other person. Listening between the lines means not just hearing what the person is saying, but understanding what the person truly means.

Listening is the ultimate deal skill. You cannot get people what they want if you are not sure what it is. You cannot overcome an objection if you do not understand it clearly. A skilled deal maker understands exactly what each side wants to achieve.

3. Identify the Less Obvious Buyers

Drilling down on the core market is the easy part. The selling company can probably come up with a list of 10 to 20 buyers without too much trouble. These are the easy ones, the obvious candidates. An important deal skill is knowing where to find the less obvious buyers.

The best buyers are usually in markets that are adjacent to the core market. All markets have adjacent markets and understanding the importance of these adjacent markets is critical because they are the most fruitful places to look for buyers. Buyers in adjacent markets will often pay the most because they will use an acquisition to enter a new market. The nuances of markets, especially at the edges, are where the real action is.

For example, a few years ago I sold an e-mail direct marketing firm. The company creates and sends e-mail newsletters and weekly updates for its corporate clients. This business touches on a number of adjacent markets—advertising agencies, direct marketing firms, Internet advertising companies, marketing research firms, customer relationship management software firms, web site analytics firms and marketing consulting firms. Companies in each one of these adjacent market sectors were promising, potential buyers.

4. Perfect Your Horse Trading

What is negotiating expertise? Is it toughness? One who never budges? No, that is not necessarily good negotiating. Good negotiating skills involve having a sense for what you can achieve, knowing how to effectively work with the other party, and reaching an agreement. Communicating clearly is an important part of negotiating. Good communication skills help build trust on both sides and keep objectives clear.

Horse trading embodies a number of skills. It involves give and take, feeling out the other side. How to go back and forth with offers and counteroffers is an important skill—knowing whether to come back with a little or a lot. Even the tone of the reply is important.

Negotiating skills are particularly valuable when the value is intangible—when there is no concrete basis for value, which is usually the case in technology and software transactions. And remember, you do not just negotiate price. Terms can be every bit as important.

5. Apply Creative Problem Solving

If there were no problems, deals would simply go together all by themselves. The best way to solve deal problems is to understand the issues clearly and to employ creativity in developing solutions. A good deal person distinguishes between real problems and phantom objections that are designed to push the price down. He knows how to make some problems go away entirely and how to minimize the other problems.

Just because the seller says he or she wants cash, that does not mean a stock deal is out of the question. What if the deal came down to a choice of $5 million in cash or $11 million in stock? Now would you consider stock? It depends, of course, on who the company is, but do not dismiss it out of hand.

Creativity can solve a lot of problems, in unique ways. Rarely are there just one or two ways to solve a problem. A clever deal maker will come up with a range of acceptable alternatives. Most of the time when deal problems create an impasse, it is because the parties are not thinking creatively enough.

In one instance, I closed a transaction that was technically a marketing agreement, not an acquisition per se. It was tantamount to a sale of the company because the customer base was the primary asset. Rather than go through the problems associated with transferring stock or assets, the transaction structure simply involved paying for the customers as they migrated to the acquiring company. This was an unusual structure but it was effective and very creative.

6. Pace the Transaction

Selling a company is like a slow dance. Managing the pace of a transaction is an art. You can control the timing to your advantage. Know when to push, when to back off, when to move it quickly, or when to slow it down. There is a rhythm to every deal, a cadence.

You can always slow the process down but you can rarely speed it up. A lot of CEOs want to go, go, go, push, push, push. Being proactive is one thing, but being impatient is another. This is not a good way to pace a transaction. Patience is a powerful deal skill.

A key to achieving the best price is getting multiple offers. However, receiving multiple offers does not do much good unless the parties show up at the table at the same time. You cannot say "just a minute" and get back to them two months later. An experienced deal maker will manage the pace of a transaction to the client's advantage, using subtle deal skills to get the parties to the table at the same time.

7. Structure the Deal Appropriately

Structuring a transaction appropriately can make the whole process productive and successful. The key to good structuring is knowing what kinds of things are workable and what are not. A good deal person can be inventive and create structures that meet the needs of both parties.

A wide variety of issues crop up during the deal process. For example, should the letter of intent be binding or not? What about certain paragraphs? What length of a no-shop clause is reasonable? Experience and judgment can pay huge dividends while handling the multitude of minor issues that can cause stumbling blocks along the way.

Many deals have been structured as earnouts that should never have been structured that way. Sometimes earnouts are great but they can also be awkward and messy. An earnout should be used when it is the appropriate structure, not because the parties simply cannot agree on price. Smart structuring solves the needs of both parties in the simplest possible way.

Many transactions get completed. However, in my experience, a good portion of these deals were not structured optimally. With a little creativity and a better understanding of the parties' objectives, many of these deals could have been structured more intelligently, so that both parties would be better off.

Additional Tips

A few additional tools that an investment banker should have in his or her bag of tricks are:

1. **Sniff Out Tire Kickers.** Figure out if the other party is serious. You can waste a lot of time and energy dealing with buyers that are not serious.
2. **Keep Plan B Alive.** You should always have a backup plan. Keep your alternatives warm. Sometimes Plan C is a good idea, too.
3. **Know How to Approach Buyers.** It is important to approach buyers effectively so they will commit the time and effort to explore an acquisition. Who should you contact at the buying company? What about confidentiality? Should you provide a lot of information initially or only a little?
4. **Communicate Effectively.** Clearly communicating a company's strengths, competencies, and opportunities is a constructive skill. Why do customers pay good money for the firm's products or services? Exaggerating is not a good idea; it will come back to bite you.
5. **See Value through the Buyer's Eyes.** Determine how valuable the company is to the buyer. Try to view value through their mindset. What would it cost them to duplicate what the seller has?
6. **Manage Expectations.** Manage the emotions and expectations of the parties—the CEO, founders, VCs, shareholders, and employees. To some degree, you can also manage the expectations of the opposing party as well.
7. **Foresee Problems.** Know where problems might crop up and which roads not to go down. The wise deal person heads off issues before they become real problems. The easiest objections to overcome are the ones that never come up.
8. **Persist.** Closing a deal can be an uphill battle. The tenacity to keep on pushing, persisting until you succeed, can make all the difference in getting a transaction closed.

Deal skills are about interacting with those pesky creatures called human beings, with all their quirks, biases, egos, and emotions. Deal skills are acquired through experience. A deal maker discovers what works and what does not work by trying things out, by interacting with many different types of people and situations. Effective deal skills are truly an art that can make all the difference in completing transactions at the best price and with the fewest problems along the way.

A Final Note

One of the best skills that has served me well over the years is the ability to suspend all assumptions. I try to never assume anything about different aspects of the transaction. Make no assumptions about seller motivations or about the deal structure. It does not have to be a certain way. A transaction can be structured in many different ways. I am always surprised by the countless and curious issues that pop up. Suspending assumptions is an ability that can have remarkably positive consequences.

FINDING THE RIGHT ATTORNEY AND ACCOUNTANT

The right attorney and accountant can make the transaction process much smoother. In addition, good counsel from these advisers can protect the company and its shareholders from both immediate problems and issues that could arise in the future.

The key to hiring the right attorney or the right accountant is experience. An attorney or an accountant with significant experience with the sale of companies will be a great help in properly addressing problems and making the transaction proceed smoothly.

Accountants

Accountants can assist with a number of tasks. They can help prepare financial projections. They can offer advice on structuring in order to minimize the tax consequences. Accountants can also help compile due diligence information for the buyer.

Is the company's financial house in order? Most intangible companies could use some help to better organize their financial state of affairs. Accurate and complete financial statements and supporting schedules can give the buyer a higher degree of comfort regarding the selling company. Good financial preparation gives the buyer confidence that the seller has its act together.

To be completely organized a company should contact an outside accounting firm six months in advance to get the financial house in order. An experienced accountant knows exactly what it means to have one's financial house in order. Getting the accountants involved early could expose problems that the selling company may want to address. It is better to discover and address any problem areas prior to the buyer's due diligence research.

If a company has been growing rapidly it may have financial issues that its in-house staff is not aware of. A company may presume that they are more profitable than they actually are. Proper cost accounting may reveal a different profitability picture. The company might improve profits if certain issues were accounted for appropriately.

Attorneys

Choose an attorney who has been through the M&A process multiple times. And by experienced, I mean experienced in mergers and acquisitions, not just general business law. Do not use your college friend who incorporated you when you founded the company years ago. Use an experienced transaction attorney. It may cost a little more, but it is well worth it.

All attorneys have experience. However, an attorney who has not been through the M&A process multiple times will not have the judgment to be an effective adviser. An experienced deal attorney knows where problems might lurk. He or she knows what things are necessary and what things are not required.

Do not let your attorney or accountant negotiate the transaction for you. Sometimes legal issues can migrate upstream toward deal points or important transaction terms. The attorney should offer advice and suggestions to the CEO and to the investment banker. He should not make decisions about the transaction; that is not his role. Lawyers enjoy the deal-making process and thrashing out the business issues. However, attorneys are not businessmen; they have a different orientation. You do not want legal issues to drive the transaction. Get the assistance of an investment banker or a board member with a good business background.

WAR STORY: THE LEGAL GAME VERSUS THE DEAL GAME

The attorney for my client wanted to continue to negotiate with the attorney for the other side. They had been going back and forth for several weeks. The other side's lawyer was slow on the draw. I sensed delaying tactics. Our lawyer insisted that she do the negotiating with the other lawyer, not me, asserting something like "that's how lawyers do things." I went to the client and overrode her and eventually instructed her to cease conversations with the other lawyer altogether because the talks were going nowhere.

If I had not stepped in, their discussions would have gone on for a number of weeks and run up the legal bill for no benefit. In the end

I discovered that my judgment was exactly right. The company was purposefully delaying in order to buy time to raise capital. Our lawyer was down in the trenches involved in the legal game; she did not see the larger picture.

Attorneys are biased toward the legal issues and accountants are biased toward the accounting issues. Their viewpoints are influenced by their professional orientations. And that is fine; that is how it should be. It is the lawyer's job to focus on the legal details of the transaction. However, sometimes attorneys focus so narrowly that they lose the sense of the overall transaction.

Part of the investment banker's role is to oversee the various advisers and make sure they are moving the transaction in the right direction and with the client's objectives in mind. I have rescued a number of transactions by stepping in and instructing the attorneys to change tactics or directions.

The selling company will need an experienced transaction attorney. Ask other sellers who they used as their attorneys. Talk with several candidates and select one with a bias toward the person with the most experience in the merger and acquisition field.

WAR STORY: A CASE OF LEGAL OVERKILL

This was a small transaction, only a $1.3 million deal. However, the deal structure was somewhat complicated. There were a lot of moving parts and several shareholder problems needed to be dealt with. I was worried that the legal fees might get out of hand so I suggested to my client, the CEO of the seller, that he ask his attorney for an estimate of the legal fees.

The company's attorney worked at a relatively large law firm and he was a very bright and experienced attorney. His approach was exceptionally thorough—every schedule must be prepared, every contingency must be covered. Everything was full blast; he did not know when to stop. Whether this was a $1 million deal or a $100 million deal, it made no difference to the attorney. The estimate for the legal fees came in at $110,000—and the attorney was not even drafting the

(Continued)

purchase agreement. (The buyer's attorney typically drafts the purchase agreement.) The $110,000 seemed excessive.

I recommended a local four-partner law firm who did the legal work for $20,000. They did a fine job and the transaction closed without a hitch. The difference was not just the hourly billing rate. It was more about the level of detail in drafting and reviewing documents. Sometimes judgment is needed regarding the appropriate amount of work for a specific situation.

SUMMARY

The assistance of an experienced adviser such as an investment banker can be invaluable. As an objective third party, he or she can assist in overcoming the inevitable deal problems and also play an important role in negotiations. We underscored the importance of hiring the right size investment banking firm given the size of the transaction.

You cannot talk about investment bankers without talking about fees. This chapter reviewed a number of the issues regarding the fee agreement and addressed a handful of questions that clients commonly ask. The key to a good fee arrangement is to closely align the terms of the agreement with the interests of the client.

Many founders and CEOs of intangible companies have not had significant experience working with investment bankers and this chapter reviewed ways to work effectively with an intermediary. Tips include viewing the banker as part of the deal team; recognizing that he is more than a finder; letting the banker handle the communications and negotiations with the buyer; and letting him negotiate the CEO's compensation package. Most importantly, let the investment banker earn his fee.

In addition, the chapter outlined seven deal skills that make an investment banker effective. We also commented on the importance of hiring an experienced accountant and an experienced attorney to assist with the transaction.

The reader might find it interesting to peruse the three appendices. Appendix A examines small acquisitions from the buyer's perspective and outlines why these deals offer a unique window into niche markets. It also reviews how small transactions differ from large deals. Appendix B presents some observations on international aspects of selling an intangible company, including comments on European buyers. Appendix C discusses the criteria for selecting an investment banker and poses 16 questions to ask prospective candidates.

Afterword

The merger and acquisition process is a fascinating one. The transaction process can be a roller coaster ride—there are many ups and downs, and many moving parts. Some problems can be solved and some problems must simply be dealt with. Overcoming problems and completing transactions brings me great satisfaction. Whether the deal is a large or small, it still counts as a closed transaction. A deal is a deal.

Writing this book and reflecting on the transaction process has given me a greater appreciation for the people skills, the soft skills, and the communication skills that come into play during the transaction process. Deals are not done between companies, deals are done between people.

What lessons have I learned in my years of selling intangible companies? What ideas can I pass on to help others in the software and technology industries? Reflecting on my years in the technology M&A business three themes come to mind.

The first theme is that a business should define itself by its customers, not by its products or services. Tech firms tend not to do this. Their mindsets, as well as their web sites, tend to focus just on the technology. This needs to change. The wise businessman gets very close to his customers and solves their problems. The technology will one day become obsolete, but the customers will always have needs.

How a business defines itself is important—in the same way that self-image defines a person. It sets the stage for what the firm should or should not do, what it can or cannot do.

The second theme is that CEOs of technology and other intangible companies need to be businessmen first and technologists second. Being a businessman means focusing on the business, making business judgments. It means being opportunistic. A technology firm is about more than just its technology; it exists to solve its customers' problems. Almost every business is a technology business these days; it is not just the computer industry.

CEOs and managers of technology firms need to learn a lesson from their non-technology brethren and improve their people skills. Running a business is about interacting with people—employees, customers, and share-holders. The most important skill any business person can have is people skills—knowing how to communicate effectively, how to listen effectively, and how to empathize with people. These are the skills that successful business people embody.

The third theme is to not do everything yourself. People who must do everything themselves misunderstand the game. The real game of business is to build the most effective company that you can. The most effective company does not do everything itself. It will outsource and bring in outside help when needed. It will build the best internal systems, get close to their customers, and solve the customers' problems. It will execute superbly. Tech people need to be more focused on building effective companies and less focused on doing everything themselves.

On a related note, entrepreneurs must learn to give up control. Trying to maintain too much control over the business severely limits the entrepreneur and it constricts the business. This management style rarely produces successful companies. To create a successful and thriving business, an entrepreneur must give up control, trust others, and delegate in order to benefit from the diverse capabilities of his or her employees.

Now that I have divulged all of my secrets about how to sell intangible companies, have I given away too much information? Have I put myself out of business? Well, actually, no. Deal skills cannot be learned in a book. They can only be learned through experience. And experience comes from many years of interacting with buyers and sellers, CEOs and founders, and other players in the merger and acquisition game.

Over the years I have come to really appreciate the art of negotiating and selling a company. Even after 25 years in this business, I still learn something new with every transaction. Actually, I still learn many things in each transaction. Sometimes I learn nuances of transaction structure, but mostly I learn about people. Every deal teaches me more about people and their psychologies. It's like I'm building a big database of human psychology in my head. Human beings are so similar and also so different. It is fascinating working with them and learning about them. People are what truly makes the deal process enthralling.

The Beauty of Small Acquisitions

A small acquisition can create shareholder value in several ways: by identifying new areas for growth, acquiring new capabilities and technologies, and helping transform a company's business model. Making a small acquisition can be an excellent strategy for an acquirer to gain a foothold in a niche market. A company can gain new customers and new talent. After the acquisition has been completed, it can serve as a platform to build upon.

What is a small acquisition? How should it be defined? Is it a $5 million deal? What about $10 million or maybe $20 million? I define a small acquisition as one with a transaction value of less than $30 million. Why is that important? It is important because the size of the typical buyer is much smaller than it is for a larger transaction. In addition, the selling process is different for a small transaction.

A $5 million or a $10 million acquisition will be important to a company with $200 million or less in revenue. To a $500 million or a $1 billion company, a $10 million acquisition is almost irrelevant. Only if the technology is highly strategic will a large company be interested in acquiring a small firm.

The market opportunity for small acquisitions is substantial. Small acquisitions are less expensive, simpler to transact and easier to integrate. Many small companies need to be part of larger companies in order to grow and thrive and to gain economies of scale in marketing and sales. Plus, the search for small acquisitions can provide a resourceful window into new growth areas. Even if an acquisition is not completed, the search process brings new market knowledge.

This appendix also reviews how small transactions are different from large transactions: the universe of buyers is different, the acquirers are smaller in size, and the sale process is different.

LOOKING OUTSIDE FOR GROWTH

A company's opportunities for growth often lie outside the confines of its current industry description. Where should a company look for small acquisitions? The best place is at the edges of a company's market space and in adjacent markets. Market spaces are always gray around the edges; there are no clear boundaries. The edges of a market offer the best opportunities. That is where the new niches are sprouting up.

Think of a small acquisition as a type of outsourced research and development. Much of the new technology that is developed is discovered by small companies. More important, however, is the application of a new technology; using it to solve a customer's problem. This is where small companies excel.

Most successful companies are continuously refining their business models. Small acquisitions are an excellent way to transform or redefine a company's business model. For example, a company can acquire a firm that provides services and gradually shift to being more of a services company.

The market opportunity for small acquisitions is significant. Many small companies need to be acquired in order to gain economies of scale and gain access to stronger sales and distribution channels. Plus, there is simply the matter of numbers. There are many more small companies, in the $5 million to $15 million range, than there are larger companies that need to be acquired.

Often the best companies to acquire are not for sale. They are chugging along, enjoying steady growth. They are not seeking to be acquired and they may be under the radar. The good news is that the market for small acquisitions has not been picked over. The bad news is that these companies will not come knocking on a buyer's door. The smart acquirer will continually be on the lookout for good acquisitions particularly for companies that are not for sale. To identify these opportunities buyers must actively seek them out.

A second reason that underscores this market opportunity is that most buyers are seeking large acquisitions, not small acquisitions. The large industry buyers and financial buyers (private equity groups or buyout funds) want acquisitions of a minimum size, usually revenues greater than $25 million and operating profit greater than $2 million or $3 million.

One software company that I conferred with about acquisitions is a typical example. This buyer was a $250 million software firm that wanted to make acquisitions to consolidate midsized software companies. In speaking to the CEO about acquisitions, he informed me that they had an active list of 60 companies that they were monitoring. Every company on their list had revenues greater than $30 million. None of these companies were for sale, at least at a reasonable price. If the buyer did acquire one of these firms it would have been for a fairly high price. As a matter of corporate policy the company was simply not interested in acquisitions less than $25 million in transaction value. The CEO did not think that smaller acquisitions were worth their time and effort. This is a typical attitude for a large or midsized acquirer; they are rarely interested in acquisitions under $25 million.

Another reason for the market opportunity in small acquisitions is that the large investment banks do not seek out small acquisitions for their clients because they typically don't work on deals less than $20 million. Their business model does not support it; the fees are simply not large enough to make it worth their while.

The smart play is to make a small acquisition, get a foothold in a niche market, and then grow it. Small companies are much more malleable and easier to grow the way the buyer wants. Their business models are not rigid. For example, a buyer can change pricing structures before the industry gets accustomed to one particular way. It can establish the service and support standards. The buyer is not inheriting a situation that can't easily be changed.

All large markets were small markets at one time. The small acquisition strategy may involve more work but it requires much less capital, and the buyer has more flexibility regarding how it chooses to grow the business.

A WINDOW INTO NICHE MARKETS

The search for small acquisitions can provide an acquirer with a window into new growth areas and niche markets. You might call it a type of market research; even if there is no resulting acquisition, the search process can provide useful insight. You may conclude that a particular market niche is too small to be of interest, but at least you'll be aware of it. And you can keep an eye on the niche in case you decide later that the sector is becoming large enough to warrant serious attention.

Small intangible companies are solving some kind of customer need with their products or services. Customers certainly must see something of value. What need is being met? What problem is being solved? Should the buyer be addressing this market need? The fact that a small company is making sales means that the larger companies are not addressing this particular area.

Companies usually prefer purchasing products and services from large suppliers. Bigger firms are more stable and often have better service and support. (This is not categorically true; some small companies offer excellent service which is why customers choose them.) The fact that small firms are in business means that the bigger companies either are not addressing the problem or their solutions are too expensive. In either case, there is a real market opportunity that the small company is addressing.

A buyer may decide not to make a particular acquisition for one reason or another. It may not like the management, for example. However, the buyer may decide to enter that market sector on its own. At a minimum, the acquisition search effort has opened the buyer's eyes to a new market opportunity.

If a buyer does decide to seek out small acquisitions there are two types of searches: specific and opportunistic. In a specific search the acquirer knows precisely what capabilities it is seeking. The goal of the specific search is to drill down into the markets to identify candidates that fit the company's criteria for specific products, technologies, or service capabilities. The search is a systematic and well-organized effort to identify, research, screen, and contact all of the companies in a particular market sector. The search for specific capabilities is very highly focused.

An opportunistic search works the opposite way. The search is not highly focused, but rather, it is a broad exploration. The buyer may discover a company that is open to being acquired. Then the buyer ponders whether or not the seller has capabilities or assets that it could capitalize on. Upon finding a potential acquisition candidate the buyer will ask itself, "Is this a niche market that we should consider?" The purpose of the opportunistic search is to push the envelope and look at deals that are not directly in the buyer's market, to expand the buyer's horizons, and to seek out companies that the buyer would not normally consider.

These types of opportunities are not usually on the buyer's radar screen. They may be in tangential markets or even one step removed. These acquisition ideas can be both creative and unusual. There is no set criterion. In fact, definitive criteria can actually constrain the search process.

In addition to actually making an acquisition, reviewing opportunistic ideas can stimulate a buyer's thinking process and aid in revitalizing its strategic plan. If it wasn't for the acquisition search the buyer may not have been aware of a particular market niche.

CRITERIA CAN BE LIMITING

Well thought-out criteria are usually a good thing for an acquirer. However, when trying to jump into new market areas, criteria can be limiting. Strict criteria almost always points to the center of a market, not to the fringes. And most buyers already know the companies in their primary market spaces.

In the opportunistic acquisition searches that I have been involved with, the key to success is not to follow the company's criteria. The first step is to investigate the acquirer and gain a good understanding of its strengths, weaknesses, capabilities, customers, and so on. The next step is to go out into the market and explore. One may run across unlikely companies that could be excellent additions that don't fit any preconceived criteria.

The notion of specific and detailed criteria is consistent with the analytical mindset of most technology companies. Tech people like to think everything through from the beginning. The opportunistic mindset is not one that I often observe in the technology sector. This can be quite limiting. The companies that succeed over the long term are those that are continually open to new opportunities and to the opportunistic mindset.

THE TROUBLE WITH SMALL ACQUISITIONS

There is one problem with small acquisitions—there are many companies to consider. The endeavor involves a significant amount of work. The process of researching, screening, and communicating with many small companies requires a considerable amount of time and effort.

The best buyers for small acquisitions (companies with revenues of $15 million to $175 million) are usually too busy running their businesses to be able to afford the time to look for acquisitions. They are resource constrained and do not usually have extra manpower to devote to an acquisition search. There are two ways to overcome this problem. One is to hire an in-house team to perform the search, screen, and communication activities. The second approach is to outsource the search to a boutique investment banking firm that will give committed attention to small acquisitions.

HOW SMALL DEALS ARE DIFFERENT

Many technology CEOs and venture capitalists have experience in the big M&A arena, either from working for a Wall Street investment bank or from working at a large technology company like Cisco, Oracle, or Computer Associates. They know how big M&A is done. Many tech CEOs and VCs assume the process is the same for selling a company for less than $30 million. It is not. The processes are very different; small M&A is a different ball game.

Why would a small transaction be any different than a large transaction? A deal is a deal. Well, that is actually not the case. Sub-30 transactions differ in a number of ways:

- The buyers are a different set of companies. Small deals have smaller buyers; say $50 million in revenues versus $500 million.

- More potential buyers must be contacted when selling a sub-30 company.
- A small technology company may be utilized by buyers in a number of different ways and thus can be a good fit with more types of buyers.
- The sale process is different. The auction method is not appropriate for sub-30 deals. A negotiated transaction is much more effective.
- Small transactions are easier to transact and easier to integrate.
- Deal structures can be more diverse for a small transaction.
- More creativity is required to delve into adjacent markets because many buyers use sub-30 acquisitions to enter new markets.
- Management and people issues can have a greater impact on a small transaction.
- The participants in a small transaction are often less sophisticated; they may never have been through the M&A process.

The Buyers are Smaller and More Numerous

The buyers for an acquisition that is less than $30 million in transaction size are relatively small firms. The typical buyer for a $5 million or $10 million acquisition is a company with $15 million to $100 million dollars in revenue. Larger companies are not usually interested in small acquisitions. So the universe of buyers for a small deal is quite different; it is not the same set of companies.

There are more potential buyers for a small transaction. For a large transaction there may be at most 40 or 50 potential industry buyers. For a sub-30 transaction it may be wise to contact 125 or more buyers. Generally, the smaller a transaction is the more potential buyers must be contacted.

In one transaction my client was a European software company that was a participant in the predictive analytics arena. This was a relatively hot market as more and more companies incorporated analytics tools into their software suites. In this transaction I contacted 165 companies. Some were large companies and some were small companies but all were reasonably good potential acquirers. The value of this company was less than $10 million. If this was a larger firm with say $75 million in revenues, there might have been only 30 reasonable buyers.

Many small acquisitions are made with market entry as a motive. As a result, the buyers are not from the core industry of the seller, but in adjacent market sectors. As a result the search process must entail more creativity in exploring these areas. Sometimes industry knowledge can blind one to potential buyers that are out of the ordinary. With small transactions the search for buyers always extends beyond the usual market participants.

Not Cast in Concrete

Small technology and software companies are not usually fully developed. They are not "cast in concrete." Any company with $100 million in revenue is fairly well-defined; it is what it is. A company with $7 million in revenue, on the other hand, is much more malleable or adaptable. From an M&A perspective a young intangible company can fit with more buyers than a larger one can.

The key asset of a small company is often its technology and technology can be used in a number of ways. Technology developed for one application can be utilized in other applications as well. It can be employed in different contexts.

A young entrepreneurial company is similar to a one-year old child: the mind is not fully developed. It can develop in different ways. Likewise, technology can be applied in different ways and the company can unfold in different ways. A specific type of security technology, for example, can be applied to many different software applications.

The Sale Process Is Different

The process for selling a sub-30 company is different than the process for selling a larger company, whether the larger company is $50 million, $100 million, or $500 million in revenues. The two-step auction process that is used for large transactions does not work well for transactions less than $30 million. A negotiated sale is much more effective for sub-30 deals. You cannot just knock off a zero or two and assume it is the same process.

Selling a small company is about working the deal process. This means contacting all the companies in a market space (including some in adjacent markets), presenting them with the acquisition opportunity, and then negotiating the best price. In Chapter 3, I explained in more detail the advantages and disadvantages of the two-step auction process versus the negotiated sale.

Easier to Transact

Sub-30 deals are easier to transact than large deals in several respects. Not only are small deals less expensive, they can have simpler transaction structures. Many sub-30 transactions are a straightforward purchase of assets. Since the stock is not being acquired, there is less concern about unknown liabilities and less due diligence is required. In addition, sub-30 acquisitions rarely face any antitrust hurdles.

The time line for small deals can be shorter than for large deals. Although most deals usually take six months to complete, I have found that if it is important, I can shorten this time frame dramatically. Occasionally, venture capital firms provide bridge loans to their portfolio companies. A venture firm may wish to conclude a sale transaction quickly in order to minimize these cash outflows, so there is pressure to conclude a deal in short order. I have completed several transactions in very short time frames (90 days) because time was critical.

Easier to Integrate

Small deals are much easier to integrate after the acquisition is completed. The seller is usually small enough that it does not have a "culture" of its own that must be dealt with and integrated. One of the biggest problems with large acquisitions is integration. With a small acquisition there are simply fewer integration issues. There are fewer people to bring on board and fewer matters that must be dealt with.

Deal Structures are More Diverse

Sometimes the transaction structure can be very straightforward on a small deal. In many small transactions the buyer will simply purchase the seller's assets and assume selected liabilities. In an asset purchase, hidden or off balance sheet liabilities do not come into play. The benefit of this approach is a very simple deal structure.

On the other hand, small deals can sometimes involve more complicated deal structures. If Microsoft acquired Yahoo for $47 billion there are probably only one or two transaction structures that are appropriate. However a small transaction can be structured in any number of ways. Typical transaction structures on a small deal can include notes, earnouts, royalties, consulting agreements, and so on. On a small transaction a consulting agreement or a noncompete agreement can account for a significant portion of the transaction value.

To further complicate matters, the intellectual property may be owned by the founder. The building may be owned by the management team. The founder's brother may own the rights to the logo and the web site. Small deals can involve all kinds of strange relationships and issues that can complicate a deal.

The purchase currency can be stock or cash. Sometimes shareholders prefer to receive stock of the acquiring company rather than cash. In this situation they still have upside potential in case the stock (whether public or private) goes up in value. Purchases of stock require more in-depth due diligence. There may be undisclosed liabilities and it takes research to discover their existence and the degree of potential liability exposure.

Greater Creativity is Required

In some ways, small transactions can be more difficult. The participants are generally less sophisticated. The buyer might be a relatively small company and as such has never made an acquisition. I have completed a number of deals in which neither the seller nor the buyer had ever been through the acquisition process.

This can be a problem because the buyer does not know what questions to ask. It may not have the experience to know which issues are important and which issues are not important. The due diligence process can be sporadic. The buyer may neglect to ask the important questions up front but may come back later and request more information at the last minute.

The company's outside advisers also may not have significant experience in the M&A process. The seller's attorney or accountant or even its investment banker may not have been involved in very many transactions. Contrast this with a large acquisition. Attorneys who work on large acquisitions are highly experienced. They specialize in this area and typically have worked on many merger and acquisition transactions. On a large transaction there is also likely to be a team of lawyers on each side.

A small glitch can be a big problem in a sub-30 deal. For example, accrued vacation pay totaling $125,000 can have a major impact on a $2 million deal. I was involved in one transaction that had exactly this problem. Shortly before closing the buyer discovered the accrued vacation pay issue. As a result, I had to renegotiate the transaction price. On a $150 million deal, $125,000 of vacation pay is an irrelevant detail.

Some people assume that small deals are just as complicated as big deals. They can certainly end up being complicated, but they do not need to be. People can make any transaction complex if they want to. In sub-30 deals the players must exercise businessman's judgment and be smart about which issues to address in-depth and which issues to pass over.

What about Large Acquisitions?

Large acquisitions can add significant value and enable a company to achieve scale rapidly. The problem is that there are not as many potential candidates to choose from. Plus, the market can be picked over. Large industry buyers and financial buyers compete aggressively for large acquisitions. Big deals are more expensive, not just in absolute terms but also in relative terms—they will have different valuation multiples. A large acquisition is priced higher per dollar of earnings. For example, a small transaction, of say $15 million, may be priced at 5 or 6 times operating earnings. On the other hand, a large transaction of $100 million or more may be priced at 10 times operating earnings.

Part of the difference between these multiples is due to different risk characteristics between small firms and large firms. Small firms generally have a higher degree of risk. Another reason for the difference in multiples is because of the competitive nature of the acquisition market—large acquisitions get bid up more than small acquisitions.

Acquisitions have been pilloried in the press in the last several years for not creating shareholder value. However, these are almost always large acquisitions: $50 million, $100 million, or even a billion dollars. Small acquisitions are a different ball game. In my experience small acquisitions have a much better record of creating shareholder value.

Large acquisitions take place in large and established markets. The fact that an acquisition is large means the seller has been in business for a number of years, addressing existing markets. Large companies are generally not players in new niche markets. If entering an up-and-coming market niche is a firm's quest, then a large acquisition is probably not the right type of acquisition. Small companies usually operate in small and growing markets and small acquisitions enable buyers to enter new market niches.

Notes on International Deals

Over the years I have worked on a number of international transactions involving the sale of software and technology companies. By no means am I an expert in the international merger and acquisition arena but I have had some experiences selling software and technology companies that might be interesting or helpful for the reader. What follows are some notes on a variety of aspects of international acquisitions.

Most of the international acquisitions that I have experience with involved a European buyer that acquired a company located in the United States. In the majority of these international transactions my firm was representing a U.S. company and the assignment was to sell the company. In a handful of transactions, my firm represented European firms or Indian firms that were seeking acquisitions of companies in the United States. I have also arranged a number of transactions with buyers located in the United Kingdom, Germany, Canada, and Australia.

There are two primary drivers for the acquisition of a U.S. company by a European company. The first is that the European firm seeks to gain products, technology, and capabilities that complement the buyer's products and services. The second reason for these acquisitions is to gain a stronger presence and distribution channels in the United States. In the case of the Indian firms, they were seeking companies in specific vertical markets. For example one Indian firm had been involved in the financial sector, primarily doing outsourced work for a U.S. company. Having developed expertise in this sector, this company was now seeking to acquire a small or midsized American company in order to capitalize on this industry expertise.

In a number of the transactions that I worked on involving European companies, many of the people that I interacted with had attended college in the United States and had worked in the United States for several years for either an American or European company. So even though they were European, they had an excellent understanding not just of the American language but of the American culture.

I have always enjoyed working on transactions with companies in other countries. Certainly there are more challenges because of the distances and because of the cultures but it is extremely interesting to deal with people with different perspectives, outlooks, and backgrounds.

FOREIGN BUYERS

Foreign buyers comprise between 10 and 20 percent of the buyers in most of the transactions that I have been involved in. On average, foreign buyers account for about 15 percent of the potential buyers. Over the years this percentage has been gradually increasing and will likely continue to climb as business becomes more international and as the technology industries mature. Companies in developing countries will seek to grow by acquisition and U.S. firms will seek additional growth through acquisition in developing countries.

LANGUAGE

Language differences are almost nonexistent. English has clearly become the lingua franca of international business. Almost all international business people speak English and their proficiency is usually quite good. Even if a European person struggles a little to speak in English they usually have no problem understanding English. This is typical of any foreign language—it is easier to comprehend the language than to speak it.

CULTURE

Cultural differences still play a very important part in any international business transaction. People in other countries have different styles of doing deals and different styles of negotiation.

In one transaction that I completed, the CEO of a California software company commented to me that prior to entering into negotiations with a French software company she bought a book on how cultural issues affect international business. She read the book and thought it was utterly old-fashioned and out-of-date. This is the new world she thought; people aren't like this anymore. As she moved forward with negotiations with the French company, almost every cultural issue or difference that was described in the book proved to be true. Cultural issues are still quite prevalent.

Another cultural issue to consider is women in business. In the United States it is not unusual at all for a woman to be CEO of a business, large or small. In Europe it is a very different situation. It is relatively rare for a woman to run a company in Europe. The French company referenced above acquired a U.S. company managed by several women. As the woman CEO told me, "The French view themselves as progressive; however during meetings they were always aware that there was a woman in the room."

NEGOTIATING STYLES

Let me contrast two different negotiating styles: the Taiwan Chinese and the French. The Chinese have a Western-style of negotiating. You say you want $10 million. They respond with "we will give you $5 million." Then you go back and forth and meet somewhere in the middle. There is no deal until both sides have agreed upon the terms. Then the deal is set. This is a comfortable style for Americans because it is similar to how Americans typically negotiate.

The French on the other hand have a very different style. They play it very close to the vest, and are likely to agree to a transaction early on. You say you want $10 million and the Frenchman says "okay, we will give you $10 million." And from there they negotiate downwards in small pieces. First "there is the problem with the distribution agreement, so we must reduce the price by $500,000." Okay, so now we agree to the $9.5 million price. But, then there is that issue with the patent rights; that's another $500,000. And so on. It is death by a thousand cuts. In the U.S., "nickel and diming" someone is viewed as irritating and possibly negotiating in bad faith, but in this transaction that is how the French chose to negotiate.

The Chinese style is more like that in the United States but with a slight difference. There is no deal until terms are fully agreed upon. But if the parties verbally agree and look each other in the eyes then the deal is set. The paperwork is almost irrelevant. In one financing transaction, the Taiwanese financier sent a portion of the funds to the U.S. company that he was investing in before the documents were even signed. The parties had verbally agreed, so the transaction was decided.

TIME ZONES

Time zones are surprisingly easy to accommodate. My firm is located on the west coast of the United States and working with a European company simply involves making phone calls in the early morning. There is a 7- to 9-hour time difference depending on the city.

Working with a client in Australia involved making phone calls in the late afternoon or early evening. There is a 5- to 7-hour time difference. The interesting thing is that instead of adding hours, one subtracts five hours and recognizes that it is the next day. So, Tuesday at 4 PM in Seattle is 11 AM on Wednesday in Sydney. One interesting aspect is that when we switch to daylight savings time, the time difference changes by two hours, not by one hour. The reason of course is that they are in the Southern hemisphere so they are going off daylight time while we are switching to daylight time. It took me a little while to figure that one out.

The best solution to time zone issues is e-mail. Almost all communications are now done with e-mail, except certain negotiating conversations that are important to be conducted by telephone.

DOLLAR VERSUS EURO

At the time of the writing of this book, the dollar has been declining markedly compared to the Euro. The effect is to give European buyers a discount—a significant discount—when acquiring U.S. companies. European buyers may be excellent buyers at this time because the Euro is at a 30 percent premium to the dollar compared to five years earlier. As of April, 2008 the exchange rate was 1.58 dollars per Euro. Five years earlier it was 1.09 dollars per Euro. This is like getting a 30 percent discount on the price of a U.S. company.

Exchange rates, of course, can move in both directions. If the dollar were to appreciate against the Euro, it would make the acquisition of a U.S. company more expensive for a European firm. In this situation, a U.S. buyer would have a greater incentive to make acquisitions in Europe because they would be less expensive.

How to Select an Investment Banker

This appendix is intended to help CEOs, entrepreneurs, and boards of directors make better decisions when hiring an investment banker for a merger and acquisition (M&A) engagement. We examine the three essential criteria for selecting an investment banker: competency, commitment, and character.

The investment banker's role is to help clients accomplish their M&A objectives. These include getting the transaction closed with the best buyer and at the best price and best terms. The client also wants to close the transaction in a timely manner, with the fewest problems and a minimum of disruption.

The key competency that an investment banker brings to a transaction is not only getting the best price for the client but creatively and effectively overcoming the obstacles that inevitably occur. Every deal will have problems of some kind. (Remember that 40 percent of all transactions blow up at least once.) The seller wants the highest price and the buyer wants the lowest price. These are diametrically opposed positions. It is no wonder that issues crop up. The broader one's base of experience, the more effective the banker will be at solving the problems that arise and closing the deal at the best price.

One of an investment banker's key skills is researching and analyzing market sectors. It is a straightforward task to research an industry and develop an in-depth understanding of the market situation. Sometimes a banker with limited experience will emphasize his industry knowledge because it is the only way he can compete with an experienced banker.

THE THREE Cs

The best investment bankers have three essential qualities that enable them to close transactions successfully and obtain the best price for their clients.

I like to call them "the three Cs":

- Competence
- Commitment
- Character

Let's examine each one of these characteristics.

Competence

Competence is the ability to get a deal done at the optimum price. Competence is closely correlated with experience; the more experience an investment banker has the more competent he will be. The investment banker with the broadest experience will have the greatest range of skills for resolving problems and getting the deal closed. He will have a history of successful solutions to draw upon and experience utilizing creativity to resolve issues.

How should one examine competence? There are six fundamental aspects of competence:

1. Competence with intangible value
2. Experience with similar sized transactions
3. Experience with technology markets
4. Negotiating competency
5. Creativity and imagination
6. Deal savvy

Competence with Intangible Value   Many people are uncomfortable with the concept of intangible value because it is vague. People seek certainty regarding value. Almost all technology M&A transactions involve value that is strategic or intangible. The dynamics of these transactions are different than the dynamics of transactions in which value can be determined objectively. The appropriate M&A advisor is one who has had significant experience selling companies in which the value is intangible.

Experience with Similar Sized Transactions   It is important to hire a firm that is the right size for your transaction. If the transaction is greater than $150 million you will be best served with a large New York investment bank. If the transaction size is between $30 million and $150 million, go with a midsized investment bank. If the transaction is less than $30 million, choose a small boutique firm.

A medium-sized investment banking firm is unlikely to give their full attention to a sub-30 transaction. They simply cannot earn a large enough fee to make it worth their while. A $10 million deal is a very different transaction from a $100 million or $500 million deal. Investment bankers who try to run an auction process on small deals are trying to put a round peg into a square hole. A negotiated transaction, on the other hand, takes more time and more effort but the results are much better. Do not assume that the process employed on large deals is also the best for smaller ones. So, select a banker who has significant experience arranging transactions that are similar in size to yours.

Experience in Technology Markets   Understanding the dynamics of technology markets is critical. These markets operate differently than other markets in our economy. They are fast-moving and fluid. An investment banker who has worked extensively in the technology markets will have a much better understanding of how to close transactions in this rapidly changing arena.

A sector that is consolidating has different dynamics than a sector in the early stages of growth. In a consolidating market, motives for acquisition change and valuation metrics change. Plus, adjacent markets are more important for technology industry acquisitions. The best banker will have experience in the various stages of development in the technology markets.

Experiences learned in one sector of the technology markets are applicable to other sectors of the technology markets. Over the years I have closed transactions in many sectors of the software industry. My understanding of the dynamics of this industry is excellent. Sellers still ask me, "Yes, but have you ever done a deal in the XYZ software micro-niche sector?" This is a case of the founder not knowing what questions to ask when hiring an investment banker. At the end of this section I present a number of good questions to ask when selecting a banker.

Negotiating Competency   Effective negotiators have three primary abilities: communication skills, people skills, and problem-solving skills. Closing a deal means working with people and overcoming their problems, issues, and emotions. Buyers have different approaches, different motivations, different opinions of value, and different negotiating styles. What are they trying to accomplish? What are their priorities? Keen listening skills help a banker understand the other party's issues. Communication skills involve not just the ability to state one's points, but to make sure the other side clearly understands them.

The experienced deal maker anticipates problems before they arise. He heads off minor problems before they fester into bigger problems. He knows what roads to go down and what roads to avoid. Every transaction has difficulties. The best banker will have significant experience overcoming problems and negotiating a successful outcome.

Imagination and Creativity Imagination and creativity are the qualities that separate the good deal doers from the great deal doers. The reason is that really difficult problems cannot be solved any other way. Tough problems demand that the investment banker step back and take a fresh, out-of-the-box approach. It is imperative to view the problem from new angles. Only then will one devise new and creative solutions. Does the banker have creative skills? Can he approach the problem with an imaginative mindset?

Deal Savvy Deal savvy is addressed last because it is the most elusive quality. It is difficult to define but you know it when you see it. Deal savvy, or street smarts, means simply knowing how to make deals happen, how to get a difficult transaction closed. It embodies instinct. You might also call this talent deal instincts or negotiating instincts.

In poker if you are good at calculating odds, you can be a reasonable poker player. However, you can never be a great poker player without the ability to effectively read people. Deal savvy enables the banker to effectively deal with bluffs, false objections, and other impediments. He will know how to discover weaknesses in the other side. An investment banker with deal savvy can juggle multiple uncertainties at one time, float a few trial balloons, and work effectively with moving targets. In the end he will find a way to get the transaction closed.

Commitment

Will the investment banker give fully committed attention to the client? Is the deal large enough to get the banker's interest? What priority will the banker give the assignment? Will he aggressively pursue all alternatives? Commitment is important because deals can reach an impasse. When the going gets tough will the investment banker fade away and move on to the next transaction? Or, will he stick with it, hang in there, scratching and clawing his way to close the deal?

During slow times, a large or midsized investment bank may reach down to take on smaller transactions to keep its people busy or use it as training ground for its junior associates. Who will be the individual working on the assignment? Is it a senior partner or will the assignment be handed off to a junior person? Many investment banks are organized this way—the senior partner brings in the deal and the junior associates do all the work. Who will be working on your deal? Senior-level attention is something every client should demand.

Committed attention is one of the most important things that an investment banker can provide to his client. The worst negative stories regarding investment bankers are those in which the banker did not give the assignment his full and committed attention.

Character

Character embodies trust, integrity, and chemistry. Integrity takes two forms in the context of a transaction. The first is integrity with respect to the client. This means communicating issues that the client needs to be aware of honestly and truthfully. The investment banker should have the integrity to inform the client about all aspects surrounding the transaction, even the bad news.

The second aspect of integrity relates to negotiating. Negotiations are more fruitful when each side trusts the other side. So, when one side states its position they don't renege on that position later; they stay true to their word. A banker who is constantly shifting his requests or positions does not generate trust. When you can't trust the other side, it makes reaching an agreement much more difficult.

The sale of a company is one of the most significant transactions in many people's business lives. The management team should enjoy and respect the people with whom they are working. In addition, good chemistry between people is an excellent foundation for discussions, should a problem arise. The principals of a company will be spending a good six months with this advisor so choose wisely.

Ask the investment banker for several references and call them. In addition, call a company or two that were not provided as references. If you are aware of a transaction that the investment banker has worked on, call the CEO and see if he or she will comment on the investment banker's performance. This is usually better than getting references from the banker himself. Many times you can read between the lines to discern if the client was pleased with the banker's performance.

16 GOOD QUESTIONS

Many CEOs, directors, and venture capitalists have a mistaken belief that industry contacts or "knowing a space" is the primary criteria for selecting an investment banker. In many cases the first question that I am asked is "Do you have any contacts in the XYZ industry?" or "What space have you worked in lately?" These questions presume that all investment bankers are the same and that the only differentiating characteristic is industry knowledge. This is certainly not the case.

The following questions are an excellent way to understand how the investment banker thinks and how he views the transaction process. The answers will give insight into his experience and competency. The questions are broken down into two sections—questions about the sale process and questions about the investment banker's experience and expertise.

Questions about the Process:

1. Describe the methodology of your sale process. How long will the process take?
2. What is your strategy for communicating with potential buyers? Do you plan to contact any of our competitors? Will you approach financial buyers?
3. How will you approach the valuation issue? What do you see as our most valuable assets or capabilities? (Don't get snowed by an investment banker who is trying to win your business by suggesting a very high valuation. Inflated expectations can lead to a number of problems.)
4. How will you manage confidentiality? When should we use an NDA?
5. Which individuals will do the actual work on our transaction? Who will draft the descriptive memorandum?
6. How much time and effort should our management team expect to devote to the sale process?
7. Who will handle the negotiations?
8. What kind of reporting to us will you do during the assignment? How frequently will you report?
9. What kinds of transaction structures would you expect? Where might you foresee any problems with the transaction?

Questions about Transaction Experience:

10. What are some transactions you have completed that might be comparable to our situation? Were these transactions handled by other people in your firm or handled by you personally?
11. Tell me about one of your more successful transactions—what made you effective? What issues did you overcome? What strengths did you bring to bear?
12. Describe a transaction that ran into a serious obstacle. How did you overcome it? Can you give me an example of how you used creativity to solve a deal problem?
13. Describe a transaction in which you were not successful in selling the company. Why didn't it sell? What would the CEO of the company say about you and your efforts?

14. What is your depth of international experience? Tell me about an international transaction that you completed. (International reach is becoming increasingly important. In my experience, 10 to 20 percent of the prospective buyers are located overseas.)
15. Do you have any conflicts of interest or other relationships with firms in our market that might impact this transaction?
16. What differentiates your firm from others?

About the Author

Thomas V. Metz, Jr. has been an investment banker for more than 27 years. He founded T.V. Metz & Co., LLC, an investment banking boutique, in 1983. His primary specialization has been selling technology, software, and service companies. Mr. Metz has closed transactions across North America as well as internationally, including clients in Paris, Vienna, Brussels, Finland, Germany, Israel, India, Australia, and Singapore. He has negotiated and closed a wide range of transactions in which the value was not tangible.

Mr. Metz has devised creative transaction structures and acted as a negotiator for difficult transactions. He has undertaken acquisition searches and arranged acquisitions on behalf of buyers. He has also raised capital, arranged leveraged buyouts, and been an expert witness on valuation matters.

Earlier in his career, he managed new business projects and invested venture capital for Gramark, a private holding company. He also worked for DeLorean Motor Company. Previously, Mr. Metz worked in computer sales with IBM.

Mr. Metz has a Bachelor of Science degree in Mathematics and Computer Science from the University of Oregon (1973). He holds an MBA from the University of California at Berkeley (1979). He has written numerous articles for business publications and is a frequent speaker on mergers, acquisitions, and entrepreneurial topics.

Mr. Metz is an avid heli-skier and squash player. One year he won the U.S. National Squash Championships and was the number one player in the country in his age group. He pilots his own airplane, a Cessna 182, to family and golf destinations.